BY BROAD POTOMAC'S SHORE

By Broad Potomac's Shore

Great Poems from the Early Days
of Our Nation's Capital

Edited by Kim Roberts

UNIVERSITY OF VIRGINIA PRESS
Charlottesville and London

University of Virginia Press
© 2020 by the Rector and Visitors of the University of Virginia
All rights reserved
Printed in the United States of America on acid-free paper

First published 2020

9 8 7 6 5 4 3 2 1

Library of Congress Cataloging-in-Publication Data

Names: Roberts, Kim, 1961– editor.
Title: By broad Potomac's shore : great poems from the early days of our
    nation's capital / edited by Kim Roberts.
Description: Charlottesville : University of Virginia Press, 2020. | Includes
    bibliographical references and index.
Identifiers: LCCN 2020014425 (print) | LCCN 2020014426 (ebook) |
    ISBN 9780813944746 (hardcover) | ISBN 9780813944753 (paperback)
    | ISBN 9780813944760 (epub)
Subjects: LCSH: American poetry—Washington (D.C.) | Washington
    (D.C.)—Poetry. | American poetry—1783–1850. | American poetry—
    19th century. | American poetry—20th century.
Classification: LCC PS548.D6 B9 2020 (print) | LCC PS548.D6 (ebook) |
    DDC 811/.008/09753—dc23
LC record available at https://lccn.loc.gov/2020014425
LC ebook record available at https://lccn.loc.gov/2020014426

Cover art (clockwise from top left): Henry Adams, c. 1885 (Harvard University
Archives); Anna Julia Cooper, c. 1901–3 (C. M. Bell Studio Collection,
Library of Congress Prints and Photographs Division); Ambrose Bierce,
1892 (Bancroft Library Portrait Collection, UC Berkeley); Frederick
Douglass, 1856 (National Portrait Gallery, Smithsonian Institution, acquired
through the generosity of an anonymous donor); James Weldon Johnson,
c. 1900–1920 (Library of Congress Prints and Photographs Division);
Walt Whitman, 1871 (Feinberg-Whitman Collection, Library of Congress
Prints and Photographs Division); Paul Lawrence Dunbar, 1905 (Library
of Congress Prints and Photographs Division); Alice Dunbar, 1902
(Schomburg Center for Research in Black Culture, Manuscripts, Archives,
and Rare Books Division, New York Public Library Digital Collections); U.S.
Capitol Building (Library of Congress Prints and Photographs Division)

❖ CONTENTS ❖

Preface   xix

Introduction   1

Part I. The Earliest Bards

Joel Barlow   25
   From The Columbiad   26
   From The Hasty Pudding   27

Thomas Law   29
   The Moth   30

John Quincy Adams   31
   To a Lady   32
   The Lip and the Heart   33
   To the Sun-Dial   33

Thomas Kennedy   34
   Ode to the Mammoth Cheese   35

James Kirke Paulding   37
   The Old Man's Carousal   37

Francis Scott Key   38
   Defense of Fort M'Henry   40
   Song   40
   To My Cousin Mary   42

Joseph Story   42
  Advice to a Young Lawyer   43
  The Druid Rites: A Fragment   43

George Washington Parke Custis   45
  Lines Written for the Centennial Anniversary of
    the Birth of Washington   46

John Agg   47
  Mrs. Adams's Ball   48

George Watterston   50
  My Native Home   51

Emma Willard   52
  Rocked in the Cradle of the Deep   53
  To a Young Lady   54
  Lafayette's Welcome   54

Part II. The Rift of the Civil War

John Pierpont   59
  A Word from a Petitioner   59
  Oft, in the Chilly Night   61

B. B. French   62
  A Short Poem on the Death of Abraham Lincoln   62
  From Fitz Clarence: A Poem   63

Albert Pike   64
  Dixie   65
  The Magnolia   66

Margaret Lucy Shands Bailey   68
  Endurance   69

William Slade   70
  The Slave to His Star   71

Arthur Bowen   72
  Farewell   73

Frederick Douglass   74
    A Parody   75
    After the Departure of a Friend   77

Walt Whitman   79
    By Broad Potomac's Shore   81
    Vigil Strange I Kept on the Field One Night   81
    The Wound-Dresser   83

Sara Clarke Lippincott (Grace Greenwood)   85
    The Leap from the Long Bridge   86

George Boyer Vashon   88
    From Vincent Ogé   88

Mary E. Nealy   89
    Arlington   90

O. O. Howard   91
    The Blue and the Gray   92

John Sella Martin   94
    From The Hero and the Slave   95
    The Sentinel of Freedom   98

Elizabeth Akers Allen   100
    Spring at the Capital   101
    Lost Light   102
    Rock Me to Sleep   103

John L. McCreery   105
    There Is No Death   105

Sarah Morgan Bryan Piatt   107
    Hearing the Battle—July 21, 1861   108
    Army of Occupation   109
    April at Washington   110

Thomas Bailey Aldrich   111
    Accomplices   111
    Fredericksburg   112
    Memory   112

Fanny Jackson Coppin   113
   The Black Volunteers   113

John Willis Menard   115
   The Negro's Lament   116

Laura Reddon Searing (Howard Glyndon)   118
   In Time of War   118
   Thomas Hopkins Gallaudet   120

John A. Joyce   121
   Grant's Mustered Out!   122
   Decoration Day Poem   122

Walter H. Brooks   126
   The Fall of Richmond, April 3, 1865   127

Jeanie Gould Lincoln   127
   My Soldier's Grave   128

T. Thomas Fortune   129
   Nat Turner   130
   Lincoln   131
   The Diamond in the Clay   131
   Slavery to the Slave!   132

Part III. Poets of Moral Persuasion

Daniel Alexander Payne   135
   From The Pleasures   136

Christopher Pearse Cranch   138
   Correspondences   138
   The Pines and the Sea   139

Jane Grey Swisshelm   140
   To George D. Prentiss   140
   November   141

Anna Hanson Dorsey   141
   From Sunset among the Alps   142

Charles Astor Bristed (Carl Benson)   143
    The Drinker's Apology   143
    The Pertinacious Toper   144

Caroline Healey Dall   145
    At a Death-Bed   146

Madeleine Vinton Dahlgren   147
    A First Pair of Spectacles   148
    The Blue Ridge   148

Solomon G. Brown   149
    God's Vengeance Is Creeping   150
    Fifty Years To-Day   153

Mary Abigail Dodge (Gail Hamilton)   156
    Note   156
    To Dr. Bailey, with a Pair of Gloves, Christmas   158

Henry McNeal Turner   159
    Hymn   160
    One Year Ago Today   160

Mary Emily Neeley Bradley   161
    Beyond Recall   162

Margaret Louisa Sullivan Burke   162
    In Spite of Fate   163

Mary Clemmer Ames   163
    The Joy of Work   164

Rose Elizabeth Cleveland   165
    From The Dilemma of the Nineteenth Century   165

Marian Longfellow O'Donoghue (Miriam Lester)   168
    Leeward   169

Newell Houston Ensley   169
    Write Thy Name   170

Wendell Phillips Stafford   170
  On the Photograph of a Lynching   171
  The Cry of the Dark   172
  Passing Mount Vernon   172

John Henry Paynter   173
  To Emperor Selassie   173

Kelly Miller   174
  The Cat   175

Isabel Likens Gates   176
  R.O.T.C., 1917   176

Bertha Gerneaux Davis   177
  At Arlington   178
  The Service Flag   178

Kendall Banning   179
  God's Puppets   179

Part IV. Poets of the American Scene

Horatio King   183
  "All's Well"   183

Anne Lynch Botta   184
  Webster   185
  The Bee   187
  To an Astronomer   188
  In the Library   188

Donn Piatt   189
  We Parted at the Omnibus   189

Jeremiah Eames Rankin   190
  From Broken Cadences: An Ode in Three Parts   191

Charles G. Halpine (Miles O'Reilly)   192
  Webster   193

Eliza Woodworth   193
    Asleep upon the Grass   194
    On the Beach   194

Edward Robert Bulwer-Lytton (Owen Meredith)   195
    The Cloud   196

John James Piatt   197
    Taking the Night-Train   197
    To Walt Whitman, the Man   198

Harriet Prescott Spofford   199
    Evanescence   199
    Reprieve   200
    A Weed   200

Mary Toles Peet   201
    Ethel's Letter   202

John Burroughs   203
    The Bobolink   203
    Waiting   204

Charlotte Forten Grimké   205
    The Gathering of the Grand Army   206
    Charles Sumner   207
    Wordsworth   208
    At Newport   209
    A Parting Hymn   209

Cincinnatus Heine Miller (Joaquin Miller)   210
    By the Pacific Ocean   211
    Sea-Blown   211

Henry Adams   212
    Prayer to the Dynamo   213
    The Capitol by Moonlight   214

John Hay   215
    The Crows at Washington   216
    Two on the Terrace   217

Esmerelda Boyle 218
    Love Me Little, Love Me Long 219

George Alfred Townsend (Gath) 219
    Cloture 220

Julia Von Stosch Schayer 221
    The Moon-Flower 221

Ambrose Bierce 222
    The Statesmen 223
    The New Decalogue 224
    A Year's Casualties 225

Alfred Islay Walden 225
    Dedicated to a Young Lady Representing the
        Indian Race at Howard University 226
    The Nation's Friend 227

Charles Warren Stoddard 229
    The First Rain 229

Emily Thornton Charles (Emily Hawthorn) 230
    Rondeau 230

William Henry Babcock 231
    Walt Whitman 232
    Edgar Poe's Grave 232

Grace Denio Litchfield 233
    The Setting Sun 233
    Good Bye 233

Robert Underwood Johnson 234
    In Tesla's Laboratory 234
    On Nearing Washington 235

William Temple Hornaday 235
    The Whispering Pine 236

Anne Kelledy Gilbert 237
    Grief 237

Arlington   238
Snow   239

Cecil Arthur Spring-Rice   239
The St. Gaudens Monument at Rock Creek Cemetery   240

Carrie Williams Clifford   241
To Howard University   242
Peril   242
Tercentenary of the Landing of Slaves at Jamestown   243
Egyptian Sphinx   243
Lincoln   244

Maud Andrews Ohl (Annulet Andrews)   244
Why Is It?   245

Richard Hovey   245
An Off-Shore Villanelle   246
Evening on the Potomac   246

John Claggett Proctor   247
Georgia Avenue   248

Helen Hay Whitney   249
Alone   250
Sapphics   250
The Seal   250

Part V. The Rise of the Personal

Paul Claudel   253
Sieste/Nap   253

Alice Archer Sewall James   255
There Is a Veil   256
The Greek Bath   256

James Weldon Johnson   256
Mother Night   257
To America   257
O Black and Unknown Bards   257

Paul Laurence Dunbar   259
    Lover's Lane   260
    Slow through the Dark   261
    Douglass   261
    We Wear the Mask   262

Leonora Speyer   262
    The Saint-Gaudens Statue in Rock Creek Cemetery,
        Washington   263
    Suddenly   263
    Ascent   264
    Measure Me, Sky   264

Mary Berri Chapman Hansbrough   264
    Debonair   265
    After Grief   265

Alice Moore Dunbar-Nelson   266
    I Sit and Sew   266
    The Lights at Carney's Point   267
    Sonnet   268
    To the Negro Farmers of the United States   268

Gertrude Simmons Bonnin (Zitkala-Ša)   269
    Winona's Aria: The Magic of the Night   270

Natalie Clifford Barney   271
    More Night!   271
    A Sonnet to My Lady with the Jaundice   272
    How Write the Beat of Love   272

Georgia Douglas Johnson   273
    The Heart of a Woman   274
    Little Son   274
    Prejudice   274
    Common Dust   274
    To John Brown   275
    Pledge   275

Eloise Bibb Thompson   276
    Tribute   276
    After Reading Bryant's Lines to a Waterfowl   277

Don Marquis   277
    The Prude's Alphabet   278
    A Politician   280

Angelina Weld Grimké   281
    A Winter Twilight   282
    The Want of You   282
    Dawn   282
    To the Dunbar High School: A Sonnet   282
    To Keep the Memory of Charlotte Forten Grimké   283

Juan Ramón Jiménez   284
    El mar/The Sea   284

Jessie Redmon Fauset   286
    Oriflamme   286
    Dead Fires   287
    Rondeau   287
    La vie c'est la vie   288

Edith B. Mirick   288
    Turn of Tide   289

Walter Everette Hawkins   289
    A Spade Is Just a Spade   290
    Where Air of Freedom Is   290
    Child of the Night   291

Louise Kidder Sparrow   293
    Hokkus in Sequence   293

Elinor Wylie   293
    Wild Peaches   294
    Sonnet   296
    Atavism   296

Mariano Brull   297
  Interior: Soneto V/Interior: Sonnet V   297

Caresse Crosby   298
  Coffin's Beach   299
  Nile-Boat   300

Archibald MacLeish   300
  Soul-Sight   301

Jean Toomer   301
  Beehive   302
  Seventh Street   303
  Her Lips Are Copper Wire   303
  Reapers   303

Otto Leland Bohanan   303
  The Washer-Woman   304

Muna Lee   304
  Methodist Revival   305
  Electors   305
  Melilot   306

Herbert Gerhard Bruncken   306
  To a Thrush at Evening   307
  Rondeau   308

Esther Popel Shaw   308
  Flag Salute   309
  Grant Me Strength   310
  Theft   311

Ruth Muskrat Bronson   312
  Sentenced: A Dirge   313
  Songs of the Spavinaw   313
  The Hunter's Wooing   314

Joseph Auslander   315
  Dawn at the Rain's Edge   316
  Home-Bound   316

Lewis Grandison Alexander   316
   Hokku   317

Frank Smith Horne   318
   To a Persistent Phantom   319

Bibliography   321
Index   329

This anthology collects poems by authors who lived in Washington, DC, during the city's early years. All the authors were born before 1800 through 1900. These poets were born in, or drawn to, the nation's capital as it grew from its founding, through such major upheavals as the Civil War, Reconstruction, and World War I. Their work spans the gamut from traditional Victorian-era sentimentality through the beginnings of literary modernism.

The city has always been home to prominent poets, including presidents and congressmen, lawyers and Supreme Court judges. These writers made their names as leaders in government, sometimes helping in the creation of the country's most important institutions and laws—but they also produced poetic works. There have also been poets who worked as foreign diplomats, professors, and scientists, as well as writers from across the country who came as correspondents for their hometown newspapers. All are represented in these pages.

I have included some of the nation's most significant authors: no book of DC poets would be complete without Francis Scott Key, James Weldon Johnson, Henry Adams, Ambrose Bierce, or Paul Laurence Dunbar. But I have taken particular pleasure in seeking out poems by lesser-known poets as well, especially women, working-class writers, and writers of color. Some poets are represented by a single poem; others who I believe deserve more critical reevaluation have been given more space.

The title of this anthology comes from a poem by Walt Whitman. Although critics now consider his work canonical, Whitman's reputation over the past nearly two centuries has waxed and waned. He is a good example of how readers' ideas of a poet's importance can change significantly over time.

How do we measure greatness? One of my favorite poets in this collection is Arthur Bowen, but would I argue his "Farewell" is as great a poem as Whitman's "The Wound-Dresser"? I would not. But Bowen's poem's connection to DC's first race riot, the infamous Snow Storm, gives "Farewell" an inarguable historical importance. And I personally find the poem—and this is no small thing—incredibly moving.

All anthologies make an argument about greatness simply by what they choose to include and what they choose to exclude; this book is no different. My desire is to offer a wide-ranging, diverse collection of noteworthy voices that present an authentic, polymorphic view of the capital city.

For each poet, I provide a short biography, placing their work within their historical context and emphasizing when they lived in Washington, DC. Although poets are presented chronologically by birth within each section, the parts are arranged by theme. So, for example, those authors in part 2 may have written about the Civil War during wartime, or long after its end. Grouping the poets thematically in this way breaks up the strict chronology, but it better represents when these poets were writing most actively, when they lived in the city, and what literary influences are seen most strongly in their poems.

I am pleased to have three significant subgroups of poets emerge. Although there are prominent politicians, such as President John Quincy Adams, Supreme Court Justice Joseph Story, Librarians of Congress George Watterston and Archibald MacLeish, and Secretary of State John Hay, I was interested in including several others who held more modest positions within the federal government. For a working-class writer, a clerkship provided much-needed stability in which to create poetry.

A second subgroup of great interest consists of the poets born enslaved. This group includes Arthur Bowen, Walter H. Brooks, Fanny Jackson Coppin, Frederick Douglass, Newell Houston Ensley, T. Thomas Fortune, John Henry Paynter, John Sella Martin, and Alfred Islay Walden. Their poems give important insight into the complexity of the lives of people of color in Washington, especially in the eras immediately after emancipation. In overcoming such traumatic beginnings to rise to become writers of note, these poets have not only enriched the city's literature, but they provide an inspirational model that helps us to better understand poetry's role in early civil rights efforts.

The third group is the largest: journalists, including a significant number of women correspondents. Both the segregated white and black newspapers hired women journalists. But the press provided another important outlet for women: poetry was regularly included alongside "hard news," and editors tended to favor poems on patriotic and religious subjects, as well as poems about family and nature, all subjects considered suitable for women's "refined sensibilities," so for many women who worked at home or had other employment, this was their first opportunity to see their work in print.

I was particularly drawn to poems that reflect the city's geography and the important events of the times: poems that could take place only in Washington. Thus you'll find an ode to the "mammoth cheese" presented to Thomas Jefferson from the "Republican" cows of New Hampshire, a love poem that takes place in the Senate chambers during cloture, poems written in memory of George Washington and Abraham Lincoln, works set at Howard University and Arlington National Cemetery, poems about the prominent grave of Henry and Clover Adams in Rock Creek Cemetery, or verses set along the banks of the Potomac River.

Taken together, the poems create a map of a particularly American landscape, and the capital city reveals something representative, something symbolic, about the identity of the country as a whole.

In my earlier book published with the University of Virginia Press, *A Literary Guide to Washington, DC: Walking in the Footsteps of American Writers from Francis Scott Key to Zora Neale Hurston*, the walking tour and "portrait" format of that book necessarily limited the number of authors I could cover. I see this anthology as a continuation of the research I did for that book, and as a companion volume.

I am grateful to the University of Virginia Press for their faith in this project, particularly Eric Brandt, Emily Grandstaff, and Helen Chandler. My gratitude also goes to the staff of Art Omi Sculpture Center in Ghent, New York, particularly Carol Frederick, D. W. Gibson, and Ruth Adams, for a writer's residency where this book was completed; and the late Pellom McDaniels and the staff at Emory University, where I was honored with a Rose Library Research Fellowship to conduct research in their collections. Other essential support came from HumanitiesDC, the Historical Society of Washington, the Library of Congress, and the Gelman Library at George Washington University.

Individuals who gave guidance and support were invaluable to me: I thank Joy Ford Austin, Jasper Collier, Teri Ellen Cross Davis, Julie R. Enszer, the late Patsy Fletcher, Michael Gushue, Jennifer King, Marya Annette McQuirter, Peter Montgomery, Martin G. Murray, Gwen Rubinstein, Myra Sklarew, and Dan Vera.

"The Fall of Richmond, April 3, 1865" by Walter H. Brooks is used with the permission of the Association for the Study of African American Life and History (www.asalh.org).

BY BROAD POTOMAC'S SHORE

Introduction

The periods this book covers were times when poetry was more accessible, more popular, and more a part of most Americans' daily lives than is true today. Newspaper and magazine outlets in the second half of the nineteenth century saw an explosive growth—in the number and types of journals, and also in readership numbers—and poetry was included from the start and is responsible in part for many of the journals' popularity.

Poems were also memorized in schoolrooms and regularly used as part of public school curricula. Poems were set to music and sung in churches and town halls; they were recited at parties, community meetings, in clubs, and at family gatherings, copied into album books, and mailed to friends. The regular meter and rhyme aided in memorization, which only added to their popularity. To modern ears, this makes much of this work sound old-fashioned, but there is also a timeless pleasure to be found in the musicality of the language. But the poetry of this era did more than simply provide pleasure: the visibility of poetry in civic forums helped Americans define themselves and their country. The poems of this era encompass an impressive range of formal variety and complex themes.

Poems of this era engaged with political and social changes in ambitious new ways, as is most evident in part 3, which covers reformers, religious poets, and radicals, what I have called "Poets of Moral Persuasion." There has been a trend since the country's founding to seek utility in the arts, to use literature to educate and inform. During the decades after the Civil War, this trend became even more prominent.

There was also a concerted effort in the post–Civil War era to employ the arts to define a clearer national identity. Many of these poems are grouped in part 4, "Poets of the American Scene."

After the failure of Reconstruction and the major political upheavals of World War I, there was a growing tendency among many poets to look inward. I cover this trend in the final section, "The Rise of the Personal." Poets in this section include some of the older Jazz Age and Harlem Renaissance–era authors, who would transform American literature in new, modernist directions.

It is impossible to understand the history of DC, and the context in which these poems were written, without examining the city's intertwined relationship with the federal government. From the start, and by design, Washington had a dual identity as both a city and the capital. Where inconsistencies between these two roles emerged (as they did almost immediately), Congress simply stepped in and took control.

Congress passed the Organic Act in 1801, to place the capital under their exclusive power. Washington City (including Georgetown and Alexandria) and the less-developed regions (designated Washington County and Alexandria County) were consolidated, and all citizens who previously could vote (when they had been citizens of Maryland or Virginia) immediately lost the franchise. Residents also had no congressional representation and no votes in the Electoral College. The U.S. president appointed a mayor, and Congress had veto power over any local legislation.

The symbolism of the capital city made it a "proving ground" for a number of social movements. More importantly, there was no local jurisdiction to appease that might stop politicians from trying out their new political ideas. Thus, for better or worse, DC has a notable number of firsts in the nation's history and became a laboratory for a wide range of reform ideals, from Prohibition to the desegregation of public transportation. As Senator Charles Sumner wrote, Washington was "an example for all the land."

There were several changes in the city's management throughout the early years that made Washington notorious as the single place in the nation most subject to antidemocratic municipal reforms. The

city's charter, enacted in 1812, formalized the tradition of imposing offi-
cials on residents through appointment rather than direct election. The
laws were amended a number of times, changing certain aspects and
functions of local governance, but by 1878, when Congress created a
municipal corporation for DC, home rule (even in a limited sense) was
removed, and the city was put once again firmly under exclusive fed-
eral control for nearly a century. Not until 1973 did District residents
enter the modern era, when they were allowed to directly elect a mayor
and city council. But even still, Congress continues to review—and
has the power to veto—all local legislation. Congress also controls the
city's budget and appoints all DC judges. Residents still have no voting
representative in the House or Senate.

It is a supreme irony not lost on any Washington resident: a lack
of democracy at the center of a democratic nation. The sting of dis-
enfranchisement was particularly galling in 1871 to African American
voters, coming so soon after their gaining universal manhood suffrage
through the passage of the Fifteenth Amendment. George Vashon, one
of the poets included here, gave an influential speech calling the change
"a base plot, designed to defraud the eight thousand freemen therein
of the elective franchise, and cheat them of their newborn freedom."

Muna Lee, in her poem "Electors," captures the spirit of white res-
idents willing to give up their own franchise to deny people of color
theirs. She characterizes a typical white voter:

> Texans, farmers, and carpet-baggers they hated;
> Feared the Negro—"This state should be lily-white,"
> And arguments to damn whatever scheme
> Were the epithets "Utopia" and "dream."

Some of the reforms Congress forced on city residents were positive.
So, for example, in the years leading up to the Civil War, when the
greater part of residents were conservative and southern (and many
constituents made their living from slave labor or slave trading), Con-
gress imposed its will to protect private schools for students of African
descent. During the war years, DC slaves were freed in 1862, before the
enactment of Lincoln's Emancipation Proclamation—although it was
also the only place in the nation where slave owners were compensated
with cash payments for their "lost property."

For good or ill, the capital remains a place where Congress tries out its ideas (before bringing them to their own constituents), and modern versions of these struggles range from blocking gun-control legislation, to denying funds for abortions to low-income women, to the establishment of charter schools. In the modern city, the local population is overwhelmingly liberal and Democratic, and during those times when Congress is controlled by Republicans, citizens once again feel put upon by unwanted federal oversight from Capitol Hill.

The first part of this anthology includes poets born before the city was established. It covers the period prior to the Civil War, when DC still had a tentative, small-town feel.

It is significant to note how quickly journalism was tied to the new city. DC's earliest newspaper, the *National Intelligencer,* began publication in 1800 (as well as a weekly version, the *Universal Gazette*), edited by Samuel Harrison Smith. Across the Potomac River, the *Alexandria Advertiser* began publication soon after. Later renamed the *Alexandria Gazette,* it remains in continuous existence. Washington is still a destination for correspondents from across the country and around the world, sent there to cover governmental affairs.

Smith moved to DC with another writer: his wife, Margaret Bayard Smith, who was the author of two novels and a biography of Dolley Madison. One of her novels was set in the city, *A Winter in Washington, or Memoirs of the Seymour Family* (1824), one of the earliest books with a DC setting. The Smiths were one of Washington's most prominent early literary couples. They were close friends with Thomas Jefferson, who visited their home nearly every night while in office to play chess or whist. Samuel was active in the American Philosophical Society, founded by Joseph Henry (who would become the first secretary of the Smithsonian Institution), and Margaret was an avid correspondent whose letters were later gathered into the posthumous volume *The First Forty Years of Washington Society* (1906). They had a house in town and a farm in what was then Washington County called Turkey Thicket, which they renamed Sidney (now the grounds of Catholic University). In addition to owning, printing, and editing the *National Intelligencer,* Samuel served as James Madison's commissioner of the revenue, secretary of the treasury, and president of the DC Branch of the Bank of the United States. The newspaper he founded would be published for almost seventy years.

The Library of Congress was established in 1800, with an initial congressional appropriation of five thousand dollars. An early librarian of Congress, George Watterston, was known primarily as a novelist, but he also wrote poems, one of which is included here. The Library was burned during the War of 1812; it was restocked with the purchase of 6,487 volumes from the personal collection of Thomas Jefferson, which included a substantial number of poets (including Homer, Virgil, Dante, Chaucer, Spenser, Milton, Philip Freneau, and Phillis Wheatley). After another devastating fire in 1852, the Library was moved to new "fireproof" quarters in the west front of the U.S. Capitol, dubbed "the largest room made of iron in the world." The library would finally move to its own independent, dedicated location in 1897. The passage of the Copyright Act of 1870 stipulated that a copy of everything deposited for copyright automatically becomes part of the collections of the Library of Congress. This ensured the continued growth and relevance of that institution.

In 1801, the Supreme Court relocated from Philadelphia, bringing with it one prominent justice, Joseph Story, who was a published poet. The Washington Navy Yard was constructed from 1800 to 1806 and became a major employer. Among the writers who worked or lived at the Yard, John Henry Paynter and Madeleine Vinton Dahlgren stand out. Michael G. Shiner, who wrote the earliest-known diary by an African American DC resident, was a Navy Yard employee and wrote a firsthand account of the burning of the Yard during the War of 1812.

Most government officials came to DC without their families until the 1840s and resided in boardinghouses, grouped into "messes" (as they were then called) by region, with southern, western, and northern men living bachelor lives together. Even the foreign diplomats tended to be single men, as Washington was considered a hardship post. The early city was a very male-dominated place.

Until churches could be built, locals and officials met at the House of Representatives or the Treasury Building for worship. St. John's Church opened across from the White House in Lafayette Square in 1816, and the church still maintains its "President's Pew." The first historically

African American church opened in 1820, when the congregants of Ebenezer Church split off to form Israel Bethel Colored Methodist Episcopal Church.

The other major public gathering places were the House and Senate chambers, where men and women treated the debates as a kind of theater. Real theater, as well as bookstores and other cultural organizations that supported writers, were thin on the ground. Some prominent citizens held cultural events in their homes (including concerts, dances, and readings, as John Agg reports in his poem included here), and there were some early clubs, such as the Washington Library Company (founded in 1811 with two hundred paying members), and the Columbian Institute for the Promotion of Arts and Sciences, a forerunner to the Smithsonian Institution, cofounded in 1815 by John Quincy Adams and Thomas Law (both of whom are included in this anthology), among others.

DC was just beginning to find its urban shape when war reached the capital in 1814. British troops burned the Capitol and White House and damaged the Navy Yard, Treasury Building, War Office, and Long Bridge (the major crossing point over the Potomac River). The War of 1812 did not end until the Treaty of Ghent was signed in December 1814. Congress authorized funds to maintain the capital in DC and rebuild, despite some sentiment among lawmakers that they should take this opportunity to rethink the location of the capital city.

The first university in the city predates the capital: Georgetown University was founded in 1789. The next institution of higher learning to open was George Washington University, in 1821. Public elementary schools were established for white students in 1806, but not for students of color until 1862 (although free African American residents' taxes still supported the white public schools their own children could not attend). One of the nation's premier private schools for the education of white girls was founded in Georgetown by Lydia English. I include two notable poets who taught at Georgetown Female Seminary in this volume: Emma Willard and Caroline Healey Dall.

The Marquis de Lafayette visited Washington in 1824 to much acclaim. Residents eager to forget the country's defeat in the War of 1812 were happy to turn their thoughts instead to the celebration of a hero of the American Revolution. The park opposite the White House, originally called President's Park, was renamed to honor Lafayette. Emma Willard's poem "Lafayette's Welcome," included here, welcomed the hero "in winter of thine age" whose "youthful valor dared the war."

Visitors to the city always noted the strange contrasts they saw. British author Harriet Martineau wrote in 1835: "The approach to the city is striking to all strangers from its oddness. I saw the dome of the Capitol from a considerable distance . . . but, though I was prepared by the description of preceding travellers, I was taken by surprise on finding myself beneath the splendid building, so sordid are the enclosures and houses on its very verge." Jane Grey Swisshelm wrote of the land "at the very foot of the Capitol, stretching out in primitive wilderness or exhausted barren wastes."

In 1830, Senator Daniel Webster of Massachusetts debated Senator Robert Hayne of South Carolina on the subject of protectionist tariffs. Webster's "Second Reply" speech was widely considered one of the most eloquent addresses ever delivered in Congress. We remember it now for his contention that government was "made for the people, made by the people, and answerable to the people," later paraphrased by Abraham Lincoln in his Gettysburg Address. Two poetic tributes to Webster can be found in this volume, written by Anne Lynch Botta, who praises his "giant mind," and Miles O'Reilly (pen name of Charles G. Halpine), who mourns the loss of his "Roman hand."

In 1831, Anne Royall and Sally Stack became two of the earliest professional women journalists in the nation when they moved to Washington to start a newspaper, *Paul Pry*, dedicated to exposing political corruption and fraud. They would become foremothers to a tradition of women journalists in the city, some of whom, such as Mary Clemmer Ames, Grace Greenwood (pen name of Sarah Clarke Lippincott), Elizabeth Akers Allen, Margaret L. S. Burke, Emily Hawthorn (pen name of Emily Thornton Charles), and Howard Glyndon (pen name of Laura Reddon Searing), were also published poets. Jane Swisshelm, a poet as well as a journalist, became the first woman admitted to the Senate Press Gallery in 1850.

DC was connected to slavery from its start. Southern congressmen were determined to place the new capital in a region far from the sway of the large industrialists of the Northeast. According to census data for 1790, approximately 55 percent of North American slave populations were centered in just two states: Maryland and Virginia. The capital city would be carved out of land from those two states at the suggestion of George Washington.

In 1808, the importation of slaves to the United States was outlawed. This did not mean the end of slave trading by any means: instead, the forced breeding of enslaved people and the illegal smuggling of free people of color into slavery went on the rise.

By 1830, DC became the nation's most important site for the inter-state slave trade. As wheat began to replace cotton as the Mid-Atlantic region's principal crop, fewer workers were needed on the plantations of Maryland and Virginia, and owners sold off enslaved people they considered "excess" to the southern states, where a cotton boom cre-ated a strong market for them. The most important slave-trading firm in the region, Franklin and Armfield, was established in Alexandria in 1828 (and the building that housed that firm, a National Historic Land-mark, still stands at 1315 Duke St). The Black Codes were adopted to regulate the movement and activities of free people of color in 1808, and in 1812 the city council formalized a system of written passes. In 1836, the codes were amended to restrict people of African descent to certain occupations, and established a permanent 10:00 p.m. curfew that was rigorously enforced. Despite these considerable impediments, residents of color built powerful institutions, particularly centered on churches and schools. Many early leaders of color were also published writers.

DC's first race riot, the Snow Storm, took place in August 1835. Among the main people involved were two poets, Arthur Bowen and Francis Scott Key. The rioting was precipitated by the alleged nighttime attack of Arthur Bowen, an enslaved nineteen-year-old, against his mistress Anna Maria Thornton, when white citizens formed mobs to destroy restaurants, schools, businesses, and homes owned by people of color. Francis Scott Key, serving as DC's district attorney, was crim-inally negligent in allowing the violence to continue for several days. By the time he called in a detachment of marines from the Navy Yard, the damage was extensive and several leading African American citizens were forced to flee for their lives.

By 1840, the majority of people of color in the city were free, making DC one of only three southern cities (along with Baltimore and St. Louis) where free African Americans outnumbered enslaved people. In July 1845, a group of approximately seventy armed male slaves escaped in Maryland, seeking sanctuary in Washington. They were engaged in a battle in Rockville, en route to their intended destination, by about two hundred white men. Although the enslaved men were recaptured, the event alarmed the local populace and polarized opinions on the institution of slavery in DC even further.

Grace Greenwood's moving poem "The Leap from Long Bridge" tells the true story of one fatal slave escape from captivity. A series of slave pens were located just south of the National Mall, where, as Greenwood writes, jailors could be found in their dungeons "to swing the red lash and rivet the chain." The most notorious slave pen, the Yellow House, was operated by William H. Williams (located on Maryland Avenue, across from today's Smithsonian Castle). That neighborhood was selected for its proximity to the Potomac River wharves and to slave markets located on Pennsylvania Avenue. Coffles of chained slaves passed the U.S. Capitol daily, a fact that was much discussed in northern newspapers. Abolitionists argued that the slave trade disgraced the nation's founding ideals.

The first petition to the U.S. Congress to abolish slavery in the city was presented in 1829. Ten years later, in contrast, more than two hundred residents signed a petition defending the "just respect due to the legal rights" of slaveholders in DC. In 1834, the American Anti-Slavery Society began a nationwide petition drive. Despite citizens' constitutional right ensured by the First Amendment "to petition the government for a redress of grievances," Congress was so overwhelmed with petitions from northern states that they passed a resolution, known as the Gag Rule, tabling all action on petitions relating to slavery from 1836 through 1844. In John Pierpont's poem "A Word from a Petitioner," he argues in response to the Gag Rule:

What! our petitions spurned! The prayer
    Of thousands,—tens of thousands,—cast
Unheard, beneath your Speaker's chair!
But ye *will* hear us, first or last.
    The thousands that, last year, ye scorned,
Are millions now. Be warned! Be warned!

DC developed a strong network of African American and white abolitionists in response to the growing slave trade. The Fifteenth Street Presbyterian Church, established in 1841 by John F. Cook Sr., took a leading role in bringing together white supporters and African American worshippers to raise funds to purchase people out of bondage, to pay legal fees, and to finance escapes through the region's Underground Railroad. Poets featured in this book who were associated with the Fifteenth Street Presbyterian Church include William Slade, John Sella Martin, and Charlotte Forten Grimké. I would have loved to include two other early DC poets of color also associated with this powerful church, the Reverend Cook and the first African American teacher to be hired by the DC Public Schools, Emma V. Brown—but as yet, none of their poems have come to light.

In 1847, Gamaliel and Margaret Bailey moved to DC to begin publication of the abolitionist newspaper the *National Era,* which frequently included poetry in its pages. The newspaper is best remembered, however, for printing the first, serialized version of Harriet Beecher Stowe's *Uncle Tom's Cabin.* The paper continued publication through 1860.

The Baileys' large downtown home was a stop on the Underground Railroad, and a regular gathering place for antislavery congressmen and white abolitionist visitors from the North. Margaret Lucy Shands Bailey also edited an abolitionist journal for youth and was a published poet herself. The family hired a series of promising young radical women writers as governesses for their children and gave many of them their first publication credits. The most prominent of these, Grace Greenwood and Gail Hamilton, became notable professional writers (and are included in this book). Margaret Bailey also supported several educational efforts for students of color in the region, volunteering as a literacy tutor in Baltimore during the Civil War and becoming an active donor to Myrtilla Miner's school for young women and girls in DC during Reconstruction.

The largest slave escape in the nation took place in Washington in April 1848, when seventy-seven people sailed north on the schooner *Pearl.* Strong winds impeded the journey, and the boat was captured near Point Lookout, Maryland, and towed back to Washington. A mob attacked the *National Era* offices in response, smashing the presses, and the Baileys were forced to flee. More significantly, slave owners sold nearly a third of the recaptured fugitives to the Deep South. Abolitionists rallied to raise funds but were only able to purchase the freedom of some of the enslaved people who had been captured. A direct descendant of two of the women fugitives, John Henry Paynter, wrote a novelization of the incident, and Frederick Douglass wrote: "Slaves escaping from the Capital of the 'model republic!' What an idea!—running *from* the Temple of Liberty to be free!"

Abolitionist leaders of color who were also poets included Bishop Daniel Alexander Payne, Bishop Henry McNeal Turner, William Slade, and the Reverend John Sella Martin, all represented in these pages. These African American men were instrumental in developing networks to support escapees, buy enslaved people, and build political autonomy.

In 1847, the part of the District located on the western side of the Potomac River was retroceded to Virginia. That portion of the original one hundred square miles that now make up Alexandria City and Arlington County constitutes about thirty-one square miles. Those living in the retroceded district regained their right to vote and their voting representatives in Congress. More significantly, when the Compromise of 1850 outlawed the slave trade in the District, those businesses west of the Potomac dealing in the sale of enslaved people were not affected.

A few nascent museums were formed in the capital's early years. Sometime after 1820, Charles Bird King opened a Gallery of Paintings at Twelfth and F Streets. In the 1840s, J. Goldsborough Bruff opened a private museum in his home in the West End neighborhood to display his collection of curiosities. In the 1830s another private collector, John Varden, opened the Washington Museum in his home, near today's Superior Court building. All of these were subsumed in 1840 with the foundation of the National Institute for the Promotion of Science and Art (which was given a congressional charter in 1842). The National Institute bought or received donations from those earlier collections. They divided their holdings into eight departments, one of which was the Department of Literature and the Fine Arts. The other major display in the city was held in the glass cases of the U.S. Patent Office, where models were lined up like a hymn to American ingenuity.

The Smithsonian Institution was founded in 1846. James Smithson, an English scientist who had never set foot in the United States, left his bequest upon his death for "an Establishment for the increase and diffusion of knowledge." Congress dithered for a decade before figuring out what to do with the money. Poetry by the institution's first African American employee, Solomon G. Brown, is included here. James Renwick's red castle was completed on the Washington Mall in 1855 to house the Smithsonian, which included a large library that was open to the public; the museum also hosted a range of public lectures.

In 1852, Congress established two other major new institutions in the city. St. Elizabeths Hospital, the first large-scale mental hospital in the nation, was built on a bluff overlooking the Anacostia River on the former farm of Thomas Blagden. One of the writers included here, Mary Berri Chapman Hansbrough, lived for forty-two years as an inmate of St Elizabeths. The government purchased another farm from George Washington Riggs for the U.S. Military Asylum (familiarly called the Old Soldiers' Home, now officially known as the Armed Forces Retirement Home), on a high rise of land in Washington County overlooking the city. The Old Soldiers' Home was used as a summer White House; President Abraham Lincoln wrote his first draft of the Emancipation Proclamation there.

The second part of this anthology covers the most major event in DC's early history, the Civil War. I include poets who served in the military during the war: Albert Pike, O. O. Howard, Ambrose Bierce, and John A. Joyce. The city was transformed by the conflict, and many major battles took place mere days' march away from the capital. A defensive system of forts, placed at half-mile intervals, was built in a ring around the city (the total by war's end was 164 forts and batteries, including 68 major enclosed forts). The forts permanently changed the city's landscape. Most forts were built of rammed earth and timber, surrounded by cut trees with sharpened ends called *abatis*. The ground in front of the forts was clear-cut for a distance of two miles, and roads were cut to connect the fortifications.

Southern congressmen left the city as their states seceded, and Justice John A. Campbell of Alabama stepped down from the Supreme Court. Many of the city's oldest and most powerful families also left, taking their slaves with them. Local residents suspected of disloyalty were imprisoned: at one point, three hundred residents were held in the Old Capitol Prison.

Prior to the war, there was only one infirmary in the city; during the war years, more than sixty military hospitals were in operation. Volunteer nurses are represented in these pages by Walt Whitman, Jane Grey Swisshelm, and Elizabeth Akers Allen. Allen's "Spring at the Capital" expresses the hope that nature will heal itself from "the war's red flood" and "the steaming wounds, the sickening scent of human blood," while Whitman's "The Wound-Dresser" notes where the soldiers' "priceless blood reddens the grass." An excerpt from that poem by Whitman is now etched into the granite entrance to the Dupont Circle Metro station. Louisa May Alcott, a volunteer nurse in DC, published her popular *Hospital Sketches* in 1863, and Walt Whitman began drafting his nonfiction book *Specimen Days*.

Julia Ward Howe wrote the "Battle Hymn of the Republic" while staying at the Willard Hotel in 1862, and the Contraband Relief Association was founded by DC resident Elizabeth Keckley (famous as the African American dressmaker and personal confidant of Mary Todd Lincoln; she was also the author of a memoir). Frederick Douglass became the first African American to have a formal meeting with a U.S. president inside the White House when he met Abraham Lincoln in July 1863 to discuss the treatment of black Union army soldiers. As Douglass wrote of white enslavers in "A Parody":

> We wonder how such saints can sing,
> Or praise the Lord upon the wing,
> Who roar, and scold, and whip, and sting,
> And to their slaves and mammon cling.

The city's population swelled during the war years, as the federal government expanded and the city became the headquarters of the Union army. Soldiers, government and military officials, and entrepreneurs seeking to profit from war contracts increased the number of residents. DC also became a mecca for contrabands, or self-emancipated African Americans escaping slavery. By late 1854, it is estimated that as many as fifty thousand contraband refugees had moved within the line of forts that surrounded Washington.

On April 16, 1862, President Abraham Lincoln signed the District of Columbia Emancipation Act. This law provided compensation to slave owners living within the boundaries of DC who could prove their loyalty to the Union. A board of three appointees evaluated each case and dispersed funds; this group included poet Horatio King. More than three thousand people were freed.

Women of color led efforts to build relief organizations for freed slaves. Many of these organizations were church-based or community mutual aid societies. Leaders included memoirists Harriet Jacobs and Elizabeth Keckley, and three poets: Emma V. Brown, Charlotte Forten Grimké, and Fanny Jackson Coppin. Some of their efforts provided freed people with housing, clothing, firewood, and food rations. Educational programs, health care, and job placement programs were also offered. As Coppin wrote so movingly in her poem "The Black Volunteers":

> Now, Freedom stands holding with uplifted face,
> Her hand, dipped in blood, on the brow of our race.
> Attest it! my country, and never again
> By this holy baptism, forget we are *men,*
> Nor dare, when we've mingled our blood in your battles,
> To sneer at our bravery and call us your "chattels."

General O. O. Howard was named commissioner of the Freedmen's Bureau from 1865 to 1873—and was also a poet. Among other reform efforts, he encouraged passage of an 1863 DC marriage law that recognized marriages made without documentation. This was an important step for emancipated slaves who were building new lives as freed people, and helped in efforts to reunify families separated by slavery or war.

There were some notable educational reforms during the war years. Gallaudet University was formed in 1864, the first national school to educate deaf and hard-of-hearing students. I include a poem written in tribute to its founder by Laura Searing, who wrote as Howard Glyndon. Emma V. Brown, an educator and poet, became the first African American teacher hired by the DC Public Schools. In 1862, Congress placed segregated public schools under a Board of Trustees of Colored Schools, whose members were appointed by the U.S. secretary of the interior. This move effectively kept the nascent system of schools for students of color out of the control of the local (usually hostile) city government.

Salons and intellectual societies increased in number during the Civil War era. These important groups included King's Reunions (1860s–70s), founded by Horatio King for readings of original works of literature; Philp and Solomon's Study (1860s–75), held in the art gallery adjacent to their bookstore on Pennsylvania Avenue; and the Washington Literary and Dramatic Association (1863–?), founded by a group of Jewish men with a private library for members, who hosted a series of soirees that included lectures, performances, and readings of original works of literature.

The assassination of Abraham Lincoln in April 1865 produced an outpouring of poetic elegies. B. B. French, who was actually present in the room where Lincoln died, was placed in charge of the president's funeral arrangements. In his tribute poem, he denounces the "life torn out by traitorous, murderous hands— / Crushed—trampled down!" But other poets, such as T. Thomas Fortune, Sarah Morgan Bryan Piatt, and Carrie Williams Clifford, focused more on his legacy than on his violent death.

The war's end, one month later, was marked with the Grand Review of the Armies, which took two days to parade through the streets of Washington. Charlotte Forten Grimké's poem "The Gathering of the Grand Army" gives a sense of the high emotion felt by those who witnessed the event, when "One thought, one purpose stirred the people's blood" to show the veterans the "silent blessings [that] from our full hearts flow."

In the postwar period, a time Mark Twain dubbed the Gilded Age, Washington became a favored seasonal home for elite white families, who migrated back to the city each winter while Congress was in session. Some of these seasonal residents built enormous mansions in the Dupont Circle and Kalorama neighborhoods (most of which are now foreign embassies). Washington was particularly attractive to the nouveau riche, who were shut out of high society in older, more established East Coast cities. The most flamboyant newcomers came from the West, once they had established their fortunes in mining, railroads, or real estate.

Older Washington families soon found themselves outspent and ignored by official society. Sometimes referred to as Cave Dwellers, this group, descendants of southern planters, often lent out their young daughters to households to instruct newcomers in etiquette and official government protocol. Some would go on to write instructional books, such as Madeleine Vinton Dahlgren, whose *Etiquette of Social Life in Washington* was revised and reissued five times.

Twain's novel *The Gilded Age*, cowritten with Charles Dudley Warner (published in 1873), features a corrupt senator, Abner Dillworthy, modeled after a real politician, Samuel C. Pomeroy of Kansas. Likewise, the villain of Henry Adams's novel *Democracy* (1880) had a real counterpart; his Silas P. Ratcliffe was a barely disguised Senator James G. Blaine of Maine. Adams hid behind anonymous publication, but the book was a publishing sensation both in the United States and in Great Britain.

In 1867, Congress chartered Howard University as a private institution of higher education for "both sexes and all colors." I include poems about Howard University by Alfred Islay Walden and Carrie Williams Clifford. Other poets in this anthology associated with the university include George Boyer Vashon, Walter H. Brooks, T. Thomas Fortune, Newell Houston Ensley, Kelly Miller, Eloise Bibb Thompson, Walter Everette Hawkins, and Lewis Grandison Alexander. Two former presidents of the university are also featured: Jeremiah Eames Rankin and the college's namesake, General O. O. Howard.

In 1870, M Street High School was established, the first permanent high school for African Americans in the nation. A public high school for white students would not open in DC until over a decade later, in 1882. M Street High maintained its reputation as the top high school in the United States for students of African descent until desegregation; poets Jessie Redmon Fauset and Angelina Weld Grimké taught there, and Jean Toomer was a student. That school is still in existence: since 1917, its name has been Dunbar High, honoring Paul Laurence Dunbar, the first African American poet to become nationally known and celebrated by both readers of color and a mainstream white audience.

Many families of color moved to the area simply for the opportunity to send their children to M Street High, where students regularly outscored their white counterparts on standardized tests. The high school could boast an unusually large number of teachers with advanced degrees, and DC was one of the only southern cities in the nation where

African American teachers were paid on par with white teachers. As Grimké writes in her sonnet to the school:

> She shall be the friend of youth for aye:
> Of quick'ning youth whose eyes have seen the gleam;
> Of youth between whose tears and laughter stream:
> Bright bows of hope.

Three of the city's most significant and lasting literary communities were organized in the postwar years. The Literary Society (1874–present) was formed by three women writers, Esmerelda Boyle (included in this book), Olive Risely Seward, and Sara Carr Upton. It was the most exclusive of the literary salons, and its membership included prominent government officials, scientists, Protestant clergy, diplomats, and authors. Members were all white (with the exception of a few foreign diplomats) and of high social standing. Meetings were held fortnightly, with programs of music or the reading of papers or literary works, followed by discussions.

The American Negro Academy (1897–1924) was founded by the Reverend Alexander Crummell as the first major national African American learned society in the nation. Limited to forty (later fifty) eminent men, the group aimed to promote "Negro culture and unity" through publications, youth scholarships, and the establishment of historical and literary archives that vindicated "the race from vicious assaults."

The Bethel Literary and Historical Association (1881–1913) was organized by Bishop Daniel A. Payne and met at Bethel Hall at the Metropolitan AME Church. A large, formal learned society that regularly attracted hundreds of African American patrons, the group met once or twice a month to hear an invited speaker, followed by a public discussion period. The discussion was lively and sometimes even confrontational. When Bishop T. Tanner visited to present "The Year 2000 and What of It," his arguments were strongly criticized in the discussion period afterward, most vocally by Kelly Miller, then just a college student. Tanner left in a fury, declaring to the organizers, "I will never read for you again." It was an important early victory for Miller, who would become a well-loved orator himself. Annual special programs marked Lincoln's Birthday, Frederick Douglass's birthday, and Founder's Day (when the society's own history was celebrated). Women were regular participants as speakers and on the organizing committee.

Housing expanded into Washington County in the 1880s, with a string of suburban developments. Congress belatedly enacted a law requiring developers to lay out streets in conformity with the plan of the inner city, to simplify the extension of water mains, sewers, and lighting. The real estate boom was on, and some residents secured their financial futures—but from this time forward, affordable housing for residents of modest incomes would remain a major, unending problem. Of course, writers were affected: gentrification in DC, as in other cities, has had ongoing negative effects on its artistic communities.

Rock Creek Park was established as public park land in 1890. The following year, Augustus Saint-Gaudens completed the Adams Memorial in Rock Creek Cemetery, where Clover Adams was entombed (and her husband, Henry Adams, would eventually be as well). The monument Adams commissioned, arguably the most significant funerary sculpture in the nation, would inspire numerous poems in response. I have included poems about the Adams Monument by Anne Kelledy Gilbert, Cecil Arthur Spring-Rice, and Leonora Speyer.

The earliest-known anthology of DC writers was published in 1895, *The Poets and Poetry of Washington*, edited by Ina Russelle Warren. One of the poets featured in that book, Eliza Woodworth, is also included here with two lovely pieces inspired by the natural world.

The DC Public Library was established in 1896 as an integrated institution. An ornate, marble-clad Carnegie Library was dedicated in the center of Mount Vernon Square in 1903; it is now home to the Historical Society of Washington, among other tenants.

The first poetry reading sponsored by the Library of Congress took place in 1897 or 1898 when Paul Laurence Dunbar, then a Library employee, read his work in a program for blind patrons. The next time a writer of color would give a public reading at the Library of Congress was not until 1962.

The first and longest-serving poet laureate at the Library of Congress was Joseph Auslander. His position, initially called the chair in poetry, was made possible by a private donor, Archer Huntington, an amateur poet and son of a wealthy industrialist. Auslander served from 1937 to 1941.

The Washington Chapter of the National Association for the Advancement of Colored People was established in 1912, the largest and most active of the organization's regional chapters. Poets in this volume associated with the NAACP include Kelly Miller, Carrie Williams Clifford, Jessie Redmon Fauset, and James Weldon Johnson, who would become the organization's executive secretary and manage national campaigns to address lynching and segregation.

Woodrow Wilson was inaugurated as the twenty-eighth U.S. president in 1913, the first statesman of southern birth elected since before the Civil War. While progressive in many areas, he argued that a physical separation of the races in federal jobs was necessary to avoid "friction," and even restrooms and lunch rooms became segregated (which persisted through the 1950s). Government employment opportunities for African Americans diminished perceptibly. The golden age for DC as the center of the nation's African American intelligentsia began its slow decline after this era, in direct response to Wilson's policies.

The city's population doubled as the country entered World War I in 1917. Washington was transformed once again into a war center, as the headquarters of the armed services, the American Red Cross, the war trade, and a range of civilian support activities, such as the Liberty Loan drives sponsored by the U.S. Treasury. The city suffered an extreme housing shortage, and the government office shortage was addressed by the placement of rows of temporary buildings constructed on the National Mall.

One of the poets in this collection, Kendall Banning, was a veteran who wrote of his war experiences. Others who wrote about the home front during World War I include Wendell Phillips Stafford, Isabel Likens Gates, Bertha Gerneaux Davis, Anne Kelledy Gilbert, John Claggett Proctor, and Alice Moore Dunbar-Nelson. Dunbar-Nelson's best-known poem, "I Sit and Sew," gives voice to the frustration of women in particular, who wait helplessly at home while men go to fight. Even though her "soul in pity flings / Appealing cries, yearning only to go / There in that holocaust of hell, those fields of woe," she is relegated to the smallest of tasks: "But—I must sit and sew."

The Red Summer race riot took place over four days in July 1919, claiming the lives of thirty residents. After the rumored arrest of an African American man for the rape of a white woman, mobs of white people randomly beat African Americans on the street and pulled others off of streetcars. When the police refused to intervene, African American citizens (including veterans who had served in World War I) fought back, defending traditionally African American neighborhoods.

A DC chapter of the Ku Klux Klan was founded in 1921 with several hundred members, a newsletter, and a baseball team. The largest Klan parade in the nation took place on Pennsylvania Avenue in 1925, with thirty thousand participants marching in their white robes. Albert Pike, a very popular poet in his day but also a KKK member, is represented here, arguing for a romanticized vision of the Old South remembered for "chivalry, loyalty, virtue . . . immortal in story."

Pennsylvania Avenue by this time had become a popular place to put protests on public display. In 1913, five thousand American feminists, led by Alice Paul, participated in a suffragist march along Pennsylvania Avenue. But women also inaugurated the idea of protesting right at the gates of the White House, connecting the president directly to their fight for voting rights and legal autonomy. The first four women arrested for picketing the White House to demand suffrage were sentenced to six months in jail in 1917. As Rose Elizabeth Cleveland, a feminist and former first lady, writes in her parody "The Dilemma of the Nineteenth Century":

> Our patient is a wretched sufferer
>   From man's injustice: you will please to note
> The cause, 'tis soon explained, and 'tis enough, sir,
>   To make a woman sick, sir, not to VOTE.
> She never told her grief, yet how it cankers!
> Give her the ballot, sir; for this she hankers.

In 1920, Congress authorized the Nineteenth Amendment, finally guaranteeing women the right to vote.

The Harlem Renaissance, despite its name, took place in multiple cities, and Washington was one of the most important for the movement—you could even argue that it began there. Howard University professor Alain Locke edited the anthology *The New Negro* in 1925, bringing a diverse group of writers of color under a single heading. As

Locke wrote, the "New Negro" rejected old ways of thinking that made him "more of a formula than a human being—something to be argued about, condemned or defended, to be 'kept down,' or 'in his place,' or 'helped up.'"

Jean Toomer published *Cane*, his stunning collection of prose sketches and poems, in 1923, when he was twenty-nine. He convinced Georgia Douglas Johnson to open her home for her acclaimed Saturday Nighters Literary Salon. Toomer and Douglas Johnson are included here, as are a generous selection of other poets from the New Negro movement: Carrie Williams Clifford, James Weldon Johnson, Alice Moore Dunbar-Nelson, Angelina Weld Grimké, Jessie Redmon Fauset, Esther Popel Shaw, Lewis Grandison Alexander, and Frank Smith Horne.

With the Great Depression, 18 percent of the population went on emergency relief. President Franklin Roosevelt's New Deal programs launched massive public works and greatly increased the number of federal jobs. The Federal Writers' Project, created in 1935, gave work to dozens of local writers with its Washington, DC, branch, which produced an *American Guide* to the city, as well as articles, pamphlets, oral history projects, and educational materials. Such major writers (and DC residents) as Sinclair Lewis, Robert Hayden, Conrad Aiken, Zora Neale Hurston, and Sterling A. Brown all worked for the Writers' Project. John Cheever, who joked that WPA stood for "We Poke Along," moved briefly to the city for a junior editor position. Though wages were modest, the program kept writers afloat during difficult years and launched some eminent careers.

By this time, modernist movements began to change Americans' taste in literature. I end my survey here, on the cusp of that transition.

❖ PART I ❖

The Earliest Bards

Joel Barlow

March 24, 1754–December 26, 1812

Joel Barlow was a diplomat who served as American consul to Algiers, where he negotiated the Tripoli Treaty; and American plenipotentiary to France, where he negotiated a commercial treaty with Napoléon Bonaparte. He was a deist who was against slavery, and he was outspoken on these controversial beliefs in both his writings and his diplomacy.

Barlow served as a Congregational Church chaplain in the Revolutionary army for three years and established a weekly newspaper in Hartford, Connecticut, the *American Mercury,* in 1784. He published several books, including *Hasty Pudding* (1793), *Conspiracy of Kings* (1792), and the patriotic epic poem *The Columbiad* (1807). He also translated books from French into English.

From 1805 to 1811, he lived in DC with his wife, Ruth Baldwin Barlow, on an estate they named Kalorama (now the site of both the embassy of Myanmar and the historic Myers House on S Street NW). The property was recommended for purchase by Thomas Jefferson, who wrote Barlow a letter in 1802, when he was in Paris, stating: "There is a most lovely seat adjoining the city on a high hill commanding a most extensive view of the Potomac now for sale. A superb house, gardens, etc., with thirty or forty acres of ground. It will be sold under circumstances of distress and will probably go for half of what it has cost."

The Barlows expanded the original mansion, adding east and west wings, a greenhouse, servants' quarters, and several outbuildings, including an entrance gate designed to look like a Greek temple. Barlow owned the largest private library in the city, and his home became a gathering place for the city's cultural elite. The mansion stood long enough to serve as a Civil War hospital and was razed in 1889, but the surrounding neighborhood retains the name (and the "beautiful view" that inspired it).

Barlow's biographer, James Woodress, writes in *A Yankee's Odyssey* (1958) that Barlow "took all knowledge for his province, interested himself in science, patronized the arts, and believed that one of man's first obligations was to do good to his fellow men." He continues: "As poet trying to articulate America's future importance, as cosmopolite trying to place his country in the world community, as enlightened defender of democracy, as promoter of cultural enterprises, and as businessman, Barlow mirrors most of the impulses and experiences that make up the United States."

From The Columbiad

Resplendent o'er the rest, the regent god
Potowmak towers, and sways the swelling flood;
Vines clothe his arms, wild fruits o'erfill his horn,
Wreaths of green maize his reverend brows adorn,
His silver beard reflects the lunar day,
And round his loins the scaly nations play.

***

Then shall your federal towers my bank adorn,
And hail with me the great millennial morn
That gilds your capitol. Thence earth shall draw
Her first clear codes of liberty and law;
There public right a settled form shall find,
Truth trim her lamp to lighten humankind,
Old Afric's sons their shameful fetters cast,
Our wild Hesperians humanize at last,
All men participate, all time expand
The source of good my liberal sages plann'd.

***

In this mid site, this monumental clime,
Rear'd by all realms to brave the wrecks of time
A spacious dome swells up, commodious great,
The last resort, the unchanging scene of state.
On rocks of adamant the walls ascend,
Tall columns heave and sky-like arches bend;

Bright o'er the golden roofs the glittering spires
Far in the concave meet the solar fires;
Four blazing fronts, with gates unfolding high,
Look with immortal splendor round the sky:
Hither the delegated sires ascend,
And all the cares of every clime attend.

From The Hasty Pudding

For endless years, through every mild domain,
Where grows the maize, there thou art sure to reign.
But man, more fickle, the bold license claims,
In different realms to give thee different names.
Thee the soft nations round the warm Levant
Polanta call; the French, of course, *Polante.*
E'en in thy native regions, how I blush
To hear the Pennsylvanians call thee *Mush!*
On Hudson's banks, while, men of Belgic spawn
Insult and eat thee by the name *Suppawn.*
All spurious appellations, void of truth;
I've better known thee from my earliest youth;
Thy name is *Hasty Pudding!* thus our sires
Were wont to greet thee fuming, from their fires;
And while they argued in thy just defense
With logic clear, they thus explained the sense:
"In *haste* the boiling cauldron, o'er the blaze,
Receives and cooks the ready powder'd maize;
In *haste* 'tis served, and then in equal *haste*
With cooling milk, we make the sweet repast.
No carving to be done, no knife to grate
The tender ear and wound the stony plate;
But the smooth spoon, just fitted to the lip,
And taught with art the yielding mass to dip,
By frequent journeys to the bowl well stored,
Performs the *hasty* honors of the board."
Such is thy name, significant and clear,
A name, a sound to every Yankee dear,

But most to me, whose heart and palate chaste
Preserve my pure, hereditary taste.

***

My father loved thee through his length of days!
For thee his fields were shaded o'er with maize;
From thee what health, what vigor he possess'd,
Ten sturdy freemen from his loins attest;
Thy constellation ruled my natal morn,
And all my bones were made of Indian corn.
Delicious grain! whatever form it take,
To roast or boil, to smother or to bake,
In every dish 'tis welcome still to me,
But most, my *Hasty Pudding,* most in thee.

***

Some with molasses line the luscious treat,
And mix, like bards, the useful with the sweet.
A wholesome dish, and well deserving praise;
A great resource in those bleak wintry days,
When the chill'd earth lies buried deep in snow,
And raging Boreas dries the shivering cow.
Bless'd cow! thy praise shall still my notes employ,
Great source of health, the only source of joy;
Mother of Egypt's god; but sure, for me,
Were I to leave my God, I'd worship thee.
How oft thy teats these pious hands have press'd!
How oft thy bounties proved my only feast!

***

Milk, then, with pudding I would always choose;
To this in future I confine my muse,
Till she in haste some further hints unfold,
Well for the young, nor useless to the old.
First in your bowl the milk abundant take,
Then drop with care along the silver lake
Your flakes of pudding; these at first will hide
Their little bulk beneath the swelling tide;

But when their growing mass no more can sink,
Then the soft island looms above the brink,
Then check your hand; you've got the portion due:
So taught our sires, and what they taught is true.

Thomas Law

October 23, 1756–July 31, 1834

Thomas Law published poetry and essays on moral philosophy, sometimes using the pseudonyms "Homo" or "Civis" for articles he wrote for the *National Intelligencer* newspaper. His books include *Ballston Springs* (1806), *Thoughts on Instinctive Impulses* (cowritten with George Watterston, 1810), and *Second Thoughts on Instinctive Impulses* (1813), as well as pamphlets and articles on the need for a national currency, among other causes. He cofounded the first theater in DC, as well as a dancing society that met monthly, and the Columbian Institute for the Promotion of Arts and Sciences, the city's first learned society and a forerunner to the Smithsonian Institution.

Law was born in Cambridge, England, the eighth son of the bishop of Carlisle, and made his fortune in India, working for the East India Company. He moved to the United States in 1794, along with two of his three mixed-race sons from his first marriage, settling first in New York and then investing heavily in early land speculation in DC, buying 445 lots on or near Capitol Hill in December 1794, prior to the city's founding. In 1796, he married Martha Washington's eldest granddaughter, Elizabeth Parke Custis, although they separated in 1804 and divorced in 1811. As Kathryn Allamong Jacob wrote in *Capital Elites: High Society in Washington, D.C. after the Civil War*: "Law and his wife, when they weren't publicly quarreling, dined with President John Adams and the Samuel Harrison Smiths and entertained neighbors and officials at their beautiful home near the riverbank. Law also frequently dined out without his wife. Apparently [he was] a sought-after guest."

Pamela Scott, in her essay "Capitol Neighbors," states that Law "was universally described as odd," and quotes another early resident, the novelist Margaret Bayard Smith, complaining that he called at her house nearly daily and "at all hours" and was perpetually restless, "the same as ever—he cannot stay still for two minutes."

Law was one of DC's wealthiest and most prominent citizens for many years before losing his fortune in land speculation (not only in DC but also in Baltimore, Philadelphia, New York, Vermont, and Illinois) and other failing business enterprises. One of his houses, known as Honeymoon House, located at 1252 Sixth Street SW, still stands and is listed on the National Register of Historic Places.

In an obituary in the *National Intelligencer*, he was praised for his "philanthropy and liberality, which, united to a nice sense of honor, were prominent traits in his character." The article goes on to state: "he has been identified with this city as one of its oldest, most zealous and enlightened citizens . . . employing himself mostly in literary labors and indulging with delight in such hospitalities as his narrowed means (for we regret to say his investments of money proved anything but lucrative) allowed him to exercise."

This poem references brooding over "Blackstone." The speaker was reading William Blackstone's *Commentaries on the Laws of England*, a book that played a key role in developing the American legal system.

The Moth
Last night in quite a sober mood,
Perhaps occasion'd by the rain,
O'er Blackstone I resolv'd to brood,
With gainful law to fill my brain;
But flutt'ring to my candle's light,
A little Moth attracts my sight.
Round and round it rapid wheels,
Now athwart the flame it reels,
And often as I push aside,
The wretch intent on suicide,

I find my efforts all in vain,
His fatal passion to restrain,
For still he tries and tries again.
At last I leave him to himself,
And angry, thus address the elf:
"Since so solicitous to die,
Indulge they strange propensity."

Too soon, alas! before my eyes,
He writhes a burning sacrifice.

A tear involuntary fell,
A sigh arose, I could not quell.
But soon a moral hence I draw,
Superior far to rules of law.
No more (said I) will I repair,
To buzz about the dang'rous fair,
My Lot and this poor Moth's the same,
Like him I should expire in flame.
Infatuation in my view,
Destructive love, adieu—adieu.

John Quincy Adams

July 11, 1767 – February 23, 1848

John Quincy Adams, the sixth U.S. president, was an ardent reader, writer, and translator. He kept a detailed diary from the age of eleven and wrote poems, many on religious subjects. His diaries, edited by his son Charles Francis Adams, were published posthumously in several volumes as *Memoirs of John Quincy Adams, Taken from His Diaries 1794–1848* (1874–77). His other books include *Letters of John Quincy Adams to His Son, On the Bible and Its Teachings* (1848), *Poems of Religion and Society* (1848), and *An Answer to Paine's Rights of Man* (1793). He published two volumes of lectures he had given as Boylston Professor of Rhetoric and Oratory at Harvard University, and his grandson Henry Adams collected his *Documents Relating to New-England Federalism, 1800–1815*.

In addition to serving as president, Adams was a diplomat, secretary of state, and congressman. His major political achievements include negotiating the Treaty of Ghent, which ended the War of 1812, negotiating with England to set the northern U.S. border with Canada, negotiating with Spain to annex Florida, and authoring the Monroe Doctrine. Yet, for all his accomplishments, he once wrote, "Could I have chosen my own genius and condition, I would have made myself a great poet."

To a Lady

Who Presented Him a Pair of Knit Gloves

Who shall say that public life
Is nothing but discordant strife?
And he whose heart is tuned to love,
Tender and gentle as the dove,
Must whet his talons, night and day,
For conflicts with the birds of prey?

This world is fashioned, Lady fair,
Of Joy and Sorrow, Ease and Care;
Of sudden changes, small and great;
Of upward and of downward fate:
And whoso bends his mood to trace
The annals of man's fallen race,
May sigh to find that nature's plan
Is ruthless war from man to man.
But nature, cruel to be kind,
Not to war only man consigned;
But gave him woman on the spot,
To mingle pleasure in his lot:
That if with man war cannot cease,
With woman reigns eternal peace.

Fair Lady, I have lived on earth
Nigh fourscore summers from my birth;
And half the sorrows I have felt
Have by my brother man been dealt;
And all the ills I have endured
By man inflicted, woman cured.
The glove from man to man, thou know'st,
Of fierce defiance is the boast;
And cast in anger on the floor,
To mortal combat shows the door:
But gloves from woman's gentle hand,
Of cordial Friendship bear this wand;

And in return a single glove
Betokens emblematic Love.

Thy gift, fair Ellen, then I take,
And cherish for the giver's sake;
And while they shelter from the storm
My hands, the heart alike shall warm;
And speed for thee to God above,
The fervid prayer of faithful love.

The Lip and the Heart

One day between the Lip and the Heart
A wordless strife arose,
Which was expertest in the art
His purpose to disclose.

The Lip called forth the vassal Tongue,
And made him vouch—a lie!
The slave his servile anthem sung,
And braved the listening sky.

The Heart to speak in vain essayed,
Nor could his purpose reach—
His will nor voice nor tongue obeys,
His silence was his speech.

Mark thou their difference, child of earth!
While each performs his part,
Not all the lip can speak is worth
The silence of the heart.

To the Sun-Dial

Under the window of the hall of the House of Representatives of the United States

Thou silent herald of Time's silent flight!
　　Say, could'st thou speak, what warning voice were thine?
　　Shade, who canst only show how others shine!
Dark, sullen witness of resplendent light

In day's broad glare, and when the moontide bright
   Of laughing fortune sheds the ray divine,
   Thy ready favors cheer us—but decline
The clouds of morning and the gloom of night.
Yet are thy counsels faithful, just and wise;
   They bid us seize the moments as they pass—
Snatch the retrieveless sunbeam as it flies,
   Nor lose one sand of life's revolving glass—
   Aspiring still, with energy sublime,
By virtuous deeds to give eternity to Time.

Thomas Kennedy

November 29, 1776–October 18, 1832

Born in Scotland, Thomas Kennedy immigrated to the United States in 1796, at age nineteen, settling in Georgetown. He worked as a bookkeeper for a merchant, for a contractor who built a bridge across the Potomac River at Little Falls, and for the Potomac Navigation Company, as well as serving as a delegate from Washington County in the Maryland state legislature.

His most prominent political cause was the revocation of a 1779 law prohibiting citizens from holding any state office, civil or military, who would not swear an oath of allegiance to Christianity. Kennedy introduced a bill to eliminate the oath, thus "placing the Jewish inhabitants of Maryland on an equal footing of Christians" in 1818, 1819, and 1820; not only was the bill defeated, Kennedy was voted out of office. Kennedy continued to petition for its passage, however, and the so-called Jew Bill was raised each session until its passage in 1826.

Kennedy established a newspaper, the *Hagerstown Mail,* and was elected to the Maryland Senate in 1827, where he served until his death from cholera. He is buried in Rose Hill Cemetery in Hagerstown in a family plot. An obelisk was added to his grave in 1918 "by a few Jewish citizens, in recognition of services rendered" to honor "one who loved his fellow man."

Kennedy published *Poems* in 1816 and *Songs of Love and Liberty* in 1817. He is remembered by the Speaker's Society of the Maryland House of Delegates, who present an annual Thomas Kennedy Award to recognize a former House member "for his or her personal courage and dedication to the principles of liberty and freedom." The Thomas Kennedy Center, in Hagerstown, Maryland, created a park and sculpture in his honor in 2018.

The Mammoth Cheese was a gift from dairy farmers, who pooled the milk of nine hundred "Republican" cows to create a wheel more than four feet in diameter, weighing 1,234 pounds. The Baptist preacher who inspired its creation, John Leland, presented it to President Thomas Jefferson, stating the cheese was but "a pepper-corn of the esteem which we bear to our chief magistrate." Jefferson accepted the gift as "extraordinary proof of the skill with which those domestic arts which contribute so much to our daily comfort are practiced." Jefferson continued to serve the cheese at White House receptions through 1804.

Ode to the Mammoth Cheese

Presented to Thomas Jefferson, President of the United States, by the Inhabitants of Cheshire, Massachusetts, January 1, 1802

I.
Most excellent, far fam'd and far fetch'd Cheese!
Superior far in smell, taste, weight and size,
To any ever form'd 'neath foreign skies,
And highly honor'd—thou wert made to please
The Man belov'd by all—but stop a trice,
Before he's prais'd, I too must have a slice.

II.
Rich too thou art, and pleasant though as large,
As any millstone, or a north-west moon;
To measure thee 'twoud take an afternoon,
Few tables can support the ponderous charge;
Into what cupboard, Mammoth, can thou enter
And where's the knife can cut thee to thy center.

III.
'Twould take a Gallatin to ascertain,
How many meals for Congress, clerks and all,

The supernumeraries about their hall,
Thy spacious limits actually contain,
What number of Welsh rabbits thou wouldst make,
How many thousand loaves there's cause to bake.

IV.
For centuries past in Europe—sometimes here,
Placemen were said to share the loaves and fishes,
(And where's the man that for a share ne'er wishes?)
But now Americans have better cheer,
And to their worthy servants 'stead of these,
They've wisely substituted Loaves and Cheese.

V.
Cheese is the attendant of a new year's day,
Cheese is the Blythmeat when a bairn is born,
Cheese—may these taste thee ne'er, who tasting scorn,
Cheese still proceeding from the milky way,
Is nature's purest, plain and simple food,
Cheese is a luxury, when like this 'tis good.

VI.
God bless the cheese—and kindly bless the makers,
The givers—generous—good, and sweet and fair,
And the receiver—great beyond compare,
All those who shall be happy as partakers,
O! may no traitor to his country's cause
E'er have a bit of thee between his jaws.

VII.
Some folks may sneer, with envy in their smiles,
And with low wit, at ridicule endeavor,
Their sense and breeding's shewn by their behavior,
Well let them use aristocratic wiles,
Do what they can, and say just what they please,
Rats love to nibble at good Cheshire cheese.

VIII.
To others leaving wealth and place and pow'r,
I'll to my home, and to my Harris hie,

Our wants are few, those industry supply,
All that we want, or wish for in life's hour,
Heaven still will grant us—they are only these,
Poetry—health—peace—freedom—bread and Cheese.

James Kirke Paulding
August 22, 1778–April 6, 1860

James Kirke Paulding moved to DC to serve on the Board of Naval Commissioners from 1815 to 1823. He was already a prolific New York writer, associated with Washington Irving and the Knickerbockers, and one of the original contributors to the *Salmagundi* essays (1807–8). While living in DC, he wrote *Koningsmarke* (1823), *Sketch of Old England by a New England Man* (1822), and a book-length poem, *The Backwoodsman* (1818), that combines patriotic sentiment with a racist tale of heroic Christians fighting against pagan Indians.

Paulding's play *The Lion of the West* (1831), about the life of Davy Crockett, was extremely popular in its day. Some of his other titles include *The Diverting History of John Bull and Brother Jonathan* (1812), *The Dutchman's Fireside* (1831), *Westward Ho!* (1832), *Letters on Slavery* (1835), *The Puritan and His Daughter* (1849), and *Life of George Washington* (1854).

In 1838, Paulding returned to DC when President Martin Van Buren appointed him secretary of the navy, but as his 1860 obituary in the *New York Times* states, "His official duties did not distract him from the pursuit of literary fame." At the end of his tenure in 1841, he moved back to his native New York to write and farm.

The Old Man's Carousal
Drink! Drink! to whom shall we drink?
To a friend or a mistress? Come, let me think!
To those who are absent, or those who are here?
To the dead that we loved, or the living still dear?
Alas! when I look, I find none of the last!
The present is barren,—let's drink to the past!

Come! here's to the girl with a voice sweet and low,
The eye all of fire and the bosom of snow,
Who erewhile, in the days of my youth that are fled,

Once slept on my bosom, and pillowed my head!
Would you know where to find such a delicate prize?
Go seek in your church-yard, for there she lies.

And here's to the friend, the one friend of my youth,
With a head full of genius, a heart full of truth,
Who traveled with me in the sunshine of life,
And stood by my side in its peace and its strife!
Would you know where to seek for a blessing so rare?
Go drag the lone sea, you may find him there.

And here's to a brace of twin cherubs of mine,
With hearts like their mother's, as pure as this wine,
Who came but to see the first act of the play,
Grew tired of the scene, and then both went away.
Would you know where this brace of bright cherubs have hied?
Go seek them in heaven, for there they abide.

A bumper, my boys! to a gray-headed pair,
Who watched o'er my childhood with tenderest care.
God bless them, and keep them, and may they look down
On the head of their son, without tear, sigh, or frown!
Would you know whom I drink to? go seek 'mid the dead,
You will find both their names on the stone at their head.

And here's—but alas! the good wine is no more,
The bottle is emptied of all its bright store;
Like those we have toasted, its spirit is fled,
And nothing is left of the light that it shed.
Then, a bumper of tears, boys! the banquet here ends.
With a health to our dead, since we've no living friends.

Francis Scott Key

August 1, 1779–January 11, 1843

A lawyer and DC's former district attorney, Francis Scott Key was a
hobbyist writer. Nonetheless, he is still revered today as the poet who
wrote the lyrics to the U.S. national anthem, "The Star-Spangled Ban-

ner." That poem (printed here under its original title) was written after Key witnessed the bombing of Fort McHenry during the Battle of Baltimore in the War of 1812. It was set to the tune of a popular British drinking song, "To Anacreon in Heaven."

I also include "Song," which honors the members of the U.S. Navy who battled Barbary pirates in the Mediterranean, especially Key's friends Commodore Stephen Decatur Jr. and Captain (later Rear Admiral) Charles Stewart.

In addition to occasional poems (collected into a book that was published fourteen years after his death), Key published a nonfiction book, *The Power of Literature, and Its Connection with Religion* (1834). Key lived at The Maples, 619 D Street SE on Capitol Hill from 1815 through 1838. That property, now converted into condominium units, is listed on the Register of Historic Places. He later moved to 3516–18 M Street NW in Georgetown, now razed, but once preserved as a museum to the author.

Key also owned a country estate, the farm where he was born, Terra Rubra (named for the red clay of its soil) in Carroll County, Maryland, a property that was added to the National Register of Historic Places in 1978, and is privately owned. Key owned slaves, most of whom worked at this farm, but during his lifetime he was considered a "racial humanitarian" who pursued dozens of legal cases to secure the freedom of enslaved families. Although he freed seven of his slaves during his lifetime, Key still owned eight enslaved people at the time of his death. He wrote that people of African descent were "a distinct and inferior race of people." Believing that African American people could never become full citizens, Key was the cofounder of the American Colonization Society, which promoted the settlement of freeborn and formerly enslaved people in Africa.

A handsome bridge over the Potomac River is named in his honor, linking the Georgetown neighborhood where he once lived with the Rosslyn neighborhood in Arlington, Virginia. A park on the DC side includes a bust of the author. In addition, Key Elementary School, part of the DC Public School system, and Key Halls at the George Washington University and at the University of Maryland at College Park are named for him. He is buried in Mt. Olivet Cemetery in Frederick, Maryland, in a crypt topped with a bronze sculpture of Key.

Defense of Fort M'Henry

O say can you see, by the dawn's early light,
What so proudly we hail'd at the twilight's last gleaming,
Whose broad stripes and bright stars through the perilous fight
O'er the ramparts we watch'd were so gallantly streaming?
And the rocket's red glare, the bombs bursting in air,
Gave proof through the night that our flag was still there,
O say does that star-spangled banner yet wave
O'er the land of the free and the home of the brave?

On the shore dimly seen through the mists of the deep
Where the foe's haughty host in dread silence reposes,
What is that which the breeze, o'er the towering steep,
As it fitfully blows, half conceals, half discloses?
Now it catches the gleam of the morning's first beam,
In full glory reflected now shines in the stream,
'Tis the star-spangled banner—O long may it wave
O'er the land of the free and the home of the brave!

And where is that band who so vauntingly swore,
That the havoc of war and the battle's confusion
A home and a Country should leave us no more?
Their blood has wash'd out their foul footstep's pollution.
No refuge could save the hireling and slave
From the terror of flight or the gloom of the grave,
And the star-spangled banner in triumph doth wave
O'er the land of the free and the home of the brave.

O thus be it ever when freemen shall stand
Between their lov'd home and the war's desolation!
Blest with vict'ry and peace may the heav'n rescued land
Praise the power that hath made and preserv'd us a nation!
Then conquer we must, when our cause it is just,
And this be our motto—"In God is our trust,"
And the star-spangled banner in triumph shall wave
O'er the land of the free and the home of the brave.

Song

When the warrior returns, from the battle afar,
　　To the home and the country he nobly defended,

O! warm be the welcome to gladden his ear,
 And loud be the joy that his perils are ended:
In the full tide of song let his fame roll along,
To the feast-flowing board let us gratefully throng,
Where, mixed with the olive, the laurel shall wave,
And form a bright wreath for the brows of the brave.

Columbians! a band of your brothers behold,
 Who claim the reward of your hearts' warm emotion,
When your cause, when your honor, urged onward the bold,
 In vain frowned the desert, in vain raged the ocean:
To a far distant shore, to the battle's wild roar,
They rushed, your fair fame and your rights to secure:
Then, mixed with the olive, the laurel shall wave,
And form a bright wreath for the brows of the brave.

In the conflict resistless, each toil they endured,
 'Till their foes fled dismayed from the war's desolation:
And pale beamed the Crescent, its splendor obscured
 By the light of the Star Spangled flag of our nation.
Where each radiant star gleamed a meteor of war,
And the turbaned heads bowed to its terrible glare,
Now, mixed with the olive, the laurel shall wave,
And form a bright wreath for the brows of the brave.

Our fathers, who stand on the summit of fame,
 Shall exultingly hear of their sons the proud story:
How their young bosoms glow'd with the patriot flame,
 How they fought, how they fell, in the blaze of their glory.
How triumphant they rode o'er the wondering flood,
And stained the blue waters with infidel blood;
How, mixed with the olive, the laurel did wave,
And formed a bright wreath for the brows of the brave.

Then welcome the warrior returned from afar
 To the home and the country he nobly defended:
Let the thanks due to valor now gladden his ear,
 And loud be the joy that his perils are ended.
In the full tide of song let his fame roll along,
To the feast-flowing board let us gratefully throng,

Where, mixed with the olive, the laurel shall wave,
And form a bright wreath for the brows of the brave.

To My Cousin Mary

For Mending My Tobacco Pouch

Thy stitches are not "few and far between,"
As other stitches very often are,
And many things beside, as I have seen,
In this sad world where good things are so rare;
But they are even, neat, and close enough
My treasured sweets to hold in purest plight;
To keep tobacco safe, and even snuff,
And thus at once eyes, nose, and mouth delight.

They're like thy smiles, fair cousin, frequent, bright,
And ever bringing pleasure in their train;
They're like thy teeth of pearl, and their pure white,
Like them, shall never know tobacco's stain.

Joseph Story

September 18, 1779–September 10, 1845

Joseph Story was a justice on the U.S. Supreme Court from 1811 to 1845 and was widely known for his writings on law and the U.S. Constitution. Story also wrote poetry, publishing his best-known poem, the book-length *The Power of Solitude*, in 1804.

Story was the youngest associate justice to the Supreme Court at the time of his nomination by President James Madison, at age thirty-two. His opinions in the areas of federal precedence over state courts, admiralty law, and patent law are considered particularly important, but his antislavery opinions, especially in the *U.S. v. The Amistad* case, are perhaps his most famous.

He later taught at Harvard University and published prolifically, mainly on legal subjects. His *Miscellaneous Writings* (1835) and *The Life and Letters of Joseph Story* (edited by his son William Wetmore Story, a sculptor and poet, and published posthumously in 1851) sold well. A residence where he rented (from 1831 to 1833), now known

as the DACOR-Bacon House, stands at 1801 F Street NW in Foggy
Bottom.

Advice to a Young Lawyer

Be brief, be pointed; let your matter stand
Lucid in order, solid, and at hand;
Spend not your words on trifles, but condense;
Strike with the mass of thought, not drops of sense;
Press to the close with vigor, once begun,
And leave, (how hard the task!) leave off, when done.
Who draws a labored length of reasoning out,
Puts straws in line, for winds to whirl about;
Who drawls a tedious tale of learning o'er,
Counts but the sands on ocean's boundless shore.
Victory in law is gained, as battles fought,
Not by the numbers, but the forces brought.
What boots success in skirmish or in fray,
If rout and ruin following close the day?
What worth a hundred posts maintained with skill,
If these all held, the foe is victor still?
He, who would win his cause, with power must frame
Points of support, and look with steady aim;
Attack the weak, defend the strong with art,
Strike but few blows, but strike them to the heart;
All scattered fires but end in smoke and noise,
The scorn of men, the idle play of boys.
Keep, then, this first great precept ever near,
Short be your speech, your matter strong and clear,
Earnest your manner, warm and rich your style,
Severe in taste, yet full of grace the while;
So may you reach the loftiest heights of fame,
And leave, when life is past, a deathless name.

The Druid Rites: A Fragment

Hah! what shrieks of anguish swell,
Recreant madness stands aghast;
Did you hear that demon's yell,
Roll on the shivering blast?

'Twas the Druid's midnight howl
To bid the fiends of sorcery meet;
Lo, wrapt in many a winding sheet,
With eye of wrath and withering scowl
Slowly rise they from the dead,
Each unveils his cowled head,
Muttering sounds of dark intent,
That tell the moody mind on schemes of murder bent.

Now the troubled rites begin,
Shouts that freeze the alarmed soul,
With dubious meaning peal their din;
The Furies burst a fitful laugh,
Loud, as the tempest rocks the sky;
Anon they seize the mystic bowl,
And holiest blood they quaff.
At length the cauldron boils, and round they fly,
Urged by no conscious will,
The boding raven hurries by,
And all again is still.

Lo, a lovely child appears,
Its cheeks suffused with scalding tears;
A mother bears the fatal knife,
To yield at witchery's doom its life,
A sacrifice of eldest birth.
Can a mother urge such deeds,
To glut the Druid's savage mirth?
Break the bondage of his spell,
Nor foul the bridal bed,
With crimes so black, as startle hell:
Monster, curses blast thy head,
He bleeds, the newborn infant bleeds!

The banquet smokes, the hags advance,
And round in wild disorder dance;
Their screams disturb the dead:
Grinning now with hideous look,

In mystery's lore supremely read,
They scan the sorcerer's Runic book:
The churchyard yawns, and many a sprite,
With hurrying step, and marble glare,
Walks the midnight's baleful air,
While livid flames betray his flight.
Pillowed on clouds of curling fire,
The fateful sisters sail behind,
Yoked to the pinions of the shuddering wind;
From wormy skulls the clotted gore
With savage ecstasy they drink,
And rolling onward slowly sink;
"Drown," they cry, "in blood your ire,
And let the orgies roar."

The cold moon, trembling with affright,
Grows pale, and reels athwart the night;
Convulsive Mona backward leaps,
And groans along her thousand steeps.
Once more they shout, "to vengeance run,
Ere morn a palsying deed of hell is done."

George Washington Parke Custis

April 30, 1781 – October 10, 1857

The adopted son of President George Washington and father-in-law of Robert E. Lee, George Washington Parke Custis (known to friends and family as "Wash") was raised at Mount Vernon and is best known as the builder of Arlington House, now on the grounds of Arlington National Cemetery. Custis carefully preserved personal items and memorabilia he inherited from his stepfather and set up an informal museum of such items in Arlington House. His collection eventually took up over half of the house.

In addition to his occasional poems, Custis was also a playwright, publishing *The Indian Prophecy; or Visions of Glory* (1827) and *Pocahontas; or The Settlers of Virginia* (1830), writings that contributed to the myth that many elite Virginians, including some of the Founding

Fathers, were direct descendants of Pocahontas. Custis's biographical essays, *Recollections and Private Memoirs of Washington,* were posthumously printed in 1860. Custis is buried in Arlington National Cemetery.

An article in the *Washington Evening Star* of May 1905, "Where Sleep the Brave," describes Custis as "hopelessly spoiled by an indulgent grandmother" as a child, and notes that the "defects of his training became apparent during his attendance at Princeton and at Annapolis College, where he displayed a deplorable lack of industry and settled purpose." The article continues: "Custis had not the slightest ambition to shine as a statesman, but chose instead the indolent life of a wealthy country gentleman."

Lines Written for the Centennial Anniversary of the Birth of Washington,

February 22, 1832

1

A Century's gone by. All hail the Day
An infant Washington first saw the light
That beamed with pure & mild benignant ray
on one whose course was destined to be bright.

2

And so it prov'd, for in his dawning youth
The favour'd auspices of life began.
And Grey beards said that courage, Wisdom, Truth
Would form the promise of the future man.

3

And now his Country calls her Savior son
To do her battle with the Savage Foe
And soon the youthful hero laurels won
That might enwreathe a veteran victor's brow.

4

Far greater trials 'wait his manhood hour
For hark. The trumpets clangor o'er the Brave
Fly to their arms against oppressive pow'r
Strike for their freedom or on honored grave.

5

And where's the Chief at this dread hour of need.
His sword late sheathed in his Vernon's Gale
Leaps from its scabbard, with lightning's speed
At the first soundings of his country's call.

6

With modest smile he accepts the high command
And well he bore him in the mighty strife
When Peace & Freedom, blest his native Land
Resigned all pow'r to seek domestic life.

7

Illustrious man. Could not ambition then
Taught thee to turn against thy Country's breast
Thy victor sword. To be like other men
And called on Heron with laurels rest.

8

Ah no. Thy laurels were by virtues won
Pure & untarnished by a single name
Freedom & Glory, claim a Washington
Millions unborn will venerate that name.

9

Thou Empire Founder, Patriot, Soldier, Sage
Centuries may pass, nations will rise & die
Thy name will flourish on from age to age
Unheeding Time. To immortality.

John Agg
1783–April 19, 1855

John Agg was born in Evesham, England, and immigrated to DC, where he became a political reporter and associate editor of the *National Journal*. He wrote poems, short fiction, and a play in addition to journalism. In 1816, he published *A Month in Town: A Satirical Novel* under the pseudonym Humphrey Hedgehog, Esq. Other works include *The Secret Memoirs of an Illustrious Princess* (1813), *The Busy Body* (1817), and *The Ocean Harp* (1819). In 1837, he published a history of the U.S.

Congress. His journalism appeared in several newspapers, including the *Washington Republican,* the *United States Gazette,* and the *New York Commercial Advertiser.* Agg and his wife owned a small farm adjacent to today's Armed Forces Retirement Home. He is buried in Rock Creek Cemetery.

In the chapter on journalism in *The Story of Washington: The National Capital* by Charles Burr Todd (1893), Agg is described as "a small, delicate-featured man, with bright, blue eyes and a musical voice, who wrote agreeable *vers de société* during the reign of Mrs. Dolley Madison, and was a great favorite with the ladies."

This gossipy poem was published in the January 8, 1824, issue of the *Washington Republican.* It reports on an event in the home of Louisa Adams in the year prior to her becoming first lady, when her husband, John Quincy Adams, was serving as secretary of state to President James Monroe. Louisa Adams was renowned as a society hostess, and her drawing room was a major cultural center in DC's early years, not only for dancing but also for theater and musical concerts.

Mrs. Adams's Ball

Wend you with the world to-night?
Brown and fair, and wise and witty,
Eyes that float in seas of light,
Laughing mouths and dimples pretty,
Belles and matrons, maids and madams,
All are gone to Mrs. Adams's.
There the mist of the future, the gloom of the past,
All melt into light at the warm glance of pleasure;
And the only regret is, lest melting too fast,
Mammas should move off in the midst of a measure.

Wend you with the world to-night?
Sixty grey, and giddy twenty,
Flirts that court, and prudes that slight,
Stale coquettes and spinsters plenty.
Mrs. Sullivan is there
With all the charms that nature lent her;
Gay M'Kim, with city air,
And charming Gales and Vandeventer;

Forsyth, with her group of graces;
Both the Crowninshields in blue;
The Pierces, with their heavenly faces,
And eyes like suns, that dazzle through;
Belles and matrons, maids and madams,
All are gone to Mrs. Adams's.

Wend you with the world to-night?
East and West, and South and North,
Form a constellation bright,
And pour a blended brilliance forth.
See the tide of fashion flowing,
'Tis the noon of beauty's reign;
Webster, Hamiltons are going,
Eastern Lloyd and Southern Hayne;
Western Thomas, gaily smiling;
Borland, nature's *protégé:*
Young De Wolfe, all hearts beguiling;
Morgan, Benton, Brown and Lee;
Belles and matrons, maids and madams,
All are gone to Mrs. Adams's.

Wend you with the world to-night?
Where blue eyes are brightly glancing,
While to measures of delight
Fairy feet are deftly dancing;
Where the young Euphrosyne
Reigns, the sovereign of the scene,
Chasing gloom and courting glee
With the merry tambourine.
Many a form of fairy bright,
Many a Hebe yet unwon;
Wirt, a gem of purest worth,
Lively laughing Pleasanton,
Vails and Taylor will be there;
Gay Monroe, so *débonnaire,*
Helen, pleasure's harbinger
Ramsay, Cottringers, and Kerr;

Belles and matrons, maids and madams,
All are gone to Mrs. Adams's.

Wend you with the world to-night?
Juno in her court presides,
Mirth and melody invite,
Fashion points and pleasure guides!
Haste away then, seize the hour,
Shun the thorn and pluck the flower.
Youth, in all its spring-time blooming,
Age, the guise of youth assuming,
Wit, through all its circle gleaming,
Glittering wealth, and beauty beaming;
Belles and matrons, maids and madams,
All are gone to Mrs. Adams's.

George Watterson
October 23, 1783 – February 4, 1854

George Watterson was born aboard a ship in New York harbor and moved to Washington with his family at age eight. He studied law and practiced briefly in Hagerstown, Maryland, before turning to journalism. Watterston edited four newspapers until appointed the third librarian of Congress by President Thomas Jefferson, serving in that position from 1815 to 1829. After the burning of the U.S. Capitol in the War of 1812, the Library of Congress was reconstituted with the purchase of more than six thousand volumes from Jefferson; Watterston received the books and catalogued them, as well as adding additional books and maps to the collection. The Library of Congress credits his tenure as planting "seeds for the expansion of the Library into a national institution."

Watterston is the author of four novels: *The Lawyer, or Man As He Ought Not to Be* (1808), *Glencarn, or the Disappointments of Youth* (1810), *The L—Family in Washington* (1822), and *Wanderer in Washington* (1827). Two of his novels are set in DC, making Watterston one of the first authors to use the city as a setting.

Watterston also wrote poems: one titled "The Wanderer in Jamaica"

(1810) was dedicated to Dolley Madison and may have influenced James Madison's decision to name him to his Library of Congress post; another is titled "Scenes of Youth" (1813). He also wrote a play, *The Child of Feeling* (1809), and several nonfiction books, including *A Memoir on the History, Culture, Manufactures, Uses, &c. of the Tobacco Plant* (1817), *Letters from Washington on the Constitution and Laws* (1818), *A Course of Study, Preparatory to the Bar or the Senate* (1823), and *Gallery of American Portraits* (1836).

On the unimpressive appearance of the early city, Watterston wrote that "citizens build houses where there are no streets, and the corporation, (which is said to be as poor as a church mouse,) makes streets where there are no houses: and so, by figuring to yourself a parcel of streets without houses, and houses without streets, you will have a pretty correct picture of the Metropolis of the United States."

Watterston was active in the city's civic affairs. He participated in the failed defense of Washington during the War of 1812, joining a local militia that fought British troops outside Bladensburg, Maryland. He served as secretary of the Washington National Monument Society from its creation in the 1830s until his death. He was also a longtime secretary of the Washington Botanical Society and wrote two early guidebooks on the capital city. His house, located at 224 Second Street SE, is now the headquarters of the National Indian Gaming Association and is listed on the National Register of Historic Places. Watterston is buried in Congressional Cemetery.

My Native Home

When storms howl around me and dark tempests roll,
And Nature seems mov'd and convulsed to each pole—
When billows o'er billows tempestuously foam,
How dear is the thought of my lov'd native home.

The Laplander's breast, cold and dreary as night,
Beats wildly with transport, and throbs with delight,
When mem'ry, sad mem'ry, once chances to roam,
And recalls the past joys of his lov'd native home.

The soldier who combats at tyranny's call,
In far distant climes, where grim terrors appall,

At the last beat of life, when he ceases to roam,
While dying, remembers his dear native home.

Grim slav'ry's poor victim, long destin'd to mourn
O'er the ruins of peace that will never return,
Views with heart-bursting grief, old Ocean's white foam,
And dies as he thinks of his lov'd native home.

Misfortune's sad child, while he wanders afar,
Still guided by Destiny's mysterious star,
Heaves a sigh, while visions of intellect roam,
And paint on his mem'ry the sweets of his home.

When sorrows the cheek of remembrance bedew,
And disease, death, and misery glare dreadful to view,
How grateful, when far from our country we roam,
Are the long cherish'd thoughts of our lov'd native home.

Who wanders o'er far distant realms to enjoy
Life baubles of pleasure and wealth's glitt'ring toy,
In his old age returns, no longer to roam,
From the long absent shades of his dear native home.

Would fortune permit me once more to return
To the cot of my youth, that is sadness I mourn,
Oh! nothing again shall induce me to roam
From the scenes, the lov'd scenes of my sweet native home.

Emma Willard

February 23, 1787–April 15, 1870

A passionate advocate for women's rights, Emma Hart Willard dedi-
cated her life to the education of girls and young women and is best
known for founding the Troy Female Seminary in Troy, New York,
America's first permanent school for young women. From 1830 to 1835,
Willard taught at Lydia English's Georgetown Female Seminary in DC,
which still stands at 1305–15 Thirtieth Street NW (now converted to
the Colonial Apartments). The building is marked by a historic plaque
that would likely have annoyed Willard: instead of listing the eminent

women who were teachers or students at the institution, it lists famous men who visited the school.

The publication of Willard's 1819 pamphlet *A Plan for Improving Female Education* was followed by an address to the New York State Legislature. She stated that "the taste of men . . . has been made into a standard for the formation of the female character" but that religion, not to mention pure reason, teaches women that "we too are primary existences . . . not the satellites of men."

Willard married a physician twenty-eight years her senior, with whom she had a son. She also raised four stepchildren. She was the author of numerous textbooks in geography, history, anatomy, and morals. She published a book of poems, *The Fulfillment of a Promise* (1831), which included her most popular poem, "Rocked in the Cradle of the Deep," which was set to music by Joseph Phillip Knight and included in several American hymnals.

Rocked in the Cradle of the Deep

Rocked in the cradle of the deep
I lay me down in peace to sleep;
Secure I rest upon the wave,
For Thou, O Lord, hast power to save.
I know Thou wilt not slight my call,
For Thou dost mark the sparrow's fall;
And calm and peaceful shall I sleep,
Rocked in the cradle of the deep.

When in the dead of night I lie
And gaze upon the trackless sky,
The star-bespangled heavenly scroll,
The boundless waters as they roll,—
I feel Thy wondrous power to save
From perils of the stormy wave:
Rocked in the cradle of the deep
I calmly rest and soundly sleep.

And such the trust that still were mine,
Though stormy winds swept o'er the brine,
Or though the tempest's fiery breath

Roused me from sleep to wreck and death.
In ocean cave still safe with Thee
The gem of immortality!
And calm and peaceful shall I sleep
Rocked in the cradle of the deep.

To a Young Lady

About to leave me, to take charge of a female academy

And dost thou leave me, Julia, and thy course
Wend far away? Go, in the name of God.
Prosper, and prove a pillar in the cause
Of woman. Lend thy aid to waken her
From the long trance of ages. Make her feel
She too hath God's own image, and the fount
Of the mind's grand and beautiful, is hers.
She, too, should learn her Maker's works and will;
Her first, best homage and obedience, *His*.
For this I would that thou should leave me, Julia.
Yet the mist gathers in mine eye, and through
My heart there comes the pang of love bereaved.
I shall not see thee more! thy pleasing smile
Will beam, but not for me; thy fond, long glance
Of sympathy will soothe, but soothe not me.
Perchance thy griefs may be unsoothed too,
Yet I would comfort, not discourage thee.
Trust God and pray to him, and I will pray;
And He, remembering all his promises,
Will hear the Widow, and the Orphan bless.

Lafayette's Welcome

And art thou, then, dear Hero, come?
    And do our eyes behold the man
Who nerved his arm and bared his breast
    For us, ere yet our life began?
For us and for our native land,
    Thy youthful valor dared the war;
And now, in winter of thine age,

Thou'st come, and left thy loved ones far.
    Then deep and dear thy welcome be,
    Nor think thy daughters far from thee,
    Columbia's daughters, lo! we bend,
    And claim to call thee Father, Friend!

But was't our country's rights alone,
    Impelled Fayette to Freedom's van?
No! t'was the love of human kind—
    It was the sacred cause of man—
It was benevolence sublime,
    Like that which sways the Eternal mind!
And, benefactor of the world,
    He shed his blood for all mankind.
      Then, deep and dear thy welcome be,
      Nor think thy daughters far from thee.
      Daughters of human kind we bend,
      And claim to call thee, Father, Friend!

❖ PART II ❖

The Rift of the Civil War

John Pierpont

April 6, 1785 – August 27, 1866

John Pierpont lived in Washington, DC, from 1861 until his death in 1866, working as a clerk in the U.S. Treasury Department. Prior to that, he was a minister, leading congregations in Boston and Medford, Massachusetts, and Troy, New York. He was also a well-regarded educator, helping to establish the English Classical School in Boston. In addition, he was involved in politics, running unsuccessfully for the office of governor of Massachusetts and for the U.S. House of Representatives. But he is best remembered as an activist, giving national voice to the temperance and abolitionist movements.

Pierpont is the author of two books of poems, *Airs of Palestine* (1816) and *Anti-Slavery Poems* (1843), and coauthor of the best-known temperance play in the nation, *The Drunkard; or, the Fallen Saved* (1844). His nonfiction includes *Phrenology and the Scriptures* (1850) and several published sermons, such as *The Burning of the Ephesian Letters* (1833), *Moral Rule of Political Action* (1939), and *National Humiliation* (1840). He regularly published nonfiction and poetry in national and regional newspapers.

"A Word from a Petitioner" was written in response to the Gag Rule, which banned debates on the abolition of slavery from the House of Representatives between 1836 and 1844, after the House was inundated by petitions sponsored by the American Anti-Slavery Society signed by more than two million American citizens. The second poem here, "Oft, in the Chilly Night," is notable as a persona poem written from the point of view of an enslaved person.

A Word from a Petitioner

What! our petitions spurned! The prayer
    Of thousands, — tens of thousands, — cast
Unheard, beneath your Speaker's chair!

But ye *will* hear us, first or last.
The thousands that, last year, ye scorned,
Are millions now. Be warned! Be warned!

Turn not, contemptuous, on your heel;—
        It is not for an act of grace
That, suppliants, at your feet we kneel,—
        We stand;—we look you in the face,
And say,—and we have weighed the word,—
That our petitions SHALL be heard.

There are two powers above the laws
        Ye make or mar:—they're our allies.
Beneath their shield we'll urge our cause,
        Though *all* your hands against us rise.
We're proved them, and we know their might;
The CONSTITUTION and the RIGHT.

We say not, ye shall snap the links
        That bind you to your dreadful slaves;
Hug, if ye will, a corpse that stinks,
        And toil on with it to your graves!
But, that ye *may* go, coupled thus,
Ye never shall make slaves of *us*.

And what, but more than slaves, are they,
        Who're told they ne'er shall be denied
The right of prayer; yet, when they pray,
        Their prayers, *unheard*, are thrown aside?
Such mockery *they* will tamely bear,
Who're fit an iron chain to wear.

***

Nay, start not from your chairs, in dread
        Of cannon-shot, or bursting shell!
These shall not fall upon your head,
        As once upon your house they fell.
We have a weapon, firmer set,
And better than the bayonet;—

A weapon that comes down as still
    As snow-flakes fall upon the sod;
But executes a freeman's will
    As lightning does the will of God;
And from its force, nor doors nor locks
Can shield you; — 't is the ballot-box.

Oft, in the Chilly Night

Oft, in the chilly night,
    Ere slumber's chain has bound me,
When all her silvery light
    The moon is pouring round me,
        Beneath her ray,
        I kneel and pray,
    That God would give some token,
        That Slavery's chains,
        On southern plains,
    Shall all, ere long, be broken.
Yes, in the chilly night,
    Though Slavery's chain has bound me,
Kneel I, and feel the might
    Of God's right arm around me.

When, at the driver's call,
    In cold or sultry weather,
We slaves, both great and small,
    Turn out to toil together,
        I feel like one,
        From whom the sun
    Of hope has long departed,
        And morning's light,
        And weary night
    Still find me broken-hearted.
Thus when the chilly breath
    Of night is sighing round me,
Kneel I, and wish that Death,
    In his cold chain, had bound me.

B. B. French

September 4, 1800–August 12, 1870

Benjamin Brown French wrote historical sketches and poems, published mostly in Masonic journals. French came to DC from New Hampshire in 1833. He was clerk of the U.S. House of Representatives and commissioner of public buildings under Presidents Franklin Pierce, Abraham Lincoln, and Andrew Johnson. Serving in the latter position, he oversaw the expansion of the U.S. Capitol and the completion of the Washington Monument, among other accomplishments. His journals are in the collections of the Library of Congress, and the Masonic lodge in the Georgetown neighborhood of DC is named for him. He is buried in Congressional Cemetery.

French is the author of *Fitz Clarence: A Poem* (1844), *Changes of Earth: A Poem* (1845), and the chapbook *A Letter and Short Poem on the Death of Abraham Lincoln* (1870). His diaries were later collected and published as *Witness to the Young Republic: A Yankee's Journal, 1828–1870*. He is best known for his associations with President Abraham Lincoln: he was present at the Gettysburg Address and in the room of the Peterson House as Lincoln lay dying, and was placed in charge of Lincoln's funeral arrangements.

Historian Margaret Leech described him in *Reveille in Washington* as "a stout, choleric old gentleman. With his arrogant mouth and his bristling gray side whiskers, brushed to the front, he resembled a cartoon of a Victorian papa."

A Short Poem on the Death of Abraham Lincoln

A jewel from our crown—
A pearl from out the Nation's diadem—
A life torn out by traitorous, murderous hands—
    Crushed—trampled down!

A people's hearts all riven
With grief—with horror—that their Chief is dead;
A nation plunged into the abyss of woe!
    A martyr gone to Heaven.

Great God! why was it done?
Thou knowest why—Thou dids't the deed permit:
And while we weep, we bow to Thy decree;
 And kneel before Thy throne—

 Humbly we kneel, and pray—
Who hold'st the power in our great Martyr's stead,
May wield it to Thy glory and our good
 For many a happy day.

 May ages still pass on,
And in one Union bind the land we love,
May blessings mark the years with happiness,
 And joy the Union crown.

From Fitz Clarence: A Poem

LVII.
The sea-breeze freshened with the rising day:
The gallant vessel on her course did keep,
Cleaving the ocean—from her prow away
In foaming whiteness did the waters leap,
While sternward whirled her pathway o'er the deep.
Ere long thy capes, Virginia, met the eye—
Soon they were passed—and, ere the hour of sleep,
While the sun's rays still tinged the western sky,
Within thy bay, broad Chesapeake, her keel did lie.

LXVI.
It was the bright and beauteous month of May,
And gaily clad Potomac's banks were seen;
The snowy dogwood spread its white array
Of blooming beauty—mid the living green
The chaste magnolia, Nature's vernal queen,
Reared its pure flower—the honeysuckle wild
Lent its bright bloom to animate the scene—
The azure violet, Flora's loveliest child,
Humble, yet fair, amid creation's glories smiled.

Albert Pike
December 29, 1809–April 2, 1891

Albert Pike was a journalist, newspaper owner, lawyer, and soldier, serving in the Mexican-American War, the Indian Wars, and in the Civil War on the Confederate side. He was allegedly a leader in the Ku Klux Klan in Arkansas and also extremely active in the Masons, attaining the rank of "Sovereign Grand Commander for the Southern Jurisdiction of the United States," and writing *Morals and Dogma of the Ancient and Accepted Scottish Rite of Freemasonry* (1871). In addition, Pike published books on Indian religions and Sanskrit, legal history, and two books of poems, *Prose Sketches and Poems Written in the Western Country* (1834) and *Hymns to the Gods and Other Poems* (1872). His poems were highly regarded in his day.

Pike falsely claimed to have attended Harvard but was instead largely self-taught; Harvard did grant him an honorary degree in 1859. He also claimed to be fluent in five languages; the truth of this claim has sometimes been questioned by modern scholars. Pike practiced law in Arkansas prior to the Civil War. He was commissioned a brigadier general in the Confederate army, and in March 1862, his brigade was defeated in the Battle of Pea Ridge, and he was forced to resign after his men were found to be scalping the bodies of the Union dead. Fellow officers later accused him of misappropriating funds, and he was briefly incarcerated, but President Andrew Johnson granted him a full pardon in 1866.

Pike separated from his wife (but did not divorce her or provide for her support, effectively abandoning her in Arkansas). He moved to DC in 1868 and remained until his death in 1891. An obituary in the *Washington Evening Star* noted his striking appearance: "He was a man of gigantic frame, with a large head of the antique mold; his face was as soft as an infant's and just as rosy, and his long, flowing beard and silken white locks, which fell gracefully over his shoulders, were much admired. His eyes were as clear and as strong as a tiger's."

He is remembered locally with a permanent exhibit at the Scottish Rite Temple at 1733 Sixteenth Street NW, where he is entombed. In October 1901, a statue of Pike was erected in Judiciary Square, making him the only Confederate military officer to be so honored in DC.

The twenty-seven-foot-tall monument of bronze and marble was paid for by the Masons and now stands on National Park Service land. In October 2017, DC's nonvoting delegate to the U.S. Congress, Eleanor Holmes Norton, filed legislation seeking congressional approval for the statue's removal.

Dixie

Southrons, hear your country call you!
Up, lest worse than death befall you!
To arms! To arms! To arms, in Dixie!
Lo! all the beacon-fires are lighted,—
Let all hearts be now united!
    To arms! To arms! To arms, in Dixie!
      Advance the flag of Dixie!
      Hurrah! hurrah!
For Dixie's land we take our stand,
    And live or die for Dixie!
      To arms! To arms!
    And conquer peace for Dixie!
      To arms! To arms!
    And conquer peace for Dixie!

Hear the Northern thunders mutter!
Northern flags in South winds flutter!
Send them back your fierce defiance!
Stamp upon the accursed alliance!

Fear no danger! Shun no labor!
Lift up rifle, pike, and sabre!
Shoulder pressing close to shoulder,
Let the odds make each heart bolder!

How the South's great heart rejoices
At your cannons' ringing voices!
For faith betrayed, and pledges broken,
Wrongs inflicted, insults spoken.

Strong as lions, swift as eagles,
Back to their kennels hunt these beagles!

Cut the unequal bonds asunder!
Let them hence each other plunder!

Swear upon your country's altar
Never to submit or falter,
Till the spoilers are defeated,
Till the Lord's work is completed.

Halt not till our Federation
Secures among earth's powers its station!
Then at peace, and crowned with glory,
Hear your children tell the story!

If the loved ones weep in sadness,
Victory soon shall bring them gladness, —
    To arms!
Exultant pride soon banish sorrow,
Smiles chase tears away to-morrow.
    To arms! To arms! To arms, in Dixie!
        Advance the flag of Dixie!
        Hurrah! hurrah!
For Dixie's land we take our stand,
And live or die for Dixie!
    To arms! To arms!
And conquer peace for Dixie!
    To arms! To arms!
And conquer peace for Dixie!

The Magnolia

What, what is the true Southern Symbol,
The Symbol of Honor and Right,
The Emblem that suits a brave people
In arms against number and might? —
'Tis the ever green stately Magnolia,
Its pearl-flowers pure as the Truth,
Defiant of tempest and lightning,
Its life a perpetual youth.

French blood stained with glory the Lilies,
While centuries marched to their grave;
And over bold Scot and gay Irish
The Thistle and Shamrock yet wave:
Ours, ours be the noble Magnolia,
That only on Southern soil grows
The Symbol of life everlasting;—
Dear to us as to England the Rose.

Paint the flower on a field blue as Heaven,
Let the broad leaves around it be seen,
'Semper Virens' the eloquent motto,
Our colors the Blue, White and Green.
Type of Chivalry, loyalty, virtue,
In Winter and Summer the same,
Full of leaf, full of flower, full of vigor—
It befits those who fight for a name.

For a name among Earth's ancient Nations,
Yet more for the Truth and the Right,
For Freedom, for proud Independence,
The old strife of Darkness and Light.
Round the World bear the flag of our glory,
While the nations look on and admire,
And our struggle, immortal in story,
Shall the free of all ages inspire.

What though many fall in the conflict,
And our blood redden many a field?
The foe's on our soil, fellow-soldiers!
And God is our strength and our shield.
Through the fire and the smoke bear our banner
Ever on, while a fragment remains!
What though we are few and they many?
THE LORD GOD OF ARMIES STILL REIGNS.

Margaret Lucy Shands Bailey

November 12, 1812–1888

Margaret Bailey was an influential white abolitionist. Born in Virginia, she married Gamaliel Bailey in 1833 and moved to DC in 1847. Her husband published the popular and successful abolitionist newspaper the *National Era*, while Margaret Bailey founded the antislavery juvenile magazine the *Youth's Monthly Visitor* (which she published from 1844 through 1852). Bailey also volunteered as a literacy teacher to soldiers of African descent at Camp Birney near Baltimore. She published poems regularly in a range of journals and wrote a popular song, "The Blind Slave Boy," published in 1844. Bailey was the mother of twelve children, half of whom died as infants. After her husband's death in 1859, she briefly took over publication of the *National Era* through 1860.

Bailey's large Washington home (now razed) became a center for the region's white antislavery activists. She hired a string of young women to live with her family and work as governesses to her children. She and her husband mentored several of them, publishing their early poems and nonfiction, and many later became professional writers. She also ran a Saturday-evening salon, frequented by local and visiting writers and Free Soil abolitionists. These events often helped locals make contacts with northerners who helped to finance slave escapes and pay legal fees.

After an unsuccessful mass slave escape from DC aboard the schooner *Pearl* in 1848, her family was targeted, and she had to briefly flee her home with her large family to avoid mob violence. Although she and her husband repeatedly stated that they were committed only to peaceful and legal methods to end slavery, such as moral suasion and political action, the couple was also active in the Underground Railroad, harboring fugitive slaves in their home. Margaret Bailey also gave financial support to create and maintain schools in DC for students of color.

After 1861, Margaret Bailey lived in Baltimore. But she is buried in DC, in Oak Hill Cemetery.

Grace Greenwood wrote of Bailey in the *Cosmopolitan* in 1890, that she "was a woman of rare loveliness and nobility of character. Gentle in all her ways, sunny and sympathetic, she yet revealed herself, in times of trial, brave and determined, a fit companion for a hero; and in times of trial did not tarry." She continued: "Mrs. Bailey was a clever woman, who took in knowledge easily, almost unconsciously. Impulsive and enthusiastic, she had also much social tact, was a rapid but usually a just, reasoned, and a witty talker. Personally she was very prepossessing, with a face fresh and fair, and a frank, pleasant voice, charming Southern *insouciance,* and unvarying cheerfulness of manner. Dr. and Mrs. Bailey were very happy in their home, wherein at that time were six beautiful children, equally balanced, as were all things in that harmonious, old-fashioned marriage."

Endurance

When, upon wings of rainbow hues,
Hope flits across thy pathway here,
And gently as the morning breeze,
Her waving pinion dries thy tear,
Oh, yield not all thy soul to joy,
Let not her blandishments allure:
Life's greenest spot hath withered flowers—
Whate'er thy lot, thou must endure.

If, on the mountain's topmost cliff,
The flag of victory seems unfurled,
And Faith, exulting, sees afar
Earth's idol, Error, downward hurled,
Deem not the triumph thou shalt share—
God keeps his chosen vessels pure;
The final reckoning is on high;
On earth thy meed is to endure.

With chastened heart, in humble faith,
Thy labor earnestly pursue,
As one who fears to such frail deeds
No recompense is due.
Wax not faint-hearted; while thou toil'st,
Thy bread and water shall be sure;
Leaving all else to God, be thou
Patient in all things to endure.

William Slade

1815–March 16, 1868

William Slade was an usher and valet for the White House during the Lincoln administration, and White House steward for President Andrew Johnson. He is believed to have been freeborn to parents of mixed ancestry; he came to DC at some point prior to 1843, with his wife, Josephine. They would have seven children, all but the eldest born in Washington, and lived in a house on Massachusetts Avenue between Fourth and Sixth Streets (now razed). His earliest jobs in the city were as a messenger for the State Department and as a porter at the Metropolitan Hotel. Slade was an elder in the Fifteenth Street Presbyterian Church, an active member of the Contraband Relief Society and the Columbian Harmony Society (a mutual aid organization), and president of the Social, Civil, and Statistical Association, an organization that collected information about segregated private schools and the amount of real estate owned by people of African descent in DC, which was used to prove the ability of people of color to thrive once emancipated. A leader in the African American community, he championed emancipation and suffrage.

This poem, written from the point of view of an enslaved person, was published in the *Anglo-African* newspaper in September 1863 and is Slade's only known poem.

In *They Knew Lincoln* by John E. Washington (1942), Slade is described as "of medium height, olive in complexion, with light eyes and straight chestnut-brown hair and wore a little goatee. He had a wonderful disposition, never became excited, always could see the bright side of things, even when Lincoln was downcast and needed a cheering, hopeful friend. Slade was a great story teller. He was known for his collection of jokes and wisecracks, and I have often heard it said that 'he had some that could make a horse laugh.' Not only did Slade serve as confidential messenger for the Lincoln family, but he also acted as valet for the President, took complete charge of the colored help, made arrangements for all public and private functions (from the standpoint of food and serving), kept a set of keys of the White House and knew every diplomat, general, and statesman." Washington also reports that Slade washed and dressed Lincoln's body after his assassination.

The Slave to His Star
Bright star, of all stars beloved,
To thee I turned from dreams erewhile;
Far up in God's free heaven unmoved,
I saw by night thy ceaseless smile,
Lighting a path of hope afar,
Freedom's high watchfire for the free—
Steadfast and solitary star,
I felt that fire was lit for me!

I gaze upon thy Northern light,
That never fails, and falters never,
But hang far over day and night,
From Heaven's wall shine down forever;
I seem to hear a voice of God
Speak through the silence down to me,
"Thy feet are strong, thy way is broad,
The star shall be my path for thee."

Hiding in darkling caves by day,
With toiling footsteps through the night,
To me came down thy guardian ray,
A burning lamp, a shining light!
The Red Sea of my pilgrim road,
Whose parted waves hung threateningly,
I traversed while that beacon glowed,
And freedom's fettered slave is free.

Star of the slave, crown of the free,
The eternal midnight's dearest gem,
My race from midnight look to thee,
As Bethlehem's star art thou to them.
Forever dear their light above,
Their path below through wood and wave,
Their evening star of trust and love,
Thou pilot of the pathless slave!

Arthur Bowen

1816?–?

Arthur Bowen was an enslaved person raised in Washington, DC, in the household of William Thornton, the architect of the Capitol, and his wife, Anna Maria Thornton. A young man of considerable intelligence, he took full advantage of his urban setting, learning how to read and write (probably at a church Sunday school), and befriending free men of color, who made up a greater proportion of DC's population than did slaves by 1830. Bowen attended public lectures and joined the Philomathean Talking Society, where national affairs and civil rights were discussed and debated by men of color.

It was after a meeting of this society, and after a few postmeeting drinks with friends, in August 1835, when Bowen first came to prominence as the person who precipitated the "Snow Storm," DC's first race riot. Bowen was then nineteen years old. Returning home late to the widow Thornton's row house on F Street (later numbered 1331 F Street NW, now the site of an office tower), Bowen entered, tripped over an ax in the front hall, and headed to Thornton's bedroom to report in. When Thornton saw her intoxicated slave, ax in hand, she called out to her neighbors for help.

Axes were common household items at this time, as all homes were heated by wood. Thornton would later swear that Bowen never raised it, and he claimed he only picked it up in order to find a better place for it. Nevertheless, realizing he was being accused of something very serious, he fled.

When Bowen returned home after three days, he was arrested and imprisoned in the city jail (located in today's Judiciary Square). The *National Intelligencer* reported on August 7, 1835, of "a circumstance of shocking character," stating that "an attempt was made on the life of Mrs. Thornton" by her slave who was "evidently induced by reading the inflammatory publications" of the abolitionist press. These reports were widely read and discussed, heightening racial tensions in the city.

A crowd of white laborers (or, as they were known at the time, "mechanics") gathered, threatening to lynch Bowen for his alleged nighttime attack. Prevented from breaching the jail, the mechanics turned their wrath instead on Beverly Snow, a free man of mixed race who owned the Epicurean Eating House. Located on the corner of Sixth

Street and Pennsylvania Avenue, the restaurant catered to the city's upper-class white population, serving such delicacies as green turtle soup and braised sheep's heads. Snow escaped unharmed into Maryland, but his business was left in ruins. He would later move to Canada.

The mob next attacked the Union Seminary, one of the earliest schools in DC for students of African descent. They destroyed all the books and furniture and tore down part of the building. The mob also burned or destroyed several private homes, a church, another school, and a whorehouse, all owned by African Americans.

Francis Scott Key, serving as DC's district attorney, belatedly called in a detachment of marines from the Navy Yard to contain the mob. After a few days, the violence finally subsided.

Bowen was brought to trial, condemned, and given the death sentence; he was scheduled to hang in February 1836. Thornton, regretting her earlier desire to punish her slave, drew up a petition for a presidential pardon and obtained thirty-four signatures of other prominent white citizens. In response to her pleading, seventeen-page letter to President Andrew Jackson, Bowen's execution was postponed. A second appeal by Thornton that summer led to Bowen's full pardon. As part of the settlement, Thornton agreed to sell Bowen to someone outside the city. He was sold for $750. Nothing more is known of Bowen's life.

Almost everything we know about Bowen comes from white people: news reporters, court records, his mistress's correspondence. This poignant poem, written from prison, is the only known written record from his own hand. In it, Bowen shows remorse and tries to sway public opinion with his poetic abilities. The poem was published in the *National Intelligencer* on February 19, 1836.

Farewell

Farewell, farewell, my young friends dear;
Oh, View my dreadful state,
Each flying moment brings me near
Unto my awful fate.

Brought up I was by parents nice,
Whose commands I would not obey,
But plunged ahead foremost into vice,
And into temptation's dreadful way.

Nothing did I ever drink
But liquor very strong
Lo I never used to think
That I was doing wrong.

To me was read the awful sentence
Oh dreadful in my ears it rang
They gave me time for my repentance
And then I must be hanged.

Good bye, good bye, my friends so dear,
May God Almighty please you all,
Do, if you please, but shed a tear
At Arthur Bowen's unhappy fall.

Frederick Douglass

February 1818? – February 20, 1895

A social reformer and leader of the abolitionist movement, Frederick Douglass was born enslaved and became a renowned orator and author. He wrote three notable autobiographies: *Narrative of the Life of Frederick Douglass, an American Slave* (1845), *My Bondage and My Freedom* (1855), and *The Life and Times of Frederick Douglass* (1881, revised 1892). He edited abolitionist newspapers, including the *North Star* and *New National Era*. He served in several government posts: as U.S. marshal, DC recorder of deeds, and consul-general to the Republic of Haiti.

His best-known poem, "A Parody," follows the form of a Christian hymn and was included at the end of *Narrative of the Life of Frederick Douglass*. The second poem, a more private meditation on loss and friendship, comes from the Douglass Papers in the collections of the Library of Congress. It references Cedar Hill, his former home, now a museum operated by the National Park Service.

Three of Douglass's DC houses still stand: Cedar Hill, at 1411 W Street SE in Anacostia; his Capital Hill home at 320 A Street NE; and the home he built and later gave to his son at 2002 Seventeenth Street NW. A bridge named in his honor was built in 1959; it takes South Capitol Street across the Anacostia River. A statue of Douglass was included in National Statuary Hall in the U.S. Capitol in 2013, representing the District of Columbia; and the University of Maryland in College Park dedicated a plaza and statue to Douglass in 2015 in front of Hornbake Library. In 2017, the U.S. Mint began issuing special-issue quarters depicting George Washington on the front, and Douglass on the reverse, with Cedar Hill depicted in the background.

A Parody
"Come, saints and sinners, hear me tell
How pious priests whip Jack and Nell,
And women buy and children sell,
And preach all sinners down to hell,
And sing of heavenly union.

"They'll bleat and baa, dona like goats,
Gorge down black sheep, and strain at motes,
Array their backs in fine black coats,
Then seize their negroes by their throats,
And choke, for heavenly union.

"They'll church you if you sip a dram,
And damn you if you steal a lamb;
Yet rob old Tony, Doll, and Sam,
Of human rights, and bread and ham;
Kidnapper's heavenly union.

"They'll loudly talk of Christ's reward,
And bind his image with a cord,
And scold, and swing the lash abhorred,
And sell their brother in the Lord
To handcuffed heavenly union.

"They'll read and sing a sacred song,
And make a prayer both loud and long,
And teach the right and do the wrong,
Hailing the brother, sister throng,
With words of heavenly union.

"We wonder how such saints can sing,
Or praise the Lord upon the wing,

Who roar, and scold, and whip, and sting,
And to their slaves and mammon cling,
In guilty conscience union.

"They'll raise tobacco, corn, and rye,
And drive, and thieve, and cheat, and lie,
And lay up treasures in the sky,
By making switch and cowskin fly,
In hope of heavenly union.

"They'll crack old Tony on the skull,
And preach and roar like Bashan bull,
Or braying ass, of mischief full,
Then seize old Jacob by the wool,
And pull for heavenly union.

"A roaring, ranting, sleek man-thief,
Who lived on mutton, veal, and beef,
Yet never would afford relief
To needy, sable sons of grief,
Was big with heavenly union.

"'Love not the world,' the preacher said,
And winked his eye, and shook his head;
He seized on Tom, and Dick, and Ned,
Cut short their meat, and clothes, and bread,
Yet still loved heavenly union.

"Another preacher whining spoke
Of One whose heart for sinners broke:
He tied old Nanny to an oak,
And drew the blood at every stroke,
And prayed for heavenly union.

"Two others oped their iron jaws,
And waved their children-stealing paws;
There sat their children in gewgaws;
By stinting negroes' backs and maws,
They kept up heavenly union.

"All good from Jack another takes,
And entertains their flirts and rakes,
Who dress as sleek as glossy snakes,
And cram their mouths with sweetened cakes;
And this goes down for union."

After the Departure of a Friend

There's gloom within my study dear.
The rosy light shines there no longer.
The green magnolia drops a tear,
The cedars sadly look, and somber.

The grass upon my wintry lawn
That joyed to feel thy lightsome tread,
The evening sky and morning dawn
Seem mournful since my hope has fled.

Fido takes illy, now, the blow
And whines to see thy gracious face,
And sable Aleck to and fro
Searches my secret woe to trace.

That something vast has touched me deep,
A thousand veils would fail to blind.
Yet its full measure, scope and sweep,
A thousand eyes would fail to find.

My spirit drops her cheerful mood
Since thy bright radiance passed away.
Though reason calls this evil good
Still feeling claims her wonted sway.

I'll not essay to settle now
Feeling's and Reason's doubled point;
Relating but the things that show
My own condition out of joint.

For Cedar Hill has lost a gem,
Brighter than morn or evening star,

More precious than the diadem
Of England's Queen or Russia's Czar.

Yet still, my muse another chord
Shall vibrate to a happier tone;
Warmly express a grateful word
For blessings here, and blessings flown.

Why should I sing disconsolate?
Battle decrees of luck and chance?
A wise man ever bows to fate,
And spares his breast her deadly lance.

And lingers not thy spirit still
Near volumes that thy hand has blest?
And is it not on Cedar Hill
Thy spirit finds its sweetest rest?

Come freely then, spirit of love
Defy the bars of space and time,
O'er these fair hills divinely rove,
Breathe them with joy and grace sublime.

No eye shall see thy form but mine,
Thy step be music but to me;
And my glad heart respond to thine,
In all a friend can do or be.

The high road by the river side,
The peaceful wood along the way,
Will oft recall the pleasant ride
We took, that warm December day.

Kate seemed to feel the dreamy state,
The light and shade that filled the air;
And calmly checked her wonted gait,
To share the bliss that lingered there.

Queen Mary sounds more soft and sweet,
Since thou wert pleased to call it fine;

My happiness would be complete
Were such approval always mine.

But never from those strings can wake
The mournful music of that song,
Without a piercing pain and ache,
Which comes to love from cruel wrong.

If what offends within them dwell,
Pray leave it to kind powers above,
See in them the sincere farewell
Of one who knows the soul of love.

Walt Whitman

May 31, 1819 – March 26, 1892

Walt Whitman lived in DC for a decade, from 1863 to 1873. He is the author of the masterpiece *Leaves of Grass,* a volume of poems he reedited and republished several times between 1855 and 1891, as well as *Drum-Taps* (1865), *Memoranda during the War* (1875), and *Specimen Days* (1882). None of his boardinghouse residences in DC still stand, but a bust of him graces the front desk of the Manuscript Reading Room at the Library of Congress, and his words are included in several public art projects: at two Metro stations (Dupont Circle and Archives/Navy Memorial), at Washington Reagan National Airport, and in the paving stones at Freedom Plaza. In addition, a two-block stretch of F Street NW in front of the Smithsonian National Portrait Gallery has been given the honorary name of Walt Whitman Way.

In December 1862, Walt Whitman read an account in the *New York Tribune* of the Fifty-First New York Regiment's casualties at Fredericksburg. Whitman's younger brother George Whitman's name was listed in the newspaper, but there were no details of the nature or severity of his injuries (and his name was even misspelled).

Whitman immediately took the train south to investigate. He was robbed in Philadelphia and arrived in Washington penniless. He was lucky to run into two friends from Boston who loaned him money, Charles Eldridge and William Douglas O'Connor. After wandering around hospitals for two days seeking news of George and fruitlessly seeking an audience with Moses Fowler Odell, his congressional representative from New York, Whitman decided to hitch a ride to the front lines in Virginia on a military transport. He found George, who had indeed been wounded in battle but not badly. (George wrote, "We have had another battle and I have come out safe and sound, although I had the side of my jaw slightly scraped with a peice [sic] of shell which burst at my feet.") Whitman shared George's tent on the front line for nine days, helping the medics and making himself as useful as possible. On December 28 he returned to the capital—and proceeded to stay on in Washington for a decade.

He found that there was a true need for his services. His initial plan, to stay in DC for a week or two, would have allowed him time to visit all the wounded Brooklyn soldiers from his brother's regiment who were now in Washington hospitals. But those soldiers introduced him to others, and Whitman could not nurse one man and refuse care to another. Whitman's voluntary work as a nurse and his close association with sick and dying soldiers gave him a deeper connection to life and a fuller understanding of human nature. As he wrote in his journal, he had "an instinct & faculty" for easing the suffering of these young men.

Two months after arriving, he wrote in a letter to his brother Jeff about why he stayed: "I cannot give up my hospitals yet. I never before had my feelings so thoroughly and (so far) permanently absorbed, to the very roots, as by these huge swarms of dear, wounded, sick, dying boys—I get very much attached to some of them, and many of them have come to depend on seeing me, and having me sit by them a few minutes, as if for their lives."

Whitman suffered his own physical decline during his Washington years. Increasingly tired and full of aches, he sought advice from a doctor at Armory Square Hospital, who recommended that he give up nursing. (We now know he had tuberculosis and lung abscesses—including a large one that was eroding his fifth rib on his right side.) He did go to Brooklyn for six convalescent months, but he returned to DC to renew his commitment to his dear soldiers. ("It is impossible for me to abstain from going to see and minister to certain cases, and that draws me into others, and so on.") He often stayed up overnight to attend dying men with whom he had forged emotional links, and his symptoms immediately returned. After a paralyzing stroke, he left DC for Camden, New Jersey, where he moved in with his brother George and his family.

Long after the end of Civil War—indeed for the rest of his life—Whitman continued to write and publish poetry and prose on the war's impact on American identity. Whitman even claimed that *Leaves of Grass* could not have been written without his wartime experiences (despite the fact that three earlier editions had been published prior to his moving to Washington). For him, the Civil War and how the nation reacted to it were more revealing, and more ennobling, than any other time. Of the years he spent in DC, Whitman concluded that "I consider [them] the greatest privilege and satisfaction, (with all their feverish excitements and physical deprivations and lamentable sights,) and, of course, the most profound lesson of my life."

By Broad Potomac's Shore
By broad Potomac's shore, again old tongue,
(Still uttering, still ejaculating, canst never cease this babble?)
Again old heart so gay, again to you, your sense, the full flush spring returning,
Again the freshness and the odors, again Virginia's summer sky, pellucid blue and silver,
Again the forenoon purple of the hills,
Again the deathless grass, so noiseless soft and green,
Again the blood-red roses blooming.

Perfume this book of mine O blood-red roses!
Lave subtly with your waters every line Potomac!
Give me of you O spring, before I close, to put between its pages!
O forenoon purple of the hills, before I close, of you!
O deathless grass, of you!

Vigil Strange I Kept on the Field One Night
Vigil strange I kept on the field one night,
When you, my son and my comrade, dropt at my side that day,
One look I but gave, which your dear eyes return'd, with a look I shall never forget,

One touch of your hand to mine, O boy, reach'd up as you lay on the
    ground,
Then onward I sped in the battle, the even-contested battle,
Till late in the night reliev'd, to the place at last again I made my way,
Found you in death so cold, dear comrade—found your body, son of
    responding kisses, (never again on earth responding,)
Bared your face in the starlight—curious the scene—cool blew the
    moderate night-wind,
Long there and then in vigil I stood, dimly around me the battle-
    field spreading,
Vigil wondrous and vigil sweet, there in the fragrant silent night,
But not a tear fell, not even a long-drawn sigh—long, long I gazed,
Then on the earth partially reclining, sat by your side, leaning my
    chin in my hands,
Passing sweet hours, immortal and mystic hours with you, dearest
    comrade—not a tear, not a word,
Vigil of silence, love and death—vigil for you my son and my soldier,
As onward silently stars aloft, eastward new ones upward stole,
Vigil final for you, brave boy, (I could not save you, swift was your
    death,
I faithfully loved you and cared for you living—I think we shall
    surely meet again,)
Till at latest lingering of the night, indeed just as the dawn appear'd,
My comrade I wrapt in his blanket, envelop'd well his form,
Folded the blanket well, tucking it carefully over head, and carefully
    under feet,
And there and then, and bathed by the rising sun, my son in his
    grave, in his rude-dug grave I deposited,
Ending my vigil strange with that—vigil of night and battle-field
    dim,
Vigil for boy of responding kisses, (never again on earth
    responding,)
Vigil for comrade swiftly slain—vigil I never forget, how as day
    brighten'd,
I rose from the chill ground, and folded my soldier well in his
    blanket,
And buried him where he fell.

The Wound-Dresser

1

An old man bending I come among new faces,
Years looking backward resuming in answer to children,
Come tell us old man, as from young men and maidens that love me,
(Arous'd and angry, I'd thought to beat the alarum, and urge
    relentless war,
But soon my fingers fail'd me, my face droop'd and I resign'd myself,
To sit by the wounded and soothe them, or silently watch the dead;)
Years hence of these scenes, of these furious passions, these chances,
Of unsurpass'd heroes, (was one side so brave? the other was equally
    brave;)
Now be witness again, paint the mightiest armies of earth,
Of those armies so rapid so wondrous what saw you to tell us?
What stays with you latest and deepest? of curious panics,
Of hard-fought engagements or sieges tremendous what deepest
    remains?

2

O maidens and young men I love and that love me,
What you ask of my days those the strangest and sudden your
    talking recalls,
Soldier alert I arrive after a long march cover'd with sweat and dust,

In the nick of time I come, plunge in the fight, loudly shout in the
    rush of successful charge,
Enter the captur'd works—yet lo, like a swift running river they fade,
Pass and are gone they fade—I dwell not on soldiers' perils or
    soldiers' joys,
(Both I remember well—many of the hardships, few the joys, yet I
    was content.)

But in silence, in dreams' projections,
While the world of gain and appearance and mirth goes on,
So soon what is over forgotten, and waves wash the imprints off the
    sand,
With hinged knees returning I enter the doors, (while for you up there,
Whoever you are, follow without noise and be of strong heart.)

Bearing the bandages, water and sponge,
Straight and swift to my wounded I go,
Where they lie on the ground after the battle brought in,
Where their priceless blood reddens the grass, the ground,
Or to the rows of the hospital tent, or under the roof'd hospital,
To the long rows of cots up and down each side I return,
To each and all one after another I draw near, not one do I miss,
An attendant follows holding a tray, he carries a refuse pail,
Soon to be fill'd with clotted rags and blood, emptied, and fill'd again.

I onward go, I stop,
With hinged knees and steady hand to dress wounds,
I am firm with each, the pangs are sharp yet unavoidable,
One turns to me his appealing eyes—poor boy! I never knew you,
Yet I think I could not refuse this moment to die for you, if that
    would save you.

3
On, on I go, (open doors of time! open hospital doors!)
The crush'd head I dress, (poor crazed hand tear not the bandage
    away,)
The neck of the cavalry-man with the bullet through and through I
    examine,
Hard the breathing rattles, quite glazed already the eye, yet life
    struggles hard,
(Come sweet death! be persuaded O beautiful death!
In mercy come quickly.)

From the stump of the arm, the amputated hand,
I undo the clotted lint, remove the slough, wash off the matter and
    blood,
Back on his pillow the soldier bends with curv'd neck and side
    falling head,
His eyes are closed, his face is pale, he dares not look on the bloody
    stump,
And has not yet look'd on it.

I dress a wound in the side, deep, deep,
But a day or two more, for see the frame all wasted and sinking,
And the yellow-blue countenance see.

I dress the perforated shoulder, the foot with the bullet-wound,
Cleanse the one with a gnawing and putrid gangrene, so sickening, so offensive,
While the attendant stands behind aside me holding the tray and pail.

I am faithful, I do not give out,
The fractur'd thigh, the knee, the wound in the abdomen,
These and more I dress with impassive hand, (yet deep in my breast a fire, a burning flame.)

4
Thus in silence in dreams' projections,
Returning, resuming, I thread my way through the hospitals,
The hurt and wounded I pacify with soothing hand,
I sit by the restless all the dark night, some are so young,
Some suffer so much, I recall the experience sweet and sad,
(Many a soldier's loving arms about this neck have cross'd and rested,
Many a soldier's kiss dwells on these bearded lips.)

Sara Clarke Lippincott (Grace Greenwood)
September 23, 1823–April 20, 1904

A poet, writer of children's literature, and journalist, Sara Clarke Lippincott, who wrote under the name Grace Greenwood, was assistant editor for the most popular woman's magazine of her time, *Godey's Lady's Book*, and a correspondent for the *New York Times*. She is the author of *Greenwood Leaves: A Collection of Sketches and Letters* (1850); *Poems* (1851); *Recollections of My Childhood and Other Stories* (1852); *Haps and Mishaps of a Tour in Europe* (1853); *A Forest Tragedy and Other Tales* (1856); a children's book, *History of my Pets* (1851); several books of travel such as *Merrie England* (1855), *Bonnie Scotland* (1861), and *New Life in New Lands* (1872); and the biography *Queen Victoria, Her Girlhood and Womanhood* (1883).

Greenwood lived in DC from 1850 to 1852, working as a governess for Gamaliel and Margaret Bailey's children and writing stories for their abolitionist newspaper, the *National Era*. She returned after her marriage, living in the city once again from 1871 to 1878.

The *Washington Evening Star* quotes her in 1904, stating: "I had none of the struggle which usually accompanies an initiation into authorship. I was promptly—perhaps too promptly—recognized. I had at first some difficulty in getting pay for what I wrote, but there was never any trouble about getting it printed. My head was not turned by my success, however. My ideal was high, and I have never been able to reach it. . . . I wrote with infinite care, for, although I first dashed off whatever was in my mind, I revised and re-revised it, frequently sending a fifth copy to the publisher. Nothing ever left my hands that was not as good as I knew how to make it, and yet I always felt that it ought to have been better."

The Long Bridge, a wooden toll bridge spanning the Potomac River between DC and Arlington, Virginia, opened in 1809. Union troops occupied the bridge during the Civil War. It is now the site of the Fourteenth Street Bridge.

The Leap from the Long Bridge

An incident at Washington

A woman once made her escape from the slave-prison, which stands midway between the Capitol and the President's house, and ran for the Long Bridge, crossing the Potomac to the extensive rounds and woodlands of Arlington Place.

No rest for the wretched. The long day is past,
And night on yon prison descendeth at last.
Now lock up and bolt.—Ha, jailer! Look here!
Who flies like a wild bird escaped from the snare?
　　A woman,—a slave! Up! Out in pursuit,
　　　　While linger some gleams of the day!
　　Ho! Rally thy hunters, with halloo and shout,
　　　　To chase down the game,—and away!

A bold race for freedom!—On, fugitive, on!
Heaven help but the right, and thy freedom is won.
How eager she drinks the free air of the plains!
Every limb, every nerve, every fibre, she strains;
　　From Columbia's glorious Capitol

   Columbia's daughter flees
  To the sanctuary God hath given,
   The sheltering forest-trees.

Now she treads the Long Bridge,—joy lighteth her eye,—
Beyond her the dense wood and darkening sky;
Wild hopes thrill her breast as she neareth the shore,—
O despair!—there are *men* fast advancing before!
  Shame, shame on their manhood!—they hear, they heed,
   The cry her flight to stay,
  And, like demon forms, with their outstretched arms
   They wait to seize their prey!

She pauses, she turns,—ah! will she flee back?
Like wolves her pursuers howl loud on her track;
She lifteth to Heaven one look of despair,
Her anguish breaks forth in one hurried prayer.
  Hark, her jailer's yell!—like a bloodhound's bay
   On the low night-wind it sweeps!
  Now death, or the chain!—to the stream she turns,
   And she leaps, O God, she leaps!

The dark and the cold, yet merciful wave
Receives to its bosom the form of the slave.
She raises,—earth's scenes on her dim vision gleam,
But she struggleth not with the strong, rushing stream,
  And low are the death-cries her woman's heart gives
   As she floats adown the river;
  Faint and more faint grows her drowning voice,
   And her cries have ceased forever!

Now back, jailer, back to thy dungeons again,
To swing the red lash and rivet the chain!
The form thou wouldst fetter a valueless clod,
The soul thou wouldst barter returned to her God!
  She lifts in His light her unmanacled hands;
   She flees through the darkness no more;
  To freedom she leaped through drowning and death,
   And her sorrow and bondage are o'er.

George Boyer Vashon

July 25, 1824–October 5, 1878

George Boyer Vashon was born free in Carlisle, Pennsylvania, and earned a BA from Oberlin College in 1844, becoming the first African American graduate of that college, and earning an MA in 1849. He had a particular aptitude for languages, studying Sanskrit, Greek, Latin, Hebrew, and Persian. Vashon was twice denied admission to the bar in Pennsylvania due to his race but was admitted in New York in 1848, making him the first African American lawyer in that state. He practiced law for three years, then turned to teaching.

From 1867 to 1874, Vashon lived in DC, working in the Solicitor's Office of the Freedmen's Bureau and in the Office of the Second Auditor of the U.S. Treasury, teaching law at Howard University, and publishing essays and poems in periodicals.

Vashon was only the third person of African descent to teach at the college level. In addition to Howard University, he taught at Avery College, New York Central College, and Alcorn University in the United States, and at Collège Faustin in Haiti. He also served on the executive committee of the Colored Men of America conference and, during Reconstruction, was appointed by the mayor of Washington as the first person of color to serve on the board of trustees of the white public schools.

Vashon died in a yellow fever epidemic and was buried in an unmarked grave in Lorman, Mississippi. In 2010, he was posthumously admitted to the bar in Pennsylvania, 163 years after being denied the right to sit for the bar examination.

His best-known poem, "Vincent Ogé," tells the epic story of the anticolonial revolt on what was then known as the island of Santo Domingo that took place from 1790 to 1791. Although the revolt was not successful, and Ogé and twenty-one others were put to death, their actions eventually led to the founding of the Republic of Haiti. Vashon lived in Haiti for two and a half years, beginning in 1849. He wrote the poem on his return to the United States.

From Vincent Ogé

And Ogé standeth in this hall;
But now he standeth not alone;—

A brother's there, and friends; and all
Are kindred spirits with his own;
For mind will join with kindred mind,
As matter's with its like combined.
They speak of wrongs they had received—
Of freemen, of their rights bereaved;
And as they pondered o'er the thought
Which in their minds so madly wrought,
Their eyes gleamed as the lightning's flash,
Their words seemed as the torrent's dash
That falleth, with a low, deep sound,
Into some dark abyss profound,—
A sullen sound that threatens more
Than other torrents' louder roar.
Ah! they had borne well as they might,
Such wrongs as freemen ill can bear;
And they had urged both day and night,
In fitting words, a freeman's prayer;
And when the heart is filled with grief,
For wrongs of all true souls accurst,
In action it must seek relief,
Or else, o'ercharged, it can but burst.
Why blame we them if they oft spake
Words that were fitted to awake
The soul's high hopes—its noblest parts—
The slumbering passions of brave hearts
And send them as the simoom's breath,
Upon a work of woe and death?

Mary E. Nealy

December 12, 1825 – February 8, 1902

Mary E. Nealy was raised in Louisville, Kentucky, and married at age seventeen to Hugh Nealy. Early in their marriage, her husband was disabled in a railroad accident, and Mary Nealy had to support the family. She began publishing poetry and commentary on visual art in such journals as the *Southern Literary Messenger, Godey's Lady's Book,* and *Home Journal.* When her two eldest sons volunteered for the Civil

War in 1861, Nealy moved the family to DC to be nearer to them. Both of those sons died in the war.

In Washington, Nealy was a special correspondent to the *Washington Evening Star* and was active in two literary groups: King's Reunions, the salon in the home of Horatio King; and the Washington Literary Society, cofounded by her close friend Madeleine Vinton Dahlgren. Two of her former homes still stand: 1712 Ninth Street NW in the Shaw neighborhood, and 1517 Twelfth Street NW in the Logan Circle neighborhood. She is buried in Glenwood Cemetery.

An obituary in the *Washington Evening Star* in 1902 called her "a prominent figure in literary and art circles of this city . . . an estimable lady, a devoted mother and a brilliant writer." The article notes that John Greenleaf Whittier "was early to recognize the merit of Mrs. Nealy's work" and says her "war poems were extensively copied and exceedingly popular because of their thoroughly patriotic sentiment."

Arlington

And while we gaze on this scene of beauty,
    And call him traitor who ruled it here,
We can but honor the sense of duty
    To which he could forfeit a home so dear.
A home so rich in its old-time splendor,
    Its templed columns and ancient trees,
And the sunset's light, which falls so tender
    On things of beauty and peace like these.
        Yet, through years of bitter chiding
           He walked boldly to his fall,
        And the ghosts of the North are gliding
           Through this lordly Southern hall.

Brilliant and bright the flag is floating
    Over this broad Parthenian home;
While the gazer's circling eye is noting
    River and city and milk-white Dome.
And the hills beyond their brilliant tinges
    Of scarlet and orange and brown and gold.
Till the heart to the spirit of Beauty cringes;
    "I never could forfeit so rich a hold."

But the strangers' feet are walking
    Each day through the ancient hall,
And the ghosts of the dead are stalking
    All around the garden wall.

O, souls of the dead! O hearts of the living!
    The Past is past. It was God's decree.
By the graves of the dead let us be forgiving:
    Let all be brothers as all are free!
There is blood enough on our plains and valleys;
    There is grief enough in our stricken land;
There is want enough in our lanes and alleys,
    Let us reach to each other the clasping hand!
        For while some forms are walking
            The olden paths tonight,
        Uncounted ghosts are stalking
            In the soft moon's sudden light.

O. O. Howard

November 8, 1830–October 26, 1909

Oliver Otis Howard was a career army soldier, nicknamed the "Christian General" because he tried to base all policy and military strategy on his deep religious belief. Howard rose through the army ranks to become a brevet major general. During the Civil War, he fought in the Union army at Bull Run, Fair Oaks, Fredericksburg, Chancellorsville, Gettysburg, Chattanooga, and in Sherman's March through Georgia. He lost his right arm at Fair Oaks, which later earned him a Medal of Honor.

After the Civil War, Howard moved to DC to accept an appointment as commissioner of the Bureau of Refugees, Freedmen and Abandoned Lands (from 1865 to 1873). He was a leader in promoting higher education for freed slaves, founding Howard University and serving as its first president from 1867 through 1873. Originally called the Howard Normal and Theological Institute for the Education of Preachers and Teachers, the school was open to students of both sexes and was highly controversial in its early years. Howard's house on the campus still stands at 607 Howard Place NW and was declared a National Historic Landmark in 1974.

After 1874, Howard served in the Indian Wars, in campaigns against Apache, Nez Perce, and Paiute warriors. His appointments included: commander of the Department of the Columbia, superintendent of the U.S. Military Academy at West Point, commander of the Department of the Platte, commander of the Division of the Pacific, and commander of the Division of the East.

Howard is the author of *The Autobiography of Oliver Otis Howard* (1907), *My Life and Experiences among Our Hostile Indians* (1907), and *Famous Indian Chiefs I Have Known* (1908), as well as biographies of Chief Joseph of the Nez Perce, General Richard Taylor, and Queen Isabella I of Castile. He also wrote occasional poems and made English translations of literature from French.

The Blue and the Gray

1.
By the flow of the inland river,
Whence the fleets of iron have fled,
Where the blades of the grave-grass quiver
Asleep are the ranks of the dead; —
Under the sod and the dew
Waiting the judgment day; —
Under the one the Blue,
Under the other the Gray.

2.
These in the robings of glory,
Those in the gloom of defeat,
All with the battle-blood gory,
In the dusk of eternity meet; —
Under the sod and the dew,
Waiting the judgment day; —
Under the laurel the Blue,
Under the willow the Gray.

3.
From the silence of sorrowful hours
The desolate mourners go,

Lovingly laden with flowers
Alike for the friend and the foe; —
Under the sod and the dew,
Waiting the judgment day; —
Under the roses the Blue,
Under the lilies the Gray.

4.
So with an equal splendor
The morning sun-rays fall,
With a touch impartially tender,
On the blossoms blooming for all; —
Under the sod and the dew,
Waiting the judgment day; —
Broidered with gold the Blue,
Mellowed with gold the Gray.

5.
So when the summer calleth,
On the forest and field of grain
With an equal murmur falleth
The cooling drip of the rain; —
Under the sod and the dew,
Waiting the judgment day; —
Wet with the rain the Blue,
Wet with the rain the Gray.

6.
Sadly, but not with upbraiding,
The generous deed was done; —
In the storm of the years that are fading,
No braver battle was won; —
Under the sod and the dew,
Waiting the judgment day; —
Under the blossoms the Blue,
Under the garlands the Gray.

7.
No more shall the war cry sever
Or the winding rivers be red,

They banish our anger forever
When they laurel the graves of our dead.
Under the sod and the dew,
Waiting the judgment day;—
Love and tears for the Blue,
Tears and love for the Gray.

John Sella Martin

September 27, 1832–August 11, 1876

John Sella Martin escaped slavery in Alabama in 1856 and made his way to Boston, where he became a minister and celebrated orator. After a lecture tour of England and select stops in the European continent, sponsored by the American Missionary Association, he moved to DC in 1869 and was a well-loved pastor of the Fifteenth Street Presbyterian Church.

In addition to sermons, he wrote journalism and poetry (his best-known poem, *The Hero and the Slave,* was published in 1870) and briefly edited the *New Era* newspaper. The *Colored American* praised him as "one of the most eloquent able platform orators of the antebellum period," and the *Washington Evening Star* called him "one of the best educated colored men in the country" and "a remarkably fluent speaker."

In 1868, he enrolled his daughter at the Franklin School, placing himself and his family at the center of Reconstruction-era debates about equal access to public accommodations. The school board allowed six-year-old Josie Martin to attend a "white" school but denied that this set a precedent for public school integration, claiming that they had agreed to consider the mixed-race child "white."

Martin was also an important voice opposing the District of Columbia Organic Act of 1871, which repealed the charters of Washington City, Washington County, and Georgetown to create a single municipal government for the entire federal district with a territorial system in which the governor and city council were appointed rather than elected. Martin wrote incisively, "In plain Anglo-Saxon, the old fogies are opposed to negro suffrage; and as they cannot withdraw it, they seek to diminish if not destroy, the opportunities for its exercise."

In 1872, Martin was elected to the state legislature of Louisiana, but he was not allowed to serve due to his race. Instead, he won an appointment as an agent to the U.S. Post Office and wrote for the *Louisianian* newspaper. He died in New Orleans in 1876 from an overdose of laudanum. It is unclear if his death was intentional or accidental.

From **The Hero and the Slave**

But just now a sable listener
Makes a passage through the crowd,
'Till he stands before the soldier—
But his presence seems a cloud;
For the listeners looked contemptuous,
As they fixed on him a stare,
And a person said in anger,
"There's a 'nigger' everywhere—
In the church, and state, and barracks,
Still his woolly head pops in";
And e'en here he comes unwelcome,
Like a Ghost upon the scene.
And as if in great amazement,
Each one from the center shrank,
As the negro neared the soldier,
Lest he soiled his skin and rank.
"Ah, my hero," spoke the negro,
As he raised his manly brow,
"Have we passed through blood and peril,
All to meet so happy now;
Thanks to Him whose love impartial,
Guards the hero and the slave,
Thanks to Him, for from *our dangers*,
He alone had power to save."
"Sir, my jaded memory fails me,"
Said the brave, with some surprise,
"But perhaps your explanation,
May remove your new disguise."
"You shall have it," said the negro,
Drawing nearer to the brave;

"From the Monumental City
I have journeyed as a slave,
And when life was ebbing from you,
Through the wounds which these deplore,
'Twas these sable hands that stayed it,
In the streets of Baltimore;
When the frenzied mob were yelling,
And with stones, and bayonet,
Crushing heads, and bodies piercing,
Of the soldiers gasping yet;
It was I who saw you falling,
And still marking where you fell,
Sought your helpless form, and dragged it
From the gates of riot's hell;
It was I who staunched your bleeding,
With the garments of my wife;
Torn from limbs by white men fettered,
To bind in a white man's life.
Even in the bondsman's prison,
Sounds mysterious sometimes came,
Telling of old Massachusetts,
First in conflict, first in fame—
First to brave king George's power,
And defend the nation's laws,
First to give the negro freedom,
And the last to leave his cause.
When I saw her son a stranger,
Helpless, wounded, and alone,
I remembered Massachusetts,
And I did what I have done.
Yes, that name so dear to bondmen,
Prompted risk of life for you,
And your safety well rewards me
For the dangerous interview."
"O, you are my life's preserver,
And whate'er my state or mood,
You shall be the constant idol

Of a soldier's gratitude.
Yes, your words awaken memory,
Which awakened, now recalls,
Every tone, and act, and feature,
Of the friend my soul extols;
O! 'twas you who proved the hero,
Mid the bloody scenes that say,
Risking life, and dealing mercy,
In the chaos of the fray;
For your acts were voluntary,
While the soldier's deeds were done
'Neath the iron spur of orders,
Which nor weak, nor brave, could shun;
And my acts should prove my feelings,
Better than my tongue can tell,
Had I wealth to guide that courage,
Which 'mid dangers shone so well.
Still these Christian men around you
Are the guardians to whose care
I commit you, as to Christians,
With a soldier's heartfelt prayer."
Then he turned to those around him,
While his eyes were growing bright,
With the gems of grateful feeling—
All too pure for vulgar sight—
And he said in tones that trembled:
"Freemen, there a freeman stands,
With his deed of manumission,
Snatched from riot's guilty hands;
From these gilded halls I journeyed
Into slavery's dark Bastille,
Thoughtless of the hearts of bondmen,
Till he taught my own to feel—
Taught me how to feel those terrors
Which our fathers' weakness gave,
Into hands to-day as murderous
To the white man as the slave.

Starting from his life-long prison,
Did this bondman make his way;
To this grand old hall of justice,
Where sweet freedom holds her sway;
I went there to lose my freedom—
He comes here in search of his;
He restored mine when I lost it,
And shall we do less than this?
In his conflict with condition,
He a double conquest gains;
Conquers hate of white-faced haters—
Conquers bondage and its chains;
Shall he now a deadlier conflict,
Wage with color's hateful ban,
Or, assisted by our justice
Stand up every inch a man.
Let us by our manly dealing
Quell the cry of prejudice,
Which drives to proscriptive darkness
Even such a gem as this;
For, though still my highest glory
Was to shed a patriot's blood,
Here I learn my highest lesson,
God's great truth of brotherhood,
And henceforth the name of negro
Loses all of its disgrace,
For the hero's deeds may blossom
From the stem of any race."

The Sentinel of Freedom

"Watchman what of the Night?"

The storm has begun, the thunders are pealing,
The lightnings of truth, like the stern, flashing eye
Of Justice, that sleeps now, of vengeance unfeeling
Are bursting from clouds in their conflict on high;
The winds of discussion like the ploughshares of terror

Sink deep 'neath the surface of slavery's dead sea;
And the monsters of crime on the billows of error,
Appear to the horrified gaze of the free.

The weepings of mercy in showers are failing
On slavery's grim altars, to dampen their blaze.
The deep tones of progress like trumpets are calling
To red revolution, who fiercens his gaze;
The earthquakes of interest are shaking with fury
The groves and high places of tyranny's power,
And molten free speech like lava will bury
Its temples and altars to rise never more.

Now stern agitation, all sleepless and busy,
Throws open the flood gates of feeling's deep sea;
And the swift rushing torrents make nations grow dizzy,
As they leap over dams built to check their wild glee.
The merciless whirlwinds of God's indignation
Are sweeping through earth disenthralled from their cave.
And reason all quenchless, in bright conflagration,
Is melting the chains from the limbs of the slave.

The champions of slavery in wild desperation,
Are cutting their flesh as the all potent charm,
And pouring their blood as the needed libation
This wrath to appease and their terrors to calm
The truth crushing genii of policy is waving,
His wand of corruption to silence the roar,
And the great fish of Mammon his Jonahs are saving
From watery destruction to die on the shore.

The altars of bondage are blazing with fire.
The slave in his chains is its grim sacrifice;
The tones of the priest rise higher and higher,
But his God now in conflict regards not his cries.
The merchant in fear brings his gift to the altar,
The statesman and jurist bring laws all in vain:
The demagogue's accents in doubt 'gins to falter
Though "Union" is sounded again and again.

But all is in vain, the heavens grow thicker
With portents of dread to oppression's weak soul,
And almighty truth flashes brighter and quicker,
While terrific reason in thunders still roll;
The earthquake is shattering their prisons to pieces
Amid the eruptions of volcanic speech
While whirlwinds and torrents in fury increases,
Though tyrants alternately curse and beseech.

And thus shall it be until freedom shall cover
With an ocean of light our nation so dark
Till justice and mercy united shall hover
O'er manhood untrammeled, in liberty's ark.
Then 'neath truth's great sun-light by conflict unfaded,
And earth renovated by fire and flood,
Shall man in his majesty stand undergraded,
The Lord of Creation, the image of God.

Elizabeth Akers Allen

October 9, 1832–August 7, 1911

Elizabeth Akers Allen (who also published under the names "Florence Percy" and "Elizabeth Akers") is the author of nine books of poems, including *Forest Buds from the Woods of Maine* (1855), *The Silver Bridge* (1885), *The High-Top Sweeting* (1891), and *The Ballad of the Bronx* (1901).

Allen grew up in Farmington, Maine. Her mother died when she was four, and she suffered repeated physical abuse from a stepmother until she was finally sent to boarding school at Farmington Academy. Allen published her first poem at age fifteen. She was an outspoken advocate of equal rights for women and against cruelty to animals. Akers earned a living as a journalist for the *Portland Transcript*, the *Boston Evening Gazette*, and the *Portland Daily Advertiser*. She came to DC in 1863 (staying for two years) to accept an appointment as a clerk in the U.S. War Office and volunteered in area Civil War hospitals as a nurse.

Her most famous poem, "Rock Me to Sleep," was the subject of a court case in 1866, when Alexander M. W. Ball claimed authorship. Allen had to bring him to court to reclaim her copyright. The poem was extremely popular with Civil War soldiers and generations of school-children.

After leaving DC, Allen lived in Richmond, Virginia; Portland, Maine; and Tuckahoe, New York, where she died at age seventy-eight. She married twice, to sculptor Benjamin Akers (who predeceased her), and to Elijah M. Allen. She had no children and continued to work as an editor and journalist throughout both marriages.

Spring at the Capital

The poplar drops beside the way
Its tasseled plumes of silver gray;
The chestnut points its great brown buds, impatient for the laggard May.

The honeysuckles lace the wall;
The hyacinths grow fair and tall;
And mellow sun and pleasant wind and odorous bees are over all.

Down-looking in this snow-white bud,
How distant seems the war's red flood!
How far remote the steaming wounds, the sickening scent of human blood!

For Nature does not recognize
This strife that rends the earth and skies;
No war-dreams vex the winter sleep of clover-heads and daisy-eyes.

She holds her even way the same,
though navies sink or cities flame;
A snow-drop is a snow-drop still, despite the Nation's joy or shame.

When blood her grassy altar wets,
She sends the pitying violets
To heal the outrage with their bloom, and cover it with soft regrets.

O crocuses with rain-wet eyes,
O tender-lipped anemones,
What do you know of agony, and death, and blood-won victories?

No shudder breaks your sunshine trance,
Though near you rolls, with slow advance,

Clouding your shining leaves with dust, the anguish-laden
   ambulance.

   Yonder a white encampment hums;
   The clash of martial music comes;
And now your startled stems are all a-tremble with the jar of drums.

   Whether it lessen or increase,
   Or whether trumpets shout or cease,
Still deep within your tranquil hearts the happy bees are humming
   "Peace!"

   O flowers! the soul that faints or grieves
   New comfort from your lips receives;
Sweet confidence and patient faith are hidden in your healing leaves.

   Help us to trust, still on and on,
   That this dark night will soon be gone,
And that these battle-stains are but the blood-red trouble of the dawn—

   Dawn of a broader, whiter day
   Than ever blessed us with its ray—
A dawn beneath whose purer light all guilt and wrong shall fade away.

   Then shall our nation break its bands,
   And, silencing the envious lands,
Stand in the search light unashamed, with spotless robe and clean
   white hands.

Lost Light

My heart is chilled and my pulse is slow,
But often and often will memory go,
Like a blind child lost in a waste of snow,
Back to the days when I loved you so—
The beautiful long ago.

I sit here dreaming them through and through,
The blissful moments I shared with you—
The sweet, sweet days when our love was new,
When I was trustful and you were true—
Beautiful days, but few!

Blest or wretched, fettered or free,
Why should I care how your life may be,
Or whether you wander by land or sea?
I only know you are dead to me,
Ever and hopelessly.

Oh, how often at day's decline
I pushed from my window the curtaining vine,
To see from your lattice the lamp-light shine—
Type of a message that, half divine,
Flashed from your heart to mine.

Once more the starlight is silvering all;
The roses sleep by the garden wall;
The night bird warbles his madrigal,
And I hear again through the sweet air fall
The evening bugle-call.

But summers will vanish and years will wane,
And bring no light to your window pane;
Nor gracious sunshine nor patient rain
Can bring dead love back to life again:
I call up the past in vain.

My heart is heavy, my heart is old,
And that proves dross which I counted gold;
I watch no longer your curtain's fold;
The window is dark and the night is cold,
And the story forever told.

Rock Me to Sleep

Backward, turn backward, O Time, in your flight,
Make me a child again just for tonight!
Mother, come back from the echoless shore,
Take me again to your heart as of yore;
Kiss from my forehead the furrows of care,
Smooth the few silver threads out of my hair;
Over my slumbers your loving watch keep;—
Rock me to sleep, mother,—rock me to sleep!

Backward, flow backward, O tide of the years!
I am so weary of toil and of tears,—
Toil without recompense, tears all in vain,—
Take them, and give me my childhood again!
I have grown weary of dust and decay,—
Weary of flinging my soul-wealth away;
Weary of sowing for others to reap;—
Rock me to sleep, mother—rock me to sleep!

Tired of the hollow, the base, the untrue,
Mother, O mother, my heart calls for you!
Many a summer the grass has grown green,
Blossomed and faded, our faces between:
Yet, with strong yearning and passionate pain,
Long I tonight for your presence again.
Come from the silence so long and so deep;—
Rock me to sleep, mother,—rock me to sleep!

Over my heart, in the days that are flown,
No love like mother-love ever has shone;
No other worship abides and endures,—
Faithful, unselfish, and patient like yours:
None like a mother can charm away pain
From the sick soul and the world-weary brain.
Slumber's soft calms o'er my heavy lids creep;—
Rock me to sleep, mother,—rock me to sleep!

Come, let your brown hair, just lighted with gold,
Fall on your shoulders again as of old;
Let it drop over my forehead tonight,
Shading my faint eyes away from the light;
For with its sunny-edged shadows once more
Haply will throng the sweet visions of yore;
Lovingly, softly, its bright billows sweep;—
Rock me to sleep, mother,—rock me to sleep!

Mother, dear mother, the years have been long
Since I last listened your lullaby song:
Sing, then, and unto my soul it shall seem

Womanhood's years have been only a dream.
Clasped to your heart in a loving embrace,
With your light lashes just sweeping my face,
Never hereafter to wake or to weep; —
Rock me to sleep, mother, — rock me to sleep!

John L. McCreery

December 2, 1835 – September 6, 1906

John McCreery's fame as an author rests on a single poem, "There Is No Death," which was written in the spring of 1863, reprinted in newspapers across the United States, and set to music by several composers. Amid the carnage of the Civil War, it's not hard to imagine why this poem would become such a sentimental favorite.

Born in rural New York State, McCreery was the son of a poor Methodist minister. He had little formal schooling. At age seventeen, he was apprenticed to a printer in Illinois, and at age twenty-one, he became an editor of the *Dubuque Times* in Iowa. He moved to DC in 1878 to take a job as a clerk in the Department of the Interior and stayed for the remainder of his life.

McCreery is the author of a single book of poems, *Songs of Toil and Triumph* (1883). He died of complications from appendicitis at age seventy-one and is buried in Glenwood Cemetery. An obituary in the *Washington Evening Star* called him "a ready speaker and gifted with a fund of wit and humor."

His final home, at 230 Eleventh Street NE on Capitol Hill, still stands.

There Is No Death

There is no death! the stars go down
To rise upon some other shore,
And bright in Heaven's jeweled crown,
They shine forevermore.

There is no death! the dust we tread,
Shall change, beneath the summer showers,
To golden grain, or mellow fruit,
Or rainbow-tinted flowers.

The granite rocks disorganize
To feed the hungry moss they bear;
The forest leaves drink daily life
From out the viewless air.

There is no death! the leaves may fall,
The flowers may fade and pass away;
They only wait, through wintry hours,
The coming of the May.

There is no death! an angel form
Walks o'er the earth with silent tread;
He bears our best-loved things away,
And then we call them dead.

He leaves our hearts all desolate,
He plucks our fairest, sweetest flowers,
Transplanted into bliss, they now
Adorn immortal bowers.

The birdlike voice, whose joyous tones
Made glad the scene of sin and strife,
Sings now its everlasting song
Amid the trees of life.

Where'er he sees a smile too bright
Or soul too pure for taint or vice,
He bears it to that world of light
To dwell in Paradise.

Born into that undying life,
They leave us but to come again;
With joy we welcome them the same
Except in sin and pain.

And ever near us, though unseen,
The dear, immortal spirits tread—
For all the boundless universe
Is Life—there are no dead!

Sarah Morgan Bryan Piatt

August 11, 1836 – December 22, 1919

Sarah Piatt married another writer but began publishing prior to her marriage. She cowrote poems with her husband but also published volumes on her own. Of the two, she is the more talented writer. Her books are *A Woman's Poems* (1871), *A Voyage to the Fortunate Isle, and Other Poems* (1874), *That New World, and Other Poems* (1876), *Poems in Company with Children* (1877), *Dramatic Persons and Moods* (1879), *An Irish Garland* (1884), *Selected Poems* (1885), *In Primrose Time* (1886), *Child's-World Ballads* (1887), *The Witch in the Glass* (1888), *An Irish Wild-Flower* (1891), *An Enchanted Castle and Other Poems* (1893), *Poems* (1894), and *Complete Poems* (1894).

Born on a plantation outside Lexington, Kentucky, to a family of slave owners, she is related on her father's side to Daniel Boone. She graduated from Henry Female College and began publishing poems in 1854. In 1861, she married John James Piatt, known to friends as J. J., a journalist who had already published a first book of poems. The young couple moved to DC, where her husband had secured a job as a clerk in the Treasury Department, and rented a home in what is today the Burleith neighborhood (now razed).

They remained in DC until 1867, when J. J. lost his job, and while there, they began to raise a large family of eleven children, although only six would survive to adulthood. The family shuttled between government jobs in DC, when her husband could get them, and newspaper jobs in her husband's native Ohio, when he could not. They returned to DC two more times when J. J. got jobs as librarian for the House of Representatives, and with the postal service. His most successful government job came in 1884, when he was appointed American consul in Ireland. The family would spend eleven years in Cork, Ireland. In 1914, J. J. was seriously injured in a carriage accident from which he never fully recovered. He died in 1917, and the widowed Sarah moved in with a son in New Jersey, where she remained until her death in 1919.

Although J. J. had published more than his wife when they first married, her poems soon eclipsed his, both in popularity and in number. He struggled to maintain the appearance of parity with her, but magazine editors distinctly preferred her work, and she published poems for adults and children regularly in leading periodicals in the United States and Great Britain, including *Atlantic Monthly, Harper's, Scribner's, Irish Monthly,* and the *Independent.*

The Piatts developed friendships with a number of other writers, including William Dean Howells and Oliver Wendell Holmes. In DC, they became part of a lively group of literary government clerks and journalists (and their spouses), making the acquaintance of Walt Whitman, John Burroughs, William Douglas O'Connor, Grace Greenwood, George Alfred Townsend (who wrote as Gath), John Willis Menard, and others.

Sarah Piatt's poems are notable for their use of dialogue and their irony, although in other ways they conform to the genteel tradition of Victorian-era poetry. She wrote often of motherhood and children but also of politics and current events, and her work expresses a strong yearning for social justice. A large number of her poems are about the devastation of the Civil War and war's aftermath; these poems are of special interest not only because they reflect her time spent in DC but because the war galvanized the poet, forcing her to rethink her assumptions about her happy southern childhood, her family's complicit role in slavery, and her era's romanticized ideals about war.

In 1915, the *Washington Herald* wrote: "There was a freshness and tenderness in her style, and a new note of Western goodness untouched by moralizing that immediately made readers recognize in it something entirely new. She was perhaps the most original poet of her generation . . . as original as any poet this country has ever known."

Hearing the Battle—July 21, 1861
One day in the dreamy summer,
On the Sabbath hills, from afar,
We heard the solemn echoes
Of the first fierce words of war.

Ah, tell me, thou veiled Watcher
Of the storm and the calm to come,
How long by the sun or shadow
Till these noises again are dumb.

And soon in a hush and glimmer
We thought of the dark, strange fight,
Whose close in a ghastly quiet
Lay dim in the beautiful night.

Then we talk'd of coldness and pallor,
And of things with blinded eyes
That stared at the golden stillness
Of the moon in those lighted skies;

And of souls, at morning wrestling
In the dust with passion and moan,
So far away at evening
In the silence of worlds unknown.

But a delicate wind beside us
Was rustling the dusky hours,
As it gather'd the dewy odors
Of the snowy Jessamine-flowers.

And I gave you a spray of the blossoms,
And said: "I shall never know
How the hearts in the land are breaking,
My dearest, unless you go."

Army of Occupation

At Arlington, 1866

The summer blew its little drifts of sound—
Tangled with wet leaf-shadows and the light
Small breath of scattered morning buds—around
The yellow path through which our footsteps wound.
Below, the Capitol rose glittering white.

There stretched a sleeping army. One by one,
They took their places until thousands met;
No leader's stars flashed on before, and none
Leaned on his sword or stagger'd with his gun—
I wonder if their feet have rested yet!

They saw the dust, they joined the moving mass,
They answer'd the fierce music's cry for blood,
Then straggled here and lay down in the grass:—
Wear flowers for such, shores whence their feet did pass;
Sing tenderly; O river's haunted flood!

They had been sick, and worn, and weary, when
They stopp'd on this calm hill beneath the trees:
Yet if, in some red-clouded dawn, again
The country should be calling to her men,
Shall the reveille not remember these?

Around them underneath the mid-day skies
The dreadful phantoms of the living walk,
And by low moons and darkness with their cries—
The mothers, sisters, wives with faded eyes,
Who call still names amid their broken talk.

And here is one who comes alone and stands
At his dim fireless hearth—chill'd and oppress'd
By something he has summon'd to his lands,
While the weird pallor of its many hands
Points to his rusted sword in his own breast!

April at Washington
O whispering Phantom and fair
Of the April of two years ago!
Rising here in the delicate air,
How strange are the pictures you show!

I see you, with Triumph that sounds
In the cannon and flashes in light,
Glide over these blossoming grounds
Through the crowded rejoicing at night.

And I see you where steel is reversed
To the funeral drum's stifled beats,
To the thought of a murder accursed,
To the bugle's long wail down the streets;

To the dust, under bells moving slow
With the weight of a people's great grief,
Among flags falling dark-draped and low,
To the dead-march behind the lost chief:

Who was wrapp'd in your beautiful hours
As he pass'd to his glory and rest,
His coffin-lid sweet with your flowers
And his last human look in your breast!

Thomas Bailey Aldrich
November 11, 1836–March 19, 1907

Thomas Bailey Aldrich was one of the many journalists who came to Washington during the Civil War, as a correspondent for the *New York Illustrated News*. He was a friend of Walt Whitman's, as well as other New York bohemians of the 1860s. He later edited a Boston publication, *Every Saturday,* and from 1881 to 1890 was editor of the *Atlantic Monthly*. Aldrich was the author of five novels, books of short fiction and travel writing, a memoir called *The Story of a Bad Boy* (1869), and eleven books of poems, including *The Ballad of Babie Bell* (1856), *Flower and Thorn* (1876), and *Wyndham Towers* (1889). He died of tuberculosis at age thirty-four.

An article in the *Washington Evening Star* in 1907 remembered him as "always witty, always brilliant, if there was anybody present capable of striking his flint at the right angle, that Aldrich was as sure and prompt and unfailing as the red hot iron on the blacksmith's anvil—you only had to hit it competently to make it deliver an explosion of sparks."

Accomplices
The soft new grass is creeping o'er the graves
By the Potomac; and the crisp ground-flower
Lifts its blue cup to catch the passing shower;
The pinecone ripens, and the long moss waves
Its tangled gonfalons above our braves.
Hark, what a burst of music from yon bower!—

The Southern nightingale that, hour by hour,
In its melodious summer madness raves.
Ah, with what delicate touches of her hand,
With what sweet voices, Nature seeks to screen
The awful Crime of this distracted land,—
Sets her birds singing, while she spreads her green
Mantle of velvet where the Murdered lie,
As if to hide the horror from God's eye.

Fredericksburg

The increasing moonlight drifts across my bed,
And on the churchyard by the road, I know
It falls as white and noiselessly as snow . . .
'Twas such a night two weary summers fled;
The stars, as now, were waning overhead.
Listen! Again the shrill-lipped bugles blow
Where the swift currents of the river flow
Past Fredericksburg: far off the heavens are red
With sudden conflagration: on yon height,
Linstock in hand, the gunners hold their breath:
A signal-rocket pierces the dense night,
Flings its spent stars upon the town beneath:
Hark!—the artillery massing on the right,
Hark!—the black squadrons wheeling down to Death!

Memory

My mind lets go a thousand things,
Like dates of wars and deaths of kings,
And yet recalls the very hour—
'Twas noon by yonder village tower,
And on the last blue noon in May
The wind came briskly up this way,
Crisping the brook beside the road;
Then, pausing here, set down its load
Of pine-scents, and shook listlessly
Two petals from that wild-rose tree.

Fanny Jackson Coppin

October 15, 1837–January 21, 1913

Fanny Jackson Coppin was born enslaved in DC and was emancipated by an aunt who purchased her freedom at age twelve. She attended Oberlin College, where she opted to take the more academically rigorous "gentleman's course," including studies in Latin, Greek, and mathematics, and distinguished herself as an exceptional scholar. After graduation, Coppin spent thirty-seven years teaching and serving as principal at the Institute for Colored Youth in Philadelphia (a forerunner of Cheyney University). The wife of a minister, she was active in the African Methodist Episcopal Church and traveled with her husband to do missionary work in South Africa. Coppin State University in Baltimore was named in her honor.

This poem appeared under her maiden name, Fanny M. Jackson, in the *Anglo African* newspaper in May 1863. The Latin phrase in the final line comes from Virgil's *Aeneid* and means "That's the path to the stars."

The Black Volunteers

We welcome, we welcome, our brave volunteers,
Fling your caps to the breeze, boys, and give them three cheers;
They have proven their valor by many a scar,
But their god-like endurance has been nobler by far.
Think ye not that their brave hearts grew sick with delay
When the battle-cry summoned their neighbors away;
When their offers were spurned and their voices unheeded,
And grim Prejudice vaunted their aid was not needed.

Till some pious soul, full of loyal devotion,
To whom flesh and muscle were more than a notion,
Proposed, that in order to save their own blood,
As "drawers of water and hewers of wood"
They should use their black brothers;—but the blacks "couldn't see"
What great magnanimity prompted the plea;
And they scouted the offer as base and inglorious,
For they knew that, through God, they should yet be victorious.

But alas! for our country, her insolent horde
Has "melted like snow in the glance of the Lord"
Aye, the face of the nation grew ghastly and white,
When the angel of death crossed her sill in the night
And her first-born were slain—then she bowed her proud head,
While in sackcloth and ashes she mourned for her dead.
Let her weep for her martial pride, weep for her noblest;
The southern plains reek with the blood of her boldest

Yet her pride is not humbled by what she has borne,
'Tis necessity's goad that is urging her on
To enlist you, my brothers. 'Tis natural, we read,
To hate whom we've injured by word or by deed.
But God's ways are just: His decrees are immutable,
Though often to us they seem dark and inscrutable.
He meant not that slavery always should last
And over his people its dark shadow cast.

Now, Freedom stands holding with uplifted face,
Her hand, dipped in blood, on the brow of our race.
Attest it! my country, and never again
By this holy baptism, forget we are *men*,
Nor dare, when we've mingled our blood in your battles,
To sneer at our bravery and call us your "chattels."
Our ancestors fought on your first battle-plains,
And you paid them right nobly with insult and chains;

You pitied not even the sad and forlorn,
You pensioned their widows and orphans on scorn!
In your hour of bitterest trial and need
You have called us once more—to your voice we give heed
No longer your treacherous faith we'll discuss:
But *let God be the witness between you and us!*
We have stout hearts among us, as well do you know,
That ne'er quailed before danger or shrank from a foe.

They have come, at your bidding, in dangers to share,
And that which is grander, to do and to dare!
Then away to the battle-field, brave volunteers,

We'll not sadden your parting with womanish tears!
Fling out to the breezes your banner of Right,
And under its broad folds assemble your might.
Go Liberty, Honor, aye, all things most dear,
Are intrusted to you to defend and to clear

From the stain of oppression, whose poisonous breath
Is less welcome to us than the black wing of death!
Tho' millions assail ye, yet fear not their might;
They shall vanish like mist in the sun's ruddy light,
For God will go with you—His word has been spoken,
His gleaming blade never in battle was broken.
With Him as your leader, your cause will fail never,
Sic itur ad astra—your watchword forever!

John Willis Menard
April 3, 1838–October 8, 1893

John Willis Menard was born in Illinois to free parents of Louisiana Creole descent and educated at Muskingum University and Iberia College. He worked as a clerk in the Department of the Interior during the Civil War and was sent to British Honduras (now Belize) in 1863 to investigate the site for a proposed colony for newly freed slaves. In 1868, he became the first African American elected to the U.S. House of Representatives, but he never served. Elected to fill the unexpired term of a Democrat who died in office (representing Louisiana's Second Congressional District), Menard was challenged by Caleb S. Hunt, the white man who lost the election, and the House, after hearing arguments from each, decided to seat neither man. In this process, Menard became the first African American to address the House chamber from the lectern.

Menard later served a term in the Florida House of Representatives and as a Florida justice of the peace. He returned to DC in 1889 to take a clerkship in the Census Office and edit the *National American* magazine, and remained until his death.

Menard was a journalist and editor for several progressive Republican newspapers, including the *Radical Standard* (LA), *Florida News*, and the *Southern Leader*. He published a book of nonfiction, *An Address* to the *Free Colored People of Illinois* (1860), and a book of poems called *Lays in Summer Lands* (1879). He lived at 1843 Seventh Street NW (still standing; now converted to a bar) and is buried in Woodlawn Cemetery in DC.

The Negro's Lament

How long, O God! how long must I remain
    Worse than an alien in my native land?
For long years past I've toiled for other's gain
    Beneath Oppression's ruthless iron hand.

Columbia! why art thou so great and fair,
    And so false and cruel to thine own?
Goodness and Beauty, a proverbial pair,
    They in thy heritage, themselves disown.

So fair and yet so false! thou art a lie
    Against both natural and human laws,—
A deformed dwarf, dropp'd from an angry sky
    To serve a selfish and unholy cause!

Ye sun-kiss'd lakes and hills of Liberty!
    And silvery flowing streams and fields!
Your teeming gold and grain are not for me,
    My birthright only ostracism yields!

My life is burdensome; year succeeds year
    With feeble hope: I try to emulate
All that conspire to ennoble manhood's sphere;
    And yet I seem to war with angry Fate!

O Liberty! I taste but half thy sweets
    In this thy boasted land of Equal Rights!
Although I've fought on land and in thy fleets
    Thy foes, by day and by dim camp-fire lights!

What more wouldst have me do? Is not my life—
    My blood, an all-sufficient sacrifice?
Wouldst thou have me transformed in the vain strife
    To change the fiat of the great Allwise?

Of what avail is life—why sigh and fret,
    When manly hopes are only born to fade?
Although declared a man, a vassal yet
    By social caste—a crime by heaven made!

Far better for me not to have been born,
    Than live and feel the frownings of mankind;
Endure its social hatred and its scorn,
    With all my blighting, forlorn hopes combined.

O, cruel fate!—O, struggle which unmans,
    And burdens every hope and every sigh!
Thou art a boundless gulf over which spans
    Only the arching, storm-foreboding sky!

Ah, woe is me! I feel my yearnings crush'd
    Ere they are born within my sighing heart;
All hopes, all manly aspirations hush'd
    As with the power of Death's fatal dart!

The nice birds sing as if in mocking glee,
    Scorn my long felt sorrows and my burning tears,
Why mock me, birds? I only crave to be
    Like you, free to roam the boundless spheres!

But still sing on! your cheerful music gives
    My fading hope a gleam of brighter days;
Why should I grieve? the eternal God still lives!—
    The sun still shines though clouds obscure his rays!

The darkest hour is just before the break
    Of dawning victory of light and life,
When Freedom's hosts with armor bright awake,
    To quell Oppression in the deadly strife!

New hope is mine! for now I see the gleam
    Of beacon lights of coming liberty!
A continent is shock'd—a crimson stream
    Of blood has paid the debt, and I am free!

Laura Redden Searing (Howard Glyndon)

February 9, 1839–August 10, 1923

Laura Redden Searing was a journalist and Civil War correspondent for the *St. Louis Republican,* writing under the pen name Howard Glyndon. She later wrote for the *New York Times, New York Evening Mail, Harper's Magazine,* and other publications. Glyndon spoke sign language, German, French, Spanish, and Italian. She published the nonfiction book *Notable Men of the House* (1862) and four books of poems, including *Idyls of Battle and Poems of the Rebellion* (1864), *Sounds from Secret Chambers* (1874), and *Echoes of Other Days* (1878). She lived in DC during the war years, from 1861 to 1864.

Searing lost her hearing at age thirteen after an illness (possibly meningitis) and completed her education at the Missouri School for the Deaf. She made sufficient money from her political and military journalism to live independently, and after the Civil War's end, she toured Europe on her own. A late marriage to Edwin Searing did not last, but she did give birth to a daughter, who moved with her to California.

Glyndon, Minnesota, is named for her, and was the only town named for a woman writer during her lifetime.

Of particular interest in this first poem are the references to newspaper coverage of the Civil War era: the "extras," or special issues that were released to report news of battles that arrived too late for the regular releases, and the crowds that gathered outside newspaper offices, where boards were posted with the latest tallies of battles, including lists of the wounded and dead.

The second poem was written for the unveiling of the statue of Thomas Hopkins Gallaudet on the grounds of what was then the Kendall School for the Deaf (now known as Gallaudet University). The statue, by Daniel Chester French, portrays Gallaudet teaching Alice Cogswell the letter A in the manual alphabet. Glyndon returned to DC to deliver the poem in a ceremony in front of the statue both in sign and orally on June 26, 1889.

In Time of War

There are white faces in each sunny street,
    And signs of trouble meet us everywhere;

The nation's pulse hath an unsteady beat,
    For scents of battle foul the summer air.

A thrill goes through the city's busy life,
    And then—as when a strong man stints his breath—
A stillness comes; and each one in his place
    Waits for the news of triumph, loss, and death.

The "Extras" fall like rain upon a drought,
    And startled people crowd around the board
Whereon the nation's sum of loss or gain
    In rude and hurried characters is scored.

Perhaps it is a glorious triumph-gleam—
    An earnest of our Future's recompense;
Perhaps it is a story of defeat,
    Which smiteth like a fatal pestilence.

But whether Failure darkens all the land,
    Or whether Victory sets its blood ablaze,
An awful cry, a mighty throb of pain,
    Shall scare the sweetness from these summer days.

Young hearts shall bleed, and older hearts shall break,
    A sense of loss shall be in many a place;
And oh, the bitter nights! the weary days!
    The sharp desire for many a buried face!

God! how this land grows rich in loyal blood,
    Poured out upon it to its utmost length!
The incense of a people's sacrifice,—
    The wrested offering of a people's strength!

It is the costliest land beneath the sun!
    'Tis priceless, purchaseless! And not a rood
But hath its title written clear and signed
    In some slain hero's consecrated blood.

And not a flower that gems its mellowing soil
    But thriveth well beneath the holy dew
Of tears, that ease a nation's straining heart,
    When the Lord of battles smites it through and through.

Thomas Hopkins Gallaudet

The mandate, "Go where glory waits,"
Was less than naught to him:
He sought the souls whose day was dark,
Whose eyes, with tears, were dim.

As yet his glory rests secure
In many a grateful mind,
First blessed by him, with knowledge sweet,
And linked into its kind.

They lay in prison, speechless, poor,
Unhearing, thralls of Fate,
Until he came, and said, "Come out!
It is not yet too late!"

He came, and lifted up, and spoke;
He set them in the sun.
The great work goes on and on
That was by him begun.

And in this bronze he lives again,
But more within each heart.
To which he said, "Be of good cheer,
Let loneliness depart."

We lift the veil, and see how Art
Has fixed his likeness there,
And placed beside him one whose life
He lifted from despair.

She stands there as the type of those
To whom he gave his all;
Those sorrows touched him till his love
Went out beyond recall!

Ah, well it was, that little fight
Was fostered by the Lord!
Ah, well it was, he loved the child
And felt her fate was hard!

Ah, well it was, he turned himself
Unto that speechless woe,
Which made the world a lonely road
One hundred years ago!

Rest here, thou semblance of our Friend
The while the world goes by!
Rest here, upon our College green,
Beneath the bending sky!

Remain, and bless the chosen work
That found its source in thee—
'Tis through thy love that ye, thy sons,
Are happy, strong, and free.

Rest here, Father of us all!
And when we pass thee by,
'Twill be with bared head and heart,
And mutely reverent eye.

Thank God, He gave thee unto us
To free us from our woe,
And put the key into thy hand
One hundred years ago.

John A. Joyce

July 4, 1842–January 18, 1915

John A. Joyce was a colonel in the Union army during the Civil War,
serving with the Twenty-Fourth Kentucky Infantry. Born in Ireland
and raised in West Virginia and Kentucky, after the war he settled in
DC, earned a law degree, and worked for the Internal Revenue Service.

He is the author of two books of poems, as well as memoirs and
books of criticism. His books include *A Checkered Life* (1883), *Jewels
of Memory* (1896), *Complete Poems* (1900), and *Beautiful Washington*
(1903), along with studies of Oliver Goldsmith, Edgar Allan Poe, William Shakespeare, and Robert Burns.

An obituary in the *Washington Times* in 1915 described his "flowing
white hair, crimson necktie, and long black coat" that "made him a

familiar figure in the Capital since war-time days. . . . Hardly an event of importance occurred in the last quarter of a century that John A. Joyce had not sought to immortalize in a poem." The article quoted him as saying that "all his writings had been to open the eyes of people, blinded with conventionality."

Joyce lived at 226 Maryland Avenue NE (now the site of the Dirksen Senate Office Building), and at 3238 R Street NW in Georgetown (still standing). He is buried at Oak Hill Cemetery, the same cemetery he celebrates in the second poem.

Grant's Mustered Out!

Half-mast the flag, a heart brave and stout
Surrenders at last; Grant's mustered out;
Toll the bell slowly, moisten his sod,
Peace to his ashes, glory to God!

Battle and trial shall never again
Harrow the hero in sunshine or rain;
He's gone to a land devoid of all doubt;
All his service is over—Grant's mustered out.

His fame, like a light, shall shine through the years,
Hallowed by memory and watered by tears—
Flags that he carried shall long flap and flout,
His record of glory we can't muster out!

Donelson, Shiloh, the Wilderness too,
Milestones immortal with deeds of the Blue:
And this is the man that never knew rout,
Till Fate told the world that Grant's mustered out.

Nations unborn shall visit his tomb,
Reared by the people, and lasting as doom—
A Mecca where manhood may kneel without doubt,
Where truth everlasting is not mustered out!

Decoration Day Poem

Oak Hill Cemetery, May 30, 1895

Grand Home of the Dead! we mourn as we tread
    Near the forms that crumble below;

How sad and how still the graves on Oak Hill,
    'Neath the sunlight in bright golden glow.

Here's a rough, rude stone, moss-grown and alone,
    Where old Time has left not a trace
Of the name it bore in the days of yore,
    After brain and body ceased race.

Vain, vain is the thought; no one ever bought
    Exemption from final decay—
To live and to rot, and then be forgot,
    The fate of the quick of today.

The soldier and sage from age unto age
    Have slept 'neath these towering trees;
The young and the old, the bright and the bold
    Are sung by the breath of the breeze.

Brave Babcock in peace here finds his surcease
    From sorrows that troubled his life;
And rests with his God, beneath the green sod,
    Away from this cold world of strife.

Here Reno retires from war's flaming fires
    To shine with immortals above,
And bivouac there, devoid of all care,
    In realms of infinite love.

Here Morris, the brave, a king of the wave,
    Doth slumber beneath the old flag;
Hero so grand, on the famed "Cumberland,"
    And bold as a tall mountain crag.

While ocean shall roar on rock-beaten shore
    The memory of Morris shall be
A great loyal light for freedom's fair fight
    On river, on land, and on sea.

And Stanton; the grand, stood out for this land,
    When Rebellion reared up its fierce face;
Calmly reposes 'neath beds of sweet roses—
    A lone hero, in war's ruin race.

His great iron arm kept the Union from harm
    While he smashed all the foes in its way—
As great Lincoln, his Chief, looked on with deep grief
    At the war 'twixt the Blue and the Gray.

As years roll along, with sorrow or song,
    His name shall grow braver and brighter—
A Puritan true, who knew what to do
    With soldiers and Grant, the great fighter.

Here sleeps fine Van Ness who knew no distress,
    While Burns expended his gold,
A Senator true, who b'lieved in the Blue,
    A gentleman honest and bold.

Great Lorenzo Dow, who never knew how
    To garnish his truth with a lie,
Sleeps under these flowers through May's golden hours,
    Illumined by the sun and the sky.

Here, Corcoran, the sage, Bishop Pinckney, broad gauge,
    Repose under marble so white;
They've gone to a land, bright, blooming, and grand,
    Where never, up there, is a night.

Here, John Howard Payne sings again that refrain
    That thrills us wherever we roam;
O'er land or o'er sea, our hearts still shall be
    The Mecca of dear Home, Sweet Home.

O'er the flight of the years, with smiles or with tears,
    The memory of Payne shall remain;
And millions unborn, in twilight and morn
    Shall sing his immortal refrain.

Let soldier and sage from age unto age
    Richly have all their merit and praise;
But the poet will be a light for the free
    To the end of our last, dawning days.

Count Bodisco sleeps here, where trees shed a tear
    O'er the grave of the Muscovite peer—

Away from all ill he rests on Oak Hill,
    A memory from year unto year.

Dick Merrick lies here, a bright, brilliant seer,
    A lawyer of lingering renown,
Who fought every wrong of the cruel and strong
    In county or city or town.

Here rests the bright Blaine, in sunshine and rain,
    Who left his imprint on the Nation,
A keen, brainy mind, devoted and kind,
    Well fitted to fill a great station.

No shaft marks his grave to tell traveler or slave
    Where that proud, loyal heart lowly lies;
Yet the tall pines of Maine sigh in sorrow for Blaine
    As they toss their green heads to the skies.

Our sweet little child, so simple and mild,
    Sleeps here under roses so fair;
Yet, soon we shall go to a clime where no woe
    Or sighs can corrode us with care.

Mother and sister, sweetheart and wife,
    Repose from their labors on earth;
Resting alone, away from all strife,
    Where the soul finds a happy, new birth.

Yet the citizens dead have always been wed
    To Liberty, Friendship, and Truth—
Must be honored as well as soldiers who fell
    In the pride of their brave, loyal youth.

Then, strew sweetest flowers o'er the soldier,
    But remember the citizen, too,
Who stood by his conscience in trouble—
    And supported the Gray or the Blue.

God bless our grand Nation forever,
    God bless every heart, fond and true;
God bless any soul that won't sever,
    The Gray from the Red, White, and Blue!

Walter H. Brooks

August 30, 1851–July 6, 1945

Born enslaved in Richmond, Virginia, Walter H. Brooks spent his first fourteen years in bondage and was traumatized as a youth when his family was broken up and sold. He remembered vividly the sale of his older sister on an auction block; he wrote about witnessing this scene in several sermons. On March 7, 1933, Brooks wrote the following poem on the torching of Richmond and shared it with his parishioners.

Brooks began his formal schooling at the end of the Civil War, earning degrees from Wilberforce Institute and Lincoln University (where he earned a BA in 1872, a BD in 1873, and a LLD in 1929), and Howard University (receiving a DD degree in 1944). He was ordained a Baptist minister in 1876 and moved to DC in 1882 to take a job as pastor of the Nineteenth Street Baptist Church, the city's oldest African American Baptist congregation, where he remained through his death in 1945. In that role, he was able to move the congregation out of debt and raise needed funds for the church's repair. Under his leadership, the church grew in membership and stature, becoming one of DC's most notable congregations, and Brooks developed a reputation as a powerful orator.

Brooks's publications include *The Pastor's Voice: A Collection of Poems* (1945), *Original Poems* (1932), *Impressions at the Tomb of Abraham Lincoln* (1926), and numerous articles for periodicals, including the influential article "The Evolution of the Negro Baptist Church" (printed in the *Journal of Negro History*, 1922). In addition, he composed hymns.

Brooks was awarded honorary degrees from Roger Williams University and Straight College (later renamed Simmons Memorial College). He was a temperance advocate and served as chaplain of the Anti-Saloon League of the District of Columbia. He was a cofounder of the American National Baptist Convention in 1895 and also chaired the Convention's Bureau of Education. Brooks served as vice president of the Bethel Literary and Historical Association, was a trustee of the National Training School for Women and Girls, and a member of the American Negro Academy and the Association for the Study of Negro Life and History. He and his first wife, Eva Holmes Brooks, were married in 1874 and had ten children; after her death in 1912, he married

Florence Swann in 1915, and Viola Washington in 1933. He is buried in Lincoln Memorial Cemetery in Suitland, Maryland.

The Fall of Richmond, April 3, 1865

Where rolls o'er rocky bed the James,
I once beheld our town in flames.

The city like a furnace burned,
Its bridges into embers turned.

Vast buildings shot up roaring fire,
That spread, and leaped up high'r and high'r,

The wildest scenes were everywhere,
Some faces darkened with despair,

While a thousand souls, bearing none ill,
Were praising God, from vale to hill,

The very heavens rang with song,
"The day has come, we've waited long."

I'll ne'er forget when Richmond fell,
My town, where still my kindred dwell.

An empire, built at such a cost
Of blood and treasure, then was lost.

I saw that empire rise and wane,
My master's loss, my people's gain.

Now they and we alike are blest,
From North to South, from East to West.

Jeanie Gould Lincoln

May 28, 1855?–August 8, 1921

Born in Troy, New York, Jeanie Gould Lincoln moved to DC after her 1877 marriage to a prominent physician, Nathan Lincoln, and became a fixture of Washington high society. She wrote poetry, romances, and historical fiction. Her books include a collection of poems, *A Chaplet of Leaves* (1869), and the historical novels *Marjorie's Quest* (1872), *A*

Genuine Girl (1896), *An Unwilling Maid* (1897), *A Pretty Tory* (1899), *A Javelin of Fate* (1905), and *Luck of Rathcoole* (1912). Of special note was her novel *Her Washington Season* (1884), comprised of letters between two characters based on herself and another prominent society figure, Mrs. Benjamin Ogle Tayloe. Gould Lincoln published in various magazines and newspapers including *Peterson's* and the *Washington Times*.

Gould Lincoln was elected a member of the Society of American Authors in 1899. Three of her former houses in Washington still stand. In the 1890s, she lived at 1717 Twentieth Street NW. She subsequently lived at 2108 E Street NW, and her final address was at 2235 Q Street NW. She is buried in Oak Hill Cemetery.

"My Soldier's Grave" was written for the first official Decoration Day (now known as Memorial Day) on May 30, 1868. John A. Logan, the commander in chief of the Army of the Republic (an organization for northern veterans of the Civil War) issued General Order Number 11, designating that day each year "for the purpose of strewing with flowers or otherwise decorating the graves of comrades who died in defense of their country during the late rebellion, and whose bodies now lie in almost every city, village, and hamlet churchyard in the land." Logan was also a DC resident, and Logan Circle includes a sculpture of him on horseback. Every Memorial Day, Logan's mausoleum at the U.S. Soldiers' and Airmen's Home National Cemetery in DC is opened to the public. Poems such as this one by Gould Lincoln helped to popularize the holiday and transform the act of mourning from a personal commemoration to a national ritual.

My Soldier's Grave

Hark! Do you hear the fife and drums?
The troops are marching down this way;
How proudly the battalion comes,
With martial pomp and panoply.

They carry flowers to deck the graves
Of those we loved,—of those who fell
For Freedom! O'er Columbia's braves
Strew laurel and the asphodel.

My eyes are brimming o'er with tears,
As, far away, a grave I see,
Where lies the buried love of years,
And stranger hands strew flowers for me.

They do not know the weary pain,
They cannot feel the grateful joy,
With which I thank them o'er again
For memory of my soldier boy!

Today I laid a fair, white rose,
Upon a grave, unclaimed, unknown,
With whispered prayer for all of those
Whose hearts are aching like my own.

O! ever let our banner bright,
Wave proudly o'er the daisied sod,
Where sleep the heroes in their might
Who died for Freedom and for God!

T. Thomas Fortune

October 3, 1856–June 2, 1928

T. Thomas Fortune would become best known as the editor of the *New York Age*, the leading African American newspaper in the United States from the 1880s to the early 1900s, but he got his start in DC, attending Howard University (although never graduating) and taking his first job as a reporter at the *People's Advocate*.

Fortune cofounded the National Afro-American League, a precursor to the Niagara Movement and the NAACP, and edited the influential weekly *Negro World*. His books include *Black and White: Land, Labor and Politics in the South* (1884), *The Kind of Education the Afro-American Most Needs* (1898), and *Dreams of Life: Miscellaneous Poems* (1905).

Fortune was active in Republican Party politics and was a longtime advisor to Booker T. Washington. His importance as a leader in Reconstruction America cannot be overstated. Born enslaved in Florida,

Fortune's writing helped lay the foundations for the modern civil rights movement.

Nat Turner

He stood erect, a man as proud
As ever to a tyrant bowed
Unwilling head or bent a knee,
And longed, while bending, to be free;

And o'er his ebon features came
A shadow—'twas of manly shame—
Aye, shame that he should wear a chain
And feel his manhood writhed with pain,
Doomed to a life of plodding toil,
Shamefully rooted to the soil!

He stood erect; his eyes flashed fire;
His robust form convulsed with ire;
"I will be free! I will be free!
Or, fighting, die a man!" cried he.

Virginia's hills were lit at night—
The slave had risen in his might;
And far and near Nat's wail went forth,
To South and East, and West and North,
And strong men trembled in their power,
And weak men felt 'twas now their hour.

"I will be free! I will be free!
Or, fighting, die a man!" cried he.
The tyrant's arm was all too strong,
Had swayed dominion all too long;
And so the hero met his end
As all who fall as Freedom's friend.

The blow he struck shook slavery's throne;
His cause was just, e'en skeptics own;
And round his lowly grave soon swarmed
Freedom's brave hosts for freedom arm'd.
That host was swollen by Nat's kin

To fight for Freedom, Freedom win,
Upon the soil that spurned his cry;
"I will be free, or I will die!"

Let tyrants quake, e'en in their power,
For sure will come the awful hour
When they must give an answer, why
Heroes in chains should basely die,
Instead of rushing to the field
And counting battle ere they yield.

Lincoln

The waves dashed high; the thunders echoed far;
The lightnings flashed into the dismal gloom
The bolts by Vulcan forged in Nature's womb,
And earth was shaken by the furious war!
The Ship of State was strained in every spar!
And strong men felt that now had come their doom;
And weak men scanned the dark heavens for a star
To save them from a fratricidal tomb.
But, one, amid the strife—collected, calm,
Patient and resolute—was firm, and trod
The deck, defiant of the angry storm,
Guiding the ship—like to some ancient god!
And high upon the scroll of endless fame,
In diamond letters, flashes Lincoln's name.

The Diamond in the Clay

The man who finds a diamond in the clay
And knows its worth from common glass
That others trod upon or blindly pass—
Their dreamful eyes uplifted from the way,
The people of that all too common class
Diogenes rebuked, as we may still, alas!
For wisdom's children yet are prone to stray
In nature's sunlight groping through life's day,
And holds it at its value true, howe'er
The common sort may taunt him for his faith,

Until it nestles in Fame's fickle ear,
Brilliant, compelling Admiration's breath,
Is more to be esteemed of men by far
Than they who praise the stone become a star.

Slavery to the Slave!
On the hills of Hayti ring
Mandates of the Frenchman's king,
And the waves the tidings bring—
"Slavery to the slave!"
Toussaint, arm thee for the fight!
Strike a blow for human right!
Crush, O crush! the tyrant's might,
And thy country save!
Stay thy arm when every foe
From thy land in haste shall go,
Sick at heart beneath the blow
On the battlefield!
Long may Hayti's banners wave!
O'er her valiant few, so brave!
Heroes worthy patriots' grave,
Who would never yield!

❖ PART III ❖

Poets of Moral Persuasion

Poets of Moral Persuasion

Daniel Alexander Payne

February 24, 1811–November 2, 1893

Born in Charleston, South Carolina, to free parents, Daniel Alexander Payne distinguished himself early by building a school where he taught slaves. Because this activity was made illegal after the Nat Turner Slave Rebellion, he had to flee South Carolina in 1835; he moved north to study for the ministry in Pennsylvania, becoming ordained as a Lutheran minister in 1839 before switching to the African Episcopal Methodist Church in 1841. Payne held pulpits in Washington and Baltimore, rising to the rank of bishop. He traveled widely to preach and train other African American preachers and helped to shape the AME Church during Reconstruction.

In his memoir, *Recollections of Seventy Years* (1888), Bishop Payne recalled moving to DC to lead Israel AME Church, where "I laid aside my books, bought a jack-plane, smoothing-plane, saw, hammer, rule, etc.; threw off my coat, and, the Society furnishing the lumber, in a few weeks" created the pews for the church. While living in DC, he also published five "Epistles on the Education of the Ministry," a series of controversial articles demanding systematic training for religious leaders. Payne reported that, as a result, "the enemies of Christian culture belched and howled forth all manner of vituperation against me." But the AME General Conference appointed him chair of their Committee on Education, and in this influential position Payne laid out a course of studies for future ministers that was adopted by the church.

Payne was also active in the Underground Railroad in the Chesapeake region. In 1862, Payne wrote: "Congress passed the bill abolishing slavery in the District of Columbia. The following Monday night I called on President Lincoln to know if he intended to sign the bill of emancipation, and thereby exterminate slavery in the District of Columbia? Having been previously informed of my intention to interview him, and having on my arrival at the White House sent in my card, he met me at the door of the room in which he and Senator [William] Washburn were conversing. Taking me by the hand, he said: 'Bishop Payne, of the African M. E. Church?' I answered in the affirmative; so with my hand in his he led me to the fire-place, introduced me to Senator Washburn, and seated me in an armchair between himself and the Senator. . . . President Lincoln received and conversed with me as though I had been one of his intimate acquaintances or one of his friendly neighbors. I left him with a profound sense of his real greatness and of his fitness to rule a nation composed of almost all the races on the face of the globe."

In 1863, Payne cofounded Wilberforce University in Xenia, Ohio, and served as university president for thirteen years, becoming the first African American college president in the country. In addition to his autobiography, *Recollections of Seventy Years*, Payne published a history of the AME Church, sermons, and a book of poems, *The Pleasures and Other Miscellaneous Poems* (1850).

From The Pleasures

Pleasures of Vice are those which most pursue,
Regarding all their promis'd joys as true;
Now will they heed the warning voice that cries,
the soul which sins, that soul in mis'ry lies.
But, like the headlong horse or stubborn mule,
Despise all truth, contemn all righteous rule,
Delight in sin as swine delight in mire,
Till hell itself entomb their souls in fire!
Thus does the Drunkard, in the sparkling bowl,
Pursue the joys which charm his brutish soul;
But soon he feels the serpent's fang is there,
The gall of wo, the demon's awful stare:
For in the visions of his crazied soul,
The furies dance and horrid monsters roll.

Some find their pleasure in tobacco wads,
Delight in them as goats in chewing cuds;
Others believe they find it quite enough,
In smoking cigars, or in taking snuff.

The glutton and the greasy epicure,
Believe they have it—for they tell us so—
In eating venison, turtle-soup and clams,
Beef a la mode and lobsters, ducks and hams;
In puddings, pound-cakes, pies and cold ice cream;
In black-strap, brandy, claret and champagne.
O who could think that men, to whom is given
Such souls as will outlive the stars of heaven,
Could hope to find in such a low employ,
The sweet pulsations of a real joy!

But dandies find it in their curled hair,
Greas'd with pomatum or the oil of bear;
In fine mustaches, breast-pins, golden chains;
In brass-capt boot-heels, or in walking canes.
Some ladies find it in their boas and muffs,
In silks and satins, laces, muslin-stuffs
Made into dresses, pointed, long and wide,
With flounces deep, and bran-bustles beside,
All neat and flowing in Parisian grace;
With small sunshades to screen their smiling face;
Then up the streets, like pea-fowls bright and gay,
They promenade on every sunny day.
Some seek for pleasure in the giddy dance,
Where Fashion smiles, and Beauty's siren glance
The soul delights and fills light bounding hearts
With dreams of love,—such dreams as sin imparts;
Not the pure streams that flow, my God, from thee:
The streams of bliss—the love of purity.
In cock-fights others find it; some, in dice;
Some in the chambers of lascivious vice.
The vile blasphemer seeks it in his shame,
Who sport like devils with the Holy Name.
O hapless wretches! fool'd and self deceiv'd!
Angels weep o'er you! God himself is griev'd!

Christopher Pearse Cranch

March 8, 1813–January 20, 1892

Christopher Pearse Cranch was born in Arlington (in what is today northern Virginia but what was, at that time, a part of the District of Columbia) and attended Columbian College, the fore-runner of George Washington University, and Harvard Divinity School. He came from a distinguished family: his father was a federal judge, his aunt was married to Noah Webster, and his grandmother was the sister of Abigail Adams. He would later marry a cousin, the great-granddaughter of John Adams.

Cranch was a Unitarian minister and associated with the Transcendentalists. He coedited the Transcendentalist journal the *Western Messenger* and contributed to the *Dial* and the *Harbinger*. Cranch spent a number of years studying painting in Italy and France and was elected to the National Academy of Design in 1864.

He is the author of three books of poems: *Poems* (1844), *The Bird and the Bell* (1875), and *Ariel and Caliban* (1887). He also published children's literature, wrote an opera libretto, and translated literature from Italian to English.

Correspondences

All things in Nature are beautiful types to the soul that will read
    them;
        Nothing exists upon earth, but for unspeakable ends.
Every object that speaks to the senses was meant for the spirit:
        Nature is but a scroll—God's hand-writing thereon.
Ages ago, when man was pure, ere the flood overwhelmed him,
        While in the image of God every soul yet lived,
Everything stood as a letter or word of a language familiar,
        Telling of truths which now only the angels can read.
Lost to man was the key of those sacred hieroglyphics—
        Stolen away by sin—till with Jesus restored.
Now with infinite pains we here and there spell out a letter;
        Now and then will the sense feebly shine through the dark.
When we perceive the light which breaks through the visible symbol,
        What exultation is ours! we the discovery have made!

Yet is the meaning the same as when Adam lived sinless in Eden,
    Only long-hidden it slept and now again is restored.
Man unconsciously uses figures of speech every moment,
    Little dreaming the cause why to such terms he is prone—
Little dreaming that everything has its own correspondence
    Folded within it of old, as in the body the soul.
Gleams of the mystery fall on us still, though much is forgotten,
    And through our commonest speech illumines the path of our
      thoughts.
Thus does the lordly sun shine out a type of the Godhead;
    Wisdom and Love the beams that stream on a darkened world.
Thus do the sparkling waters flow, giving joy to the desert,
    And the great Fountain of Life opens itself to the thirst.
Thus does the word of God distil like the rain and the dew-drops,
    Thus does the warm wind breathe like to the Spirit of God,
And the green grass and the flowers are signs of the regeneration.
    O thou Spirit of Truth; visit our minds once more!
Give us to read, in letters of light, the language celestial,
    Written all over the earth—written all over the sky:
Thus may we bring our hearts at length to know our Creator,
    Seeing in all things around types of the Infinite Mind.

The Pines and the Sea

Beyond the low marsh-meadows and the beach,
Seen through the hoary trunks of windy pines,
The long blue level of the ocean shines.
The distant surf, with hoarse, complaining speech,
Out from its sandy barrier seems to reach;
And while the sun behind the woods declines,
The moaning sea with sighing boughs combines,
And waves and pines make answer, each to each.
O melancholy soul, whom far and near,
In life, faith, hope, the same sad undertone
Pursues from thought to thought! thou needs must hear
An old refrain, too much, too long thine own:
'Tis thy mortality infects thine ear;
The mournful strain was in thyself alone.

Jane Grey Swisshelm
December 6, 1815–July 22, 1884

Jane Grey Swisshelm was an abolitionist, a feminist, and the Washington correspondent for the *New York Tribune* and the *St. Cloud Democrat*. Swisshelm sometimes published poems under the pseudonym Jennie Deans.

Swisshelm was the first woman to be granted a seat in the Senate Press Gallery. She appealed directly to President Millard Fillmore for the privilege and wrote: "He was much surprised and tried to dissuade me. The place would be very unpleasant for a lady, and would attract attention. I would not like it; but he gave me the seat. I occupied it one day, greatly to the surprise of the Senators, the reporters, and others on the floor and in the galleries; but felt that the novelty would soon wear off, and that women would work there and win bread without annoyance."

During the Civil War, Swisshelm worked as a clerk in the quartermaster general's office and a volunteer nurse in army hospitals in DC. She published a memoir, *Half a Century* (1880).

In an obituary notice in the *Washington Evening Star,* she was noted as "one of the earliest champions of woman's property rights, one of the apostles of abolition. . . . [A]lways shrewd, aggressive, active, generally engaged in some kind of warfare, she certainly led an eventful life, and did an amount of work, against heavy odds, that few of the stronger and more combative sex can boast of."

The first poem reprinted here was published in the *Pittsburgh Saturday Visiter,* a newspaper Swisshelm published from 1847 to 1851 for "the promotion of moral and social reform." The poem was written to answer an outspoken critic who complained, "She is all man but the pantaloons." This poem was reprinted in other newspapers and widely commented upon at the time.

To George D. Prentiss
Perhaps you have been busy
Horsewhipping Sal or Lizzie,
Stealing some poor man's baby,
Selling its mother, may-be.

You say—and you are witty—
That I—and, tis a pity—
Of manhood lack but dress;
But you lack manliness,
A body clean and new,
A soul within it, too.
Nature must change her plan
Ere you can be a man.

November

The dead leaves, their rich mosaics,
Of olive and gold and brown,
Had laid on the rain-wet pavements,
Through all the embowered town.

They were washed by the autumn tempest,
They were trod by hurrying feet,
And the maids came out with their brooms,
And swept them into the street.

To be crushed and lost forever
'Neath the wheels, in the black mire lost,—
The summer's precious darlings,
She nurtured at such cost!

O words that have fallen from me!
O golden thoughts and true!
Must I see the leaves as a symbol
Of the fate which awaiteth you?

Anna Hanson Dorsey

December 12, 1815–December 26, 1896

Anna Hanson Dorsey wrote poetry, novels, and drama. Her works include *May Brook* (1856), *Oriental Pearl* (1857), *Warp and Woof* (1887), and *Palms* (1887). She was born in Georgetown and lived her entire life in DC. A convert to Catholicism in 1840, her writing is noted for its Catholic themes. She married Lorenzo Dorsey in 1837 and had four children; her only son was killed while serving in the Union army during the Civil War. One daughter, Ella Dorsey, also became a writer (of journalism and novels).

Dorsey was active in a number of organizations, including the Colonial Dames, the Daughters of the American Revolution, and the Washington Literary Society. The University of Notre Dame honored her in 1889 with a Laetare Medal for writing that "illustrates the ideals of the Catholic Church and enriches the heritage of humanity."

From **Sunset among the Alps**
The valleys rest in shadow and the hum
Of gentle sounds, and low-toned melodies
Are stilled, and twilight spreads her misty arms
In broader sadness o'er their happy scenes,
And creeps along the mountains' snowy sides,
Until the setting sun's last mellow beams
Wreathe up in many a gold and purple ring
Around the highest Alpine peaks.
                              So bright
Were these fair coronals, of brilliance, snow,
And mist—so sparkling was the rose-like hue
Which shed sweet halos round the far-off beams;
So spirit-like each whisper of the winds;
So solemn was the wild magnificence
Of their high solitudes, that every peak
And avalanche, whose rest is like the sleep
Of hungry giants, seemed the ministers
Of Him who reared those altars to himself!
But listen! 'twas no echo of the winds—
I heard a voice from yonder lofty height—
Again—
          "Praise ye the Lord"—"Praise ye the Lord!"
In accents loud the tones demand, and then
From Alp to Alp, men's voices catch the note
And swelling onward rolls the chorus sweet,
Until the valleys dim, and air and sky,
And mountain caverns tremble with the song.
The chamois pauses on his cloud-girt cliff
And listens with his head upturned—intent,

And conscious;—the wild gazelle, half startled
From her rest, which full of constant peril
Is but light, with one foot poised in air
Stands ready for a leap beyond man's reach;
But soon distinguishing those blessed sounds
From hunter's shout and bugle note, returns
Again, and closes her soft eyes in peace,
As swelling past the *jubilate* rings!

Charles Astor Bristed (Carl Benson)
October 6, 1820–January 14, 1874

Charles Astor Bristed was an American scholar who sometimes wrote under the pen name Carl Benson. Bristed earned degrees from Yale College and Trinity College in Cambridge, England. He contributed articles and translations to *Galaxy*, the *American Review*, and other journals and edited the school textbook *Selections from Catallus* (1849). His other books include *The Upper Ten Thousand: Sketches of American Society* (1852); the four-volume *Pieces of a Broken-Down Critic* (1858); *Now Is the Time to Settle It: Suggestions on the Present Crisis* (1862); *The Interference Theory of Government* (1867); *American Beauty Personified as the Nine Muses* (1870); a book of poems, *Anacreontics* (1872); a memoir, *Five Years in an English University* (1873); and a novel, *Prosper* (1874).

Bristed was the nephew and heir of John Jacob Astor, making him independently wealthy. He married twice and had two sons. Bristed was one of the founders of the Astor Library, a free public library in Manhattan. He moved to DC in his later years and lived and entertained lavishly in a large house at 1325 K Street NW opposite Franklin Square (now razed) until his death at age fifty-three. An advocate of horse racing, Bristed also served as president of the Washington Turf Association. The two poems here align him with the temperance movement.

The Drinker's Apology

from the French

Come now! If I drink, where's the crime? Can you tell?
Look round us! All Nature is drinking as well.

The Earth drinks the dew, and the Sun, floating free,
Stoops to drink of the wave from the cup of the sea.
The tree, as he plunged his roots in the ground,
Through numberless mouths drinks the torrent profound.
All drink—but man only, that Scion divine,
While others drink water, knows how to drink wine;
And, measureless tippler, can boast, he alone,
Having once drunk enough, that he still can drink on.

The Pertinacious Toper

from the German

In the coolest cellar here I rest,
Near a full cask of liquor,
Right glad at heart, since of the best
I for myself can pick here.
The butler puts the spigot in,
Obedient to my winking,
Gives me the cup; I hold it up,
I'm drinking, drinking, drinking!

A demon plagues me, thirst to wit,
And so, to scare the fellow,
I take my glass and into it
Let flow the Rhine-wine mellow.
The whole earth smiles upon me then,
With ruddy, rosy blinking;
I could hurt the worst of men,
While drinking, drinking, drinking!

But ah! my thirst grows fiercer still
With every flask I ope here,
Which is th' inevitable ill
Of every genuine toper.
Yet this my comfort, what at last
From chair to floor I'm sinking,
I always kept my purpose fast
Of drinking, drinking, drinking!

Caroline Healey Dall

June 22, 1822–December 17, 1912

Famous for her associations with the American Transcendentalists, Caroline Healey Dall was active in the National Woman's Rights Convention and the New England Women's Club and was cofounder of the American Social Science Association, which advocated for improvements in the condition of prisons and insane asylums. Dall lived most of her life in Boston. She married Charles Dall, a Unitarian minister, and had two children, but her husband soon proved himself mentally unstable. When he finally abandoned the family in 1855 to take a post as a missionary in Calcutta, Dall was released to do the work to which she felt most naturally drawn: to write and give public lectures on women's rights and abolitionism. She cofounded the pioneering feminist journal *Una* with Paulina Davis.

Dall's books include *Woman's Right to Labor, or Low Wages and Hard Work* (1860); *Historical Pictures Retouched: A Volume of Miscellanies* (1861), a revisionist feminist history; *Women's Rights under the Law* (1861); *The College, the Market, and the Court; or Woman's Relation to Education, Labor, and Law* (1867); *Egypt's Place in History* (1868); *The Romance of Association* (1875); *My First Holiday; or, Letters Home from Colorado, Utah, and California* (1881); *What We Really Know about Shakespeare* (1885); *Barbara Fritchie* (1892); *Margaret and Her Friends: Ten Conversations with Margaret Fuller* (1895); *Transcendentalism in New England* (1897); and her memoir, *Alongside* (1900). She contributed articles to such publications as the *Springfield Republican*, the *Cambridge Tribune*, and the *Nation*.

From 1842 to 1844, Dall lived in the Georgetown neighborhood and was vice principal at Miss Lydia English's School for Young Ladies (now converted to the Colonial Apartments, 1305–11 Thirtieth Street NW). She returned to DC upon her retirement in 1879, to live with her son, a naturalist and curator at the Smithsonian Institution. Their house (1526 Eighteenth Street NW in the Dupont Circle neighborhood) still stands and is now the Turkish American Assembly. Dall became close friends with First Lady Frances Cleveland, and was a guest lay-preacher in Unitarian churches. Alfred University awarded her an honorary doctorate in 1877.

At a Death-Bed

Dear eyes that never looked reproach
    Dear lips that always smiled,
Dear heart of grace, that never lacked
    The sweet thought of a child!

How shall my life go on, when yours
    Is wrapped in fuller light?
How dream a sun shall ever rise
    Upon so drear a night?

"Come, lead me," once you gently said,
    "Lead onward to the end"
Putting my hand in yours, I see
    "My Father is my Friend."

My darling, I am led in turn
    Along the sweet green way;
Bless God for all the light you give
    With thoughts that never stray.

Close to that Father's arm you cling,
    Your dear eyes seek his face,
Your loving lips still chant his praise,
    Your heart accepts his grace.

My darling, as I see you go,
    I scarce can stay alone:
The glory from the Godhead draws
    Both waiting spirits on.

Good-night! we say who linger here;
    But you, a glad Good-morrow!
The joy that angels feel, you *know*—
    Their peace we feebly borrow.

Madeleine Vinton Dahlgren

July 13, 1825–May 28, 1889

Madeleine Vinton Dahlgren published journalism and some early poems under the pen names "Corinne" and "Cornelia." She also translated literature from French, Spanish, and Italian into English.

Dahlgren was associated with powerful men in DC: she was the daughter of Representative Samuel Finley Vinton (D-OH). She married and was widowed twice: first to Daniel Convers Goddard, first assistant secretary to the U.S. Department of the Interior (with whom she had two children), then to U.S. Navy Admiral John A. Dahlgren, commander of the Washington Navy Yard during the Civil War and famous for advances in gunnery (with whom she had three children).

In the 1870s, Dahlgren was one of the acknowledged leaders of DC's high society. Henry James wrote a thinly fictionalized portrait of her in his short story "Pandora." Her extremely successful nonfiction book *Etiquette of Social Life in Washington* established her as the primary expert on manners, decorum, and protocol, and was published in five editions, from 1873 through 1881. The book combines advice on such matters as proper attire, seating arrangements at formal dinners, and how and when to make social calls, with Dahlgren's personal philosophy of integrity and subdued gentility.

In addition to her guide book, Dahlgren is best known for her *Memoir of John A. Dahlgren, Rear Admiral United States Navy* (1882), and *Thoughts on Female Suffrage* (1871), in which she argued *against* extending the vote to women. She also wrote several novels, including *South-Mountain Magic* (1882), *A Washington Winter* (1883), *The Lost Names* (1886), *Lights and Shadows of Life* (1887), *Divorced* (1887), and *South Sea Sketches* (1891). Her poems and short fiction appeared in newspapers, and she was a correspondent to the *Washington Evening Star.*

Dahlgren cofounded the Washington Literary Society and served as its vice president; she also served as president of the Ladies' Catholic Missionary Society of Washington. In addition to her city home on Massachusetts Avenue NW (now razed), she lived at the historic Commandant's Headquarters in the Navy Yard and maintained a country estate at South Mountain, Maryland, where she commissioned a

Gothic revival stone chapel that still stands, and where she is buried in the family crypt.

A First Pair of Spectacles
No romance in this light we ween,
The useful only may be seen,
Yet visions of the past will rise,
Like Banquo's ghost, thro' faded eyes.

Of golden hair now pale of hue,
Of red, red lips, now wan and blue,
Of rounded cheek now puckered in,
Of swan-like neck, now wizened thin.

Once willowy form all bent with age,
Past happy hours of youth's closed page;
These now, are retrospective joys,
Of life, the unsubstantial toys.

Again, we look these glasses through,
No vistas of the past we view,
The length'ning shades have vanished all,
That swept o'er nature like a pall.

But in their place, translucent rise,
The enlarged vision of the skies,
Nor things of Earth fill up the view,
For grander pageants form anew.

MORAL.
'Tis hope immortal in these "specs,"
That mirrors heaven in light reflex.

The Blue Ridge
When God's avenging angel hurled
Our primal parents from their world
Of blissful loveliness and rest,
And cast them forth sad and unblessed,

Our mother Eve, yet lingering, brought
The veil of Isis, which she sought

To hold from angry Nature's grasp,
Her shrinking form from view to clasp.

And thus this boon of Heavenly gift,
A glimpse of Eden sent adrift,
Still rests o'er Blue Ridge craggy height,
And shadows forth a brighter light.

Empurpled mists float to the skies,
Translucent, glorious, they arise,
While Nature's heart amid these hills,
With mystic throbs, enraptured thrills.

Solomon G. Brown

1829?–June 26, 1906

Born of free parents in DC, Solomon G. Brown worked in the U.S. Post Office beginning in 1844 when he was fifteen years old. In 1845 he was detailed to assist in the construction of the first telegraph system from Baltimore to Washington. (Brown later stated that he was the messenger who carried the first telegraph message to the White House.) His next job was as a packer for Gillman & Brothers chemical manufacturing, through 1852.

In 1852, at age twenty-three, Brown began work in the Transportation Department of the new Smithsonian Institute, making him their first African American employee. He was subsequently appointed to the Foreign Exchange Division, where he would serve as a highly regarded clerk, and in 1869 he became the institution's first African American registrar. In addition, Brown was an avid amateur scientist; he provided scientific and educational illustrations for many lectures and publications. Brown remained in the employ of the Smithsonian Institution for fifty-four years, retiring in 1906 at the age of seventy-seven. He died in his home just a few months later.

Brown helped found the Hillsdale neighborhood of Anacostia and served three consecutive terms during the Reconstruction era as a delegate to the Territorial Government of the District of Columbia. His house on Elvans Road in Anacostia no longer stands. He was buried in Hillsdale Cemetery, near today's Suitland Parkway, which is also no longer extant.

Individual poems of Brown's were published in African American newspapers across the United States but were not collected until 1983, when the Smithsonian Institution published a pamphlet, *Kind Regards from Solomon G. Brown.*

His poem "Fifty Years To-Day" was written for a special ceremony honoring Brown's long service to the Smithsonian Institution. It mentions by name the first three directors of what was then called the United States National Museum, under whom Brown served: Joseph Henry, a physicist; Spencer Fullerton Baird, an ornithologist; and George Brown Goode, an ichthyologist. The poem also refers to William Temple Hornaday, the zoologist who founded the National Zoological Park and served as its first director.

God's Vengeance Is Creeping

God's vengeance is creeping, this Nation must pay,
For lives that are wasted, the crimes of our day;
We are cheated in election, denied every right,
The sin's unrepented, not hid from God's sight.

This Nation is dreaming, mid wrong and despair,
Our brothers' blood streaming, their groans fill the air;
The blood that's being wasted, will cry unto God,
This Nation, He measures by a just holy rod.

The North is protesting against this great shame,
No murderers are arrested, and none are arraigned;
Still onward they murder, untrammeled by laws.
These crimes become bolder; without any cause.

They charge men with arson, they charge them with rape,
No chance to disprove it, no chance for escape;
They'll hang without mercy, without trial or proof,
Not waiting for jurors, for witness, nor truth.

Most all of such charges, are brought up for spite,
To drive off some leaders who must fly to-night;
None but these demons, have heard of these crimes,
The pretended outraged one, is deranged in her mind.

It's strange all this outrage, occurs in the South,
The Rapers are Negroes, with hell in their mouths,
The white men are Angels, with power to slay,
They need no tribunal, but have all one way.

The justice won't know them, pretends they are strange.
So none are arrested and none are arraigned.
He can not indite them, without he has proof;
Just who hung these negroes, he can't get the truth.

Each week as it passes, fresh victims we see,
A ghastly cold body's found hung from some tree.
With cards pinned down upon it, "this negro has raped,
The people of Pineville, provided this tape."

The Nation's unable, to care for black sons,
Her Courts are too feeble, and so are her guns,
Her dark sons are bleeding, and swinging from trees
While thousands are pleading, and mourning for these.

The Church of this Nation, why don't it arise,
And cry from each station appeal to the skies:
By calling for justice, demanding what's right,
Like they did in slavery, "arise in their might."

No tide can withstand you, though hell may arise.
Should the North be united, and cry to the skies,
Demand from this Nation, these murders must cease,
that the sons of this country, may live here in peace.

Your millions are bowing to some kind of God,
We ask, whom you worship, and who is your Lord?
Is your God, our Creator, the Father of all?
That God you have told us, that all men must call?

We must say, "Our Father, for all are His Sons;
Do hear your own children, for we are all one."
"Forgive us our Father, as we do each other—
And grant us our Father, what we give to our brother."

How can we as neighbors, still worship one Lord,
And own that Christ Jesus, as the only true God;
How can they approach Him, and feel He is pleased,
Yet run down our brothers, and swing them from trees?

Do stop these foul murders, this lynching of men,
God hunt out these wretches, and purge our fair land;
Make up large meetings, unite everywhere,
Let Christians, while greeting, discuss this affair.

There are millions of Northmen, whose voice must be heard,
Loyal Southern Christians, who honor God's Word;
And Western brave farmers, who believe in what's right,
With Eastern Mayflowers, who in justice delight.

Then cry from your pulpits, your altars, and stand
How can you now falter, and not take a hand?
For mercy and justice, for law and for right,
Arrest these masked demons, who travel by night.

Your pulpits are silent, our priests are tied down,
The Southern church members, have blood on their gown
They sit in their places, pretending to pray,
With long pious faces, How Holy are they?

Oh! God what pretentions, of blood thirsty souls,
Whose priests dare not mention; what they do behold;
Oh! let loose Thy vengeance, and take up our cause,
We have no protection, under what they call laws.

God! visit this Nation, begin at its head,
Go down through each station, and purge every grade,
Move sin from high stations, move misery and crime,
To crush out such murderers, let Heavens combine.

God's vengeance is creeping, the time's near at hand,
A justice long sleeping, will burst o'er this land.
The pride and the hatred, against the black race;
Is a curse to this Nation, yes! a country's disgrace.

Fifty Years To-Day

'Mid all the changes I have seen
Since fifty years have rolled between,
My eyes can rest on only few—
Whose faces once could daily view,
And kindly greet on passing.

My mind goes back to hallowed spots
Fraught by memories by some forgot;
Which bring up friends most dear to me
Who've long since gone beyond the sea—
It seems I'll not forget them.

Many I've known are dead and gone
Many are here who've since been born;
Some's resigned and changed their home
Others through foreign countries roam,
And these are—

—Sending gems to you and me
They've gathered from the land and sea
These, too, were young, now growing old;
But many facts are yet untold,
To be revealed by others.

Every year since here I'd stay,
Some much loved friend's been called away,
Younger men in every case—
Have come right up and filled their place
And suggesting some improvements.

We'll now call up our first main chief
Whose history may be told in brief;
A pleasant man so meek and mild
Was great, yet gentle as a child,
A man whom all regarded

A man of pious, Godly fear
Affording all his friendly care;
'Twas he who first appointed me

Since then he's gone beyond the sea—
We never can forget him.

Since then new generations born,
Take his research and move them on;
Are treasured by great men of thought,
Received the credit such research ought,
Thus adding much to knowledge.

By Henry the electric plans were laid,
His mind this grand conception made;
By him was launched out on the sea—
Which now brings news to you and me,
In the shortest space of time.

I've been impressed o'er fifty years
By Henry's brain and patient cares;
The honors given F. B. Morse
Were wholly done at Henry's cause
Which all his friends regretted.

By Henry, I always will believe
The telegraph was first conceived.
The part he played upon the staff—
Made complete the telegraph,
Which is our greatest blessing.

Our second chief who filled his place
Was one of justice, truth and grace;
A scientist of great renown
No greater naturalist could be found,
In this, or other countries.

My highest tribute to these names
My comrades here will do the same;
To Henry, Baird, and G. Brown Goode—
Each in his place wherein they stood—
Long may their fame be honored.

Wisdom from these minds would flow
Increasing knowledge more and more;

Now younger men can easily learn
Just how these great men were concerned
In diffusing useful knowledge.

From precious seeds these men have sown
Gigantic plants and trees and grown;
The Weather Bureau was planted here
From observations made each year,
And studies out by Henry—

The nation's museum had its growth;
The Fish Commission was brought forth;
The exchange of books began to breathe—
By Baird and Henry these were conceived
And carried into practice.

I've lived to hail the third learned chief,
Whose election brought us much relief;
While we greatly missed the two then gone
Yet every branch moves smoothly on,
With many great improvements.

With our present chief the Zoo did start
And other additions for his part;
He also gained that splendid park
A place once dangerous, wet and dark,
Is now a splendid county.

Improvements seen on every hand
The costly, desirable, stretch of land;
See how grand since he begun
The work our honored chief has done—
To beautify this city.

Since eighteen hundred and fifty-two,
This may seem far back to you;
But much has passed I have not told—
Then I was young but now I'm old,
But still I am observing.

Mary Abigail Dodge (Gail Hamilton)
March 31, 1833–August 17, 1896

Mary Abigail Dodge, who wrote under the pen name Gail Hamilton, was born in Massachusetts and came to DC in 1856 to be governess to the children of Gamaliel and Margaret Bailey. Hamilton wrote poetry, essays, and journalism, published in Bailey's *New Era* and other progressive publications, and her work was notable for its wit and strong feminist and antislavery stances.

Hamilton coedited *Our Young Folks* with Lucy Larcom, managed *Wood's Household Magazine*, and wrote a biography of Senator James G. Blaine, whose wife was her cousin (1895). Her other nonfiction books include *Woman's Wrongs, a Counter Irritant* (1868), *Woman's Worth and Worthlessness* (1872), and *A Battle of the Books* (1870). In addition, she published a novel, *First Love Is Best* (1873); a travel book, *Wool Gathering* (1867); and a book of poems, *Chips, Fragments, and Vestiges* (published posthumously, 1902).

An obituary in the *Washington Morning Times* in 1896 states, "She had vigorous convictions which she expressed in graceful, witty and forceful language."

This first poem was written in response to a poem by her friend John Greenleaf Whittier, accusing Hamilton of possessing "measureless ridicule" as "she wields a pen / Too sharply nibbed for thin-skinned men."

Note
Oh! My!
A little fly
Folding her wings
On a fly-leaf
Brief,
Suddenly sings
Exclamation-points and things
To see a poet
Painting her picture so that all the world will know it
And receive it—
But won't more than half believe it;
For the beauty dear is all in your eyes

And doesn't belong to flies
Of my size!

Paint a bee in your bonnet,
Paint a wasp alighting on it;
Paint a devil's darning needle:
And don't wheedle
All the good folk into spying
And trying
To find where I am lying
Underneath the glory
Of your story,
Whereas before a drawing
Of a hornet with a sting,
They would say with quick ha-ha-ing
"On my word, 'tis just the thing!
Heaven mend her faults"—Oh!
The wicked little Quaker,
To go and make her
Break her
Heart, talking about faults
When thee know I haven't any—
Or not many—
Nothing to hurt you,
Only just enough to keep
Me from dissolving into a tasteless pap of virtue—
Or to be loved with holy fervor
By the *New York Observer*,
And the apostles of that shoddy
Sort of gospel now springing up from Oregon to Passamaquoddy,
Which teaches with a din,
Very pleasant to the din-ner
Not to save the world from sin,
But to fill the world with sinners!

Come now in good sooth,
Little friend, speak the truth—
Thy love for me such is

Thee put in those touches
Of rebuke and restriction
To quiet thy conscience, not speak thy conviction,
For thee know, heart and hand
I'm as good as thee can stand!
Am I not as sweet as maple molasses
When thee scold me for fingering thy brasses?
And did not the poet say of yore,
Angels could no more?
Ah, would not angels pity her
To be scolded by the "Saintly Whittier"?
That's Mrs. Hannaford—
And cannot a man afford
When pulpits preach him
And the women screech him
Up for a saint,
Not to throw stones at them that—ain't?

Ah, dear poet, and dear friend,
One whole sheet of paper has come to an end,
And the saucy fly with her jests and jeers
Shall stop her buzzing about my ears.
She folds her wings, she droops her eyes
And feels with an innermost glad surprise
The amber glory in which she lies—
The joy and beauty and wonder wrought
In the golden glow of a poet's thought.

To Dr. Bailey, with a Pair of Gloves, Christmas
I fear it will seem an Hibernian stroke
    To mark the sincerest of loves
By begloving a man whose great glory it is
    That he handles all sin without gloves.
But remember, I pray, that the glove in old times
    Was a signal of mortal defiance—
And in these evil days if a man can be found
    On whom Christendom places reliance—
Who always stands ready to shiver a lance,

For the love of the right, not renown, —
It is surely the least his admirers can do
To provide him with gloves to throw down.

Henry McNeal Turner

February 1, 1834–May 8, 1915

Henry McNeal Turner was the twelfth consecrated bishop of the African Methodist Episcopal Church. Born free in South Carolina, he was self-educated until enrolling in Trinity College in Baltimore, where he received his first formal education. He led pastorates in St. Louis, Baltimore, Washington, DC, and Savannah, and was appointed by President Abraham Lincoln to serve as the first African American chaplain to the U.S. Colored Troops during the Civil War.

Turner moved to DC in 1862 to lead Union Bethel Church. While in the city, he befriended powerful Reconstruction-era politicians, including Charles Sumner and Thaddeus Stevens. After the war, Turner became politically active in the Republican Party and was elected to the Georgia legislature in 1868. When he was expelled from that body along with all the other delegates of color, he gave a famous speech, declaring: "I shall neither fawn nor cringe before any party, nor stoop to beg them for my rights. . . . I am here to demand my rights and hurl thunderbolts at the men who dare to cross the threshold of my manhood." He was finally restored to his seat by the federal government in 1870. He held other notable political appointments: President Ulysses S. Grant named him postmaster of Macon in 1869, and in 1876 he was appointed president of Morris Brown College in Atlanta.

Turner edited two Black Nationalist newspapers: the *Voice of Missions* (1893–1900) and the *Voice of the People* (1901–4). He was also a correspondent for the *Christian Reporter*. He founded the International Migration Society and organized two ships that traveled to Liberia, resettling black Americans in two expeditions in 1895 and 1896. Turner was also a vocal supporter of prohibition and women's suffrage. He wrote *The Genius and Theory of Methodist Polity* (1885); his collected writings and speeches were published posthumously in 1971 under the title *Respect Black*.

A 1915 eulogy published in the *Crisis* stated: "Turner was the last of his clan: mighty men, physically and mentally, men who started at the bottom and hammered their way to the top by sheer brute strength, they were the spiritual progeny of African chieftains, and they built the African church in America."

The second poem, read on April 16, 1863, at the Fifteenth Street Presbyterian Church and reprinted in the *Liberator* newspaper, commemorates DC's special status as the first place slavery was officially ended (and the only place where slave owners were compensated financially). Nine months before the Emancipation Proclamation took effect, nearly 3,100 people held in bondage in DC became the nation's "First Freed."

Hymn

Kind Lord, before thy face
Again with joy we bow,
For all the gifts and grace
Thou dost on us bestow.
Our tongues would all Thy love proclaim,
And chant the honors of Thy name.

Here in Thine earthly house,
Our joyful souls have met;
Here paid our solemn vows,
And felt our union sweet.
For this our tongues Thy love proclaim,
And chant the honors of Thy name.

Now may we dwell in peace
Till here again we come;
And may our love increase
Till Thou shalt bring us home.
Then shall our tongues Thy love proclaim,
And chant the honors of Thy name.

One Year Ago Today

Dedicated to the Emancipated Slaves of the District of Columbia

Almighty God! we praise thy name
For having heard we pray;

For having freed us from our chains
One year ago today.

We thank thee for thy arm has stayed
Foul despotism's sway
And made Columbia's District free
One year ago today.

Give us the power to withstand
Oppression's baleful fray;
That right may triumph as it did
One year ago today.

Give liberty to millions yet
'Neath despotism's sway,
That they may praise thee as we did
One year ago today.

O! Guide us safely through this storm;
Bless Lincoln's gentle sway,
And then we'll ever praise thee, as
One year ago today.

Mary Emily Neeley Bradley
November 29, 1835 – April 24, 1898

Born in Easton, Maryland, Bradley began publishing in periodicals while still an adolescent, encouraged by her schoolteacher father. Her younger sister was also a writer, as were her husband's two sisters, giving her a supportive family environment in which to create.

Bradley published one book of poems, *Hidden Sweetness* (1886), and several books of short fiction for girls, including *Bread upon the Waters* (1855), *Douglass Farm* (1856), *Birds of a Feather* (1868), *A Wrong Confessed Is Half Redressed* (1870), and *The Story of a Summer* (1873). Much of her fiction and poetry for juveniles appeared in religious journals such as the *American Missionary*, but she also published poems in *Century*, *Harper's*, *Appleton's*, and *Scribner's Magazine*. Bradley lived in New York and in Washington, DC.

Beyond Recall

There was a time when Death and I
Came face to face together:
I was but young indeed to die,
And it was summer weather;
One happy year a wedded wife,
And I was slipping out of life.

You knelt beside me, and I heard,
As from some far-off distance,
a bitter cry that dimly stirred
My soul to make resistance.
You thought me dead; you called my name;
And back from Death itself I came.

But oh! that you had made no sign,
That I had heard no crying!
For now the yearning voice is mine,
And there is no replying:
Death never could so cruel be
As Life—and you—have proved to me!

Margaret Louisa Sullivan Burke

February 1836–March 16, 1917

Originally from Evansville, Indiana, Margaret Louisa Sullivan Burke graduated from Butler University, married twice, and had four children. Burke was a cofounder and first president of the League of American Pen Women in 1897. Working as a freelance journalist for the *Philadelphia Item,* she became the first woman to qualify for entry into the Press Gallery at the U.S. Capitol in 1890 under new rules limiting membership to those who derived their primary salary as dispatchers to daily newspapers (rules intended to professionalize journalism and to exclude lobbyists, women, and people of color from obtaining press passes).

She is the author of *The Story of Hercules, or the Truth about Financial Legislation of the Republican Party* (undated) and *The Truth about Our Finances* (1892). Her essays and poetry were printed in major newspapers across the United States, sometimes under the gender-neutral name of M. S. Burke, and sometimes under Maggie Lute Burke.

Her house at 1602 Fifteenth Street NW still stands. She is buried in Glenwood Cemetery.

In Spite of Fate

A troubled star was glowing red,
Upon the zenith's brow, they said,
    When I was born;
A baleful eye amid the gray,
That seemed to scan a rugged way,
    'Mid brake and thorn.

Beside my cradle Sorrow, pale,
Her ditty crooned, a broken wail,
    My lullaby;
And even childhood's summer land
Grew dull, with clouds on every hand,
    To veil the sky.

Love beckoned me, then turned away;
And Fame, when sought, had gone astray,
    And left no trace;
Misfortunes, like a harpy brood,
Have snatched away my spirit's food
    Before my face.

Yet, with a heart grown strong by strife,
I'll fight the battle still with life,
    Though growing late,
Till on its battlements I'll stand
The victor's bay within my hand,
    In spite of Fate.

Mary Clemmer Ames

May 6, 1831–August 18, 1884

Mary Clemmer Ames was a journalist best known for her "Woman's Letter from Washington," a column in the *New York Independent* that appeared for nearly two decades. Ames also wrote poetry and novels. She was one of the foremost women Washington correspondents in the period following the Civil War.

Her books include *Victoria* (1864), *Eirene* (1870), the nonfiction collection *Ten Years in Washington* (1871), *Outlines of Men, Women and Things* (1873), *His Two Wives* (1874), and *Poems of Life and Nature* (1886). Her journalism was also published in the *Utica Morning Herald* and the *Brooklyn Daily Union* in New York, the *Springfield Republican* in Massachusetts, and the *Cincinnati Commercial* in Ohio.

Unlike many women journalists of her time who reported only society news, Ames was a keen critic of politics. She was strong advocate for women's economic independence and right to work for equal pay. She also supported civil rights for newly emancipated African Americans. Her column regularly exposed members of Congress who used their positions for personal enrichment or whose behavior evidenced weak morals or corruption.

Ames was married twice; her first marriage to Reverend Daniel Ames, a Methodist minister, ended in divorce in 1874, and she married Edmund Hudson, editor of the *Army and Navy Register*, in 1883. Her DC home, no longer standing, was a literary and social center. She is buried in Rock Creek Cemetery.

The Joy of Work

The promise of delicious youth may fail;
The fair fulfillment of our Summer-time
May wane and wither at its hour of prime;
The gorgeous glow of Hope may swiftly pale;
E'en Love may leave us spite our piteous wail;
The heart, defeated, desolate may climb
To lonely Reason in her height sublime;
But one sure fort no foe can e'er assail.
'Tis thine, O Work,—the joy supreme of thought,
Where feeling, purpose, and long patience meet;
Where in deep silence the ideal wrought
Bourgeons from blossoming to fruit complete.
O crowning bliss! O treasure never bought!
All else may perish, thou remainest sweet.

Rose Elizabeth Cleveland

June 13, 1846 – November 22, 1918

Best remembered as first lady for her bachelor elder brother President Grover Cleveland during the first two years of his term, Rose Elizabeth Cleveland found her official duties so tiresome that she was said to conjugate Greek verbs during White House receptions. She was the first first lady to publish while residing in the White House, and an advocate of temperance and women's rights.

Cleveland worked as a schoolteacher and editor of the Chicago-based magazine *Literary Life*. She published a popular volume of essays, *George Eliot's Poetry and Other Studies* (1885, which went into seven editions); a book of social commentary, *You and I: Or Moral, Intellectual, and Social Culture* (1886); a novel, *The Long Run* (1886); and a translation, *The Soliloquies of St. Augustine* (1910).

In 1910, she moved to Italy to live with her lover, a wealthy widow named Evangeline Simpson Whipple, and died there during the 1918 influenza pandemic while working as a volunteer nurse to Italian World War I refugees.

From The Dilemma of the Nineteenth Century

Judith Von Stump fell sick, or fell to ailing, —
    That was as clear as day to any one, —
And it was settled Judith's health was failing,
    That something was the matter, something must be done;
And so a meeting of the wise physicians
    Of either sex was called upon to sit
In counsel upon Judith's sad condition
    And charged to find a speedy cure for it:
From far and near they came, and saw, and—sat!
Of conquering I speak not: you shall judge of that.

'Twas marvelous indeed how many doctors,
    Of every school and age, of either sex,
Came at the call, —from fierce concoctors
    Of potions blue the gastric juice to vex,
To those exponents of a dispensation
    Whose sugar-coatings, redolent with ease,

Soothing and pleasant in their application,
    Outside or in, can never fail to please.
Nor lacked there those astute manipulators
Who charge upon disease like gladiators.

***

And thus it briefly ran: "We find this woman
    Existing without life, at twenty-one;
Possessing all those forces which a human
    Nature can boast. The patient should be one
In robust health. Upon investigation,
    We find the nervous centers and the brain
A little strained: local ossification
    Threatens the heart, and yet no trace of pain
Is to be found. In fact, we are not sure
Of cause, and therefore find, as yet, no cure."

On this a doughty doctor rose, and, calling
    For silence, said, "The cause, sir, was a fall.
The woman fell in love, sir, and in falling,
    Got hurt a little in the head, — that's all.
And as to all your stuff about the heart, sir,
    Nonsense! Among all woman-kind you can't
Single out one who don't possess the art, sir,
    To make her heart as hard as adamant
If it suits her. Now bother all this chatter!
The woman is in love, — that's what's the matter."

In a great heat and much exasperation,
    A little burly doctor then cried out,
"You're wrong, sir, — wrong! The proper explanation
    Is quite the contrary, I have no doubt:
The woman's not in love, and *that's* the trouble.
    Give her a husband, sir, a house to keep,
Children to rear, and this romantic bubble
    Will soon collapse. Why, you must be asleep!
A woman, sir, is an absurd anomaly
Found anywhere but in the house and family."

At this a murmur of shrill indignation
    Arose from where the crinoline was dense.
A female here cried with determination
    "Sir, we insist on *truth* and *common sense*
And *science*, sir. The musty old traditions
    Left to us by the elders will not do.
In seeking to improve the sad condition
    Of our sick sister, we must learn to view
Her case in the broad light of progress, which advances
Beyond the pale of these effete romances."

Amidst the tumult, one, with face exuding
    With fat complacence, smiling pleasantly,
Said, "My dear friends, I hope I'm not intruding.
    Our fair friend's sickness, it is clear to me,
Is one caused by unwholesome agitation
    Of thought: in truth, her history
Makes clear that fact: it is an aberration
    From woman's law. The patient must be free
From all brain-labor. It is foul, inhuman,
And out of nature, sir, for lovely woman."

Then up there jumped, with jovial air and bustle,
    A little man, rubbing his hands with glee,
Who said, "The cause of all disease is lack of muscle.
    Turn out the patient; let her climb a tree;
Feed her with bran; teach her to roar with laughter
    All day; pack her in air at night;
Burn up her books, spill all her ink, and after
    Ten months I'll warrant her all right.
A woman's proper sphere is vegetation
In air and sunshine, with good cultivation."

The next who gained a hearing was a woman
    Of visage resolute and purpose fell,
Who now proclaimed, in accents superhuman,
    "The true cause of this illness I can tell,
And will. Our patient is a wretched sufferer

From man's injustice: you will please to note
The cause, 'tis soon explained, and 'tis enough, sir,
    To make a woman sick, sir, not to VOTE.
She never told her grief, yet how it cankers!
Give her the ballot, sir; for this she hankers."

Immense applause, tremendous acclamation,
    Followed the speaker. Quickly then arose
Another voice, which said, "This explanation
    Is good enough, and true, as far as it goes.
Our Radical Committee of Research, however,
    Are happy to assure you that they can
Announce the final cause. Our patient never
    Can hope for perfect health until she is a MAN;
Which metamorphosis our noble science
Hopes soon to reach, bidding to doubt defiance."

Marian Longfellow O'Donoghue (Miriam Lester)
April 1, 1849–January 23, 1924

Marian Longfellow O'Donoghue was born in Maine, the niece of Henry Wadsworth Longfellow and a direct descendant of Anne Bradstreet. She published poetry and short fiction in the *Boston Transcript, Boston Herald, Washington Post,* and other newspapers, sometimes under the pen name Miriam Lester, and some of her poems were set to music. She also translated literature from French to English.

O'Donoghue was a charter member of the Daughters of the American Revolution and served on the board of the Washington Choral Society. She was active in the National Society of New England Women and the International League of Press Clubs (where she was named the only woman on the Board of Governors). But she is perhaps best known as one of three cofounders of the League of American Pen Women in 1897, along with Margaret Sullivan Burke and Anna Sanborn Hamilton, a group formed in response to the Washington Press Club's refusal to admit women as members. O'Donoghue originated the idea, wrote the organization's bylaws and constitution, and served as first secretary.

O'Donoghue is the author of the books *Seven Stories for Christmas* (1884), *The Lily of the Resurrection* (1885), *Snow Crystals* (1885), and *Contrasted Songs* (1904). She married twice and had three children.

Leeward

O for the bounding wave, and the salt, salt spray on my face!
For the sweep of the filling sail, and its free, untrammelled pace!
For the life that hath no bound to its path but the open sea;
For the soul as free as air, that by right belongs to me!
For the power to cast aside these fetters dark and strong,
To bound over heaving deep—and no more to feel the throng
That cuts through the quivering heart and the restless soul, as well!
I yearn for a full life, with a might I cannot quell!
O for the bounding wave, and the salt, salt spray on my face!
For the strength to grasp and hold the plan of a waning race.
For might to compel the tide in its turn to serve my will,
That my heart of the fountain deep, may drink to the brim its fill!

Newell Houston Ensley

August 23, 1852–May 23, 1888

Newell Houston Ensley was born enslaved in Nashville, Tennessee, and was educated at Roger Williams University and Newton Theological Seminary. He taught at Shaw University in North Carolina and Howard University in Washington, DC, before taking a position as professor of rhetoric, natural sciences, and vocal music at Alcorn University in Lorman, Mississippi. Ensley was fluent in Latin, Greek, and Hebrew.

He was also in demand as a popular orator on issues of education, the Baptist Church, women's rights, and civil rights. William J. Simmons, in *Men of Mark* (1887), praised "the music of his voice and his graphic style" of speaking, which "have held audiences spell-bound." Simmons continues, "In his lectures he does not follow old stereotyped phrases nor hackneyed expressions, but his humor bubbles up like a pure rill at the foot of a mountain."

Ensley lived in DC from 1879 through 1882. He died young, at age thirty-five. This is his most famous poem, originally published in 1886 in the Roger Williams University *Record*.

Write Thy Name

Write your name upon the sand,
The waves will wash it out again.
Trace it on the crystal foam,
No sooner is it writ than gone.
Carve it in the solid oak,
'Tis shattered by the lightning's stroke.
Chisel it in marble deep,
'Twill crumble down—it cannot keep.

Seeker for the sweets of fame,
On things so frail, write not thy name.
With thee 'twill wither, die, rot;
On things so frail, then, write it not.
Would'st thou have thy name endure?
Go, write it in the Book of Life,
Engrave it on the hearts of men,
By humble deeds performed in love.

Wendell Phillips Stafford

May 1, 1861–April 21, 1953

Wendell Phillips Stafford was born in Vermont and attended St. Johns-
bury Academy and Boston University. He was admitted to the Vermont
bar in 1882 and worked in private practice until appointed a federal
judge on the United States District Court for the District of Columbia.
He received a recess appointment from President Theodore Roosevelt
in 1904. He also became a professor at George Washington University
School of Law in 1908. Stafford served on the bench until his retire-
ment on May 4, 1931. His houses at 1725 Lamont Street NW and 1661
Crescent Place NW both still stand.

Stafford's books of poems include *North Flowers* (1902); *Dorian
Days* (1909); and *The Land We Love* (1916). He was named the first
poet laureate of Vermont in 1922.

Stafford once stated, "There are lawyers by nature, as there are po-
ets by nature, endowed with two gifts, one to perceive the true relations
of things and the other the disposition to see justice done."

The poem "Passing Mount Vernon" was published in the *Washington Post* on July 12, 1917, three months after the American entry into World War I.

On the Photograph of a Lynching

This is the fruit of that forbidden tree
Whereof the nation that doth eat shall die—
The tree of hate whose fruit is cruelty.
This nation eateth, and the feet are by
Of them that bore its brothers to the tomb:

The grave is ready and the dead make room.
This is the end of Justice and of Law:
the ages travailed and have brought forth this!
Here closes the sweet dream the prophet saw.
The seraph's song ends in the serpent's hiss.
The phoenix mounts refurnished from the fire:
The swine returns to wallow in the mire.

See these fanged faces leering round their prey!
Are these the sons of unforgotten sires
That hewed the wilderness for Freedom's way,
And lit the midnight with her beaconing fires?
Not sons, but bastards, howsoever named!
In these ghoul forms the shape of man is shamed.

Here in this picture let the black man read
The noble white man's view of what is just!
His fathers were the victims of white greed;
His mothers were the victims of white lust;
And if he learned his lesson but too well,
Pupil or teacher—which deserved this hell?

Thousands of readers, but no heart is stirred.
Hundreds of statesmen, but no move is made.
Ten thousand prophets, but no trumpet word.
Millions of men, cold, cruel, or afraid.
No brave blood burns with anger at the sight.
God ring the curtain down—put out the light!

No, no, my country, no! Thou shalt not die;
The grave was never made that shall hide thee.
The old brave wind will yet come blowing by
And thou wilt leap to life and liberty,
And, striding o'er the obscene monster's maw,
Bring on resplendent brows thy down-slipped crown of Law!

The Cry of the Dark

God's wrath is kindling. Fear it, each false priest
Of law and justice! He will surely smite
People and priest guilty against the light.
Tremble, you Christians who deny the least
Of Christ's own brothers! Justice has not ceased,
If "Justices," misnamed, see black and white.
The whisper of the wronged rolls up heaven's height
In thunder; his avengers are released
Ere yet the crime is finished. Surely He
That led the fathers through a land blood-dewed
Will not desert the children when betrayed.
Think you God is a white man, He that made
Three quarters of the whole earth darker-hued?
There are no bastards in His family.

Passing Mount Vernon

The slowing speed—the ship-bell's toll—
The plain white porch outstanding clearly—
The sloping lawn—the wooded knoll
Within whose shade he lies austerely—

So on we pass. How peacefully
The Pater Patriae reposes,
With fresh returns of fleur-de-lis
And tribute late of British roses!

Today his Roman mask must wear
A smile that might be called complacent:
England and France, a loving pair,
Before his modest tomb obeisant!

But still he sleeps, unroused by wrong,
Unmoved amid a world's commotion,
While his old river glides along
To where his war birds breast the ocean.

Yet is it true to say he sleeps?
For still his ghost, august and splendid,
Its march around our border keeps;
And by his faith are we defended.

To us his voice is speaking clear,
And sounds across the seas in thunder;
And 'tis the hand that crumbles here
Which yet shall cleave the thrones asunder.

John Henry Paynter

February 15, 1862–January 18, 1948

John Henry Paynter is best known for *Fugitives of the Pearl* (1930), a novelization of a historic, unsuccessful slave escape from DC (and the largest-known mass escape attempt of enslaved people in the United States). Paynter was a direct descendant of two of the *Pearl* fugitives. His other books are *Joining the Navy: Or, Abroad with Uncle Sam* (1895), *Fifty Years After* (1940), and *Horse and Buggy Days with Uncle Sam* (1943).

Paynter served in the U.S. Navy and worked as a clerk at the U.S. Treasury. He lived at 322 A Street NE on Capitol Hill in the early 1900s (still standing), then moved to 701 Fifty-First Street NE in the Deanwood neighborhood (razed). He was active in St. Luke's Protestant Episcopal Church, the Oldest Inhabitants' Association (Colored), and served as board chair for the Universal Land Company, which created a popular amusement park for African Americans in Deanwood called Suburban Gardens (now the site of Merritt Elementary School). He is buried in Arlington National Cemetery.

To Emperor Selassie

Listen, Selassie, Oh, King of Kings,
With prideful joy to thee I bring

A united voice of praise that rings
Full-throated from thy Negro kin.

Thy griefs are borne with regal poise
That scorns a bandit's bluff and noise;
His fateful thrust to "muscle-in"
On thy heritage is unpardoned sin.

The peoples dark, on alien shores
Acclaim thy culture and share thy woes
And summon through prayer Jehovah's aid
To turn back those who would invade.

So shall we hope thy lengthened Line
Of sovereigns' lustrous since Solomon's time
Shall ages hence thy praises sing
Who kept the faith and fought, as should a King.

Kelly Miller

July 18, 1863–December 29, 1939

Kelly Miller was born in South Carolina to an enslaved mother less than a year after the Emancipation Proclamation, narrowly escaping slavery. He described himself as one of the "first fruits of the Civil War, one of the first African Americans who learned to read, write and cipher in public schools." He was the first African American to attend Johns Hopkins University, where he studied advanced mathematics, physics, and astronomy.

A professor and administrator at Howard University for more than forty years, Miller served as a math professor (1890), a sociology professor (1895–1934), and dean of the College of Arts and Sciences (1907–19). Miller wrote a syndicated column that was published in more than one hundred African American newspapers in the 1920s and 1930s. His most prominent book, *Race Adjustment* (1908), was a crucial early text challenging racist notions of black inferiority. Miller was a prolific writer; some of his other books include *The Education of the Negro* (1902), *From Servitude to Service* (1905), *The Ultimate Race Problem* (1910), *Out of the House of Bondage* (1914), *An Appeal to Con-*

science: America's Code of Caste a Disgrace to Democracy (1918), *The Negro in the New Reconstruction* (1919), and *Is Race Difference Fundamental, Eternal and Inescapable?* (1921).

Miller was one of the leading advocates in the nation for public education for students of African descent. In an essay in *Opportunity Magazine* published in 1928, he wrote: "The Washington Negro has the only complete school system in the country practically under his own control. . . . The colored high and normal schools enroll over three thousand pupils above the eighth grade level. This number of secondary students cannot be approximated in any other city—not even New York, Philadelphia and Chicago, with a much larger total Negro population. . . . The Negroes of Washington have reached the point of complete professional self sufficiency. Howard has turned out an army of physicians, lawyers, teachers and clergymen. . . . The capital furnishes the best opportunity and facilities for the expression of the Negro's innate gayety of soul. Washington is still the Negro's Heaven, and it will be many a moon before Harlem will be able to take away her scepter."

Miller was a founding member of the American Negro Academy, the first major African American learned society, and a coeditor of the *Crisis*, the journal of the NAACP. He is remembered in DC with a public housing development in the LeDroit Park neighborhood and a DC public middle school named in his honor. One of his daughters, May Miller, also became a writer of note.

The Cat
I hate a cat. The very sight
   Of feline form evokes my wrath;
When'er one goes across my path,
   I shiver with instinctive fright.

And yet there is one little kit
   I treat with tender kindliness
The fondled pet of my darling Bess:
   For I love her and she loves it.

In earth beneath, as Heaven above,
   It satisfies the reasoning,

That those who love the self-same thing
    Must also one another love.

Then if our Father loveth all
    Mankind, of every clime and hue,
Who loveth Him must love them too;
    It cannot otherwise befall.

Isabel Likens Gates

December 1, 1868 – February 6, 1942

Isabel Likens Gates is the author of *The Land of Our Dreams* (1938). She also published a textbook, *Synopsis of Grammar and Rules of Syntax* (1931); a play, *Modernity, or Latter Days* (1932); *Little Rhymes for Little People* (1939); and various song lyrics, including the official 1920 GOP campaign song, "Harding We Want You, Yes We Do."

Gates was born in Nevada and spent the first twenty years of her life in silver mining camps. But she proudly traced her lineage to the earliest Swedish settlers of Delaware in 1632. Gates began to write poetry at a young age and would later publish widely in newspapers and journals, including the *Washington Post, Washington Evening Star, Washington Daily News, National Tribune, Forest Life Magazine,* and *American Motorist.* She married Robert Woodland Gates and seems to have had no children; they lived in DC. She was active in the League of American Pen Women. Gates is buried in Rock Creek Cemetery.

Fort Myer, referenced in the following poem, was a military post in Arlington, Virginia, which was a staging area for a large number of regiments during World War I. The Reserve Officers' Training Corps (ROTC) is a program of the U.S. Air Force.

R.O.T.C., 1917

An R.O.T.C. gala picture
    Of the first training camp at Fort Myer,
When a pall hung over the nation
    And hearts were aflame with desire.

An R.O.T.C. flashlight picture,
    With its steamers and banners gay,

And its stalwart young forms and glad faces,
    And maidens in dainty array.

A farewell entertainment and supper,
    An evening without alloy,
Music and dancing and flirting,
    And favors and flowers and joy.

O heart, is it only a vision,
    A picture on memory's screen?
Is there never a Delphan to whisper
    The fate of those on the scene?

They were there, then gone on the morrow,
    And never a word to tell
How they fared, or living or wounded,
    Or how many fighting fell.

Unanswered, forever unanswered,
    Alive, or beneath the sod,
Wounded, missing or dying—
    They are known in the home of God.

Bertha Gerneaux Davis

1873–February 14, 1952

Bertha Gerneaux Davis was born in New York but moved to DC while still young and attended DC Public Schools. She wrote poetry, short stories, and articles on natural history and contributed to the *Washington Post, New York Independent, Chicago Advance,* and several Christian and children's journals.

Davis published six books of poems: *Verses* (1903), *Verses by Three Generations* (1921, with son Mark Winton and mother, Harriet Winton Davis), *The Guest* (1926), *Patient Scientists* (1928), *Opening into Nature, Humanity, Life* (1935), and *World Communion* (1943).

Davis was active in the literary salon of Frances Hodgson Burnett and a member of the League of American Pen Women. Davis married in 1898 and had four sons. She lived in DC until 1910, then moved to Minnesota, where her husband, Albert Fred Woods, was employed as a dean at the University of Minnesota through 1917. When he was offered a job as the first president of what was then the Maryland State College of Agriculture (later renamed the University of Maryland), the family returned to the area. Under his tenure, the college grew to include undergraduate and graduate programs in seven schools, changing the focus from agriculture to the liberal arts, and gaining accreditation by the Association of American Universities. She published actively in journals through 1947; her papers are now in the archives of the University of Maryland at College Park.

At Arlington

The trolley brought them out by scores today—
Our boys from nearby camps, to go away
So soon to blood-stained fields. I watched one lad
Who stood apart a little—not quite sad,
Yet somewhat grave for one so young. (I doubt
If he were twenty!) He was looking out
Upon the fair Virginia hills, the trees,
The river flowing by. A gentle breeze
Made fragrance from the clover fill the air.
He wandered out to those green acres where
The thousands lie in sleep—such endless rows!
'Twas early evening, overhead the crows
Were darkening the sky. (In wearied flight
They wing their way to Arlington each night.)
Among those countless grass-grown graves he stood,
This soldier boy, his young face clean and good,
His stiff-brimmed hat in one slim hand—(Because
The day was warm and close? Or did he pause
In honor of those dead?) Then toward the sky
He turned his face. (To see the crows drift by,
Or was it something else, unseen by me?)
I only know his smile was sweet to see!

The Service Flag

Only yesterday I passed it, small and commonplace and gray!
No one would have turned to give a second look—until today.

Now that little house seems altered—still the same low, sagging
   stairs,
Still the dingy paint, and yet what odd new dignity it wears!
For a tiny silken flag is pressed against the window-glass,
One blue star within its center—message mute, to all who pass.
Little house, the ones you shelter, are unknown to me and mine,
And though I am fain to linger, I go by and make no sign.
But I whisper this: "God bless them, whosoever they may be,
Dwelling in that star-marked cottage, but with hearts across
   the sea!"

Kendall Banning

September 20, 1879 – December 27, 1944

Kendall Banning is the author of more than a dozen books of poetry
and nonfiction, including books on the history of Annapolis and West
Point. A graduate of Dartmouth College, he was a major in the U.S.
Army Signal Corps during World War I. He subsequently became ed-
itor of such magazines as *Cosmopolitan, Popular Radio, Snappy Stories,*
and *Hearst Magazine.*

Banning's books include *Submarine: The Story of Undersea Fighters*
(1942), *The Fleet Today* (1940), *Censored Mother Goose Rhymes* (1929,
written in protest of U.S. Customs obscenity laws), and the poetry
books *Mon Ami Pierrot* (1917), *Bypaths in Arcady* (1914), *Songs of the
Love Unending: A Sonnet Sequence* (1912), and *Songs for a Wedding Day*
(1907). He is buried in Arlington National Cemetery.

God's Puppets
The curtain falls, the lights go out,
   And silence ends the play,
And Columbine and Harlequin
   In dust are laid away,
And Pierrot of the nimble heart,
   And frail Pierrette, the star;
So we must dance and go, my lass,
   God's puppets that we are!

Who knows but that their little tricks
    Still live, and still amuse?
And Columbine still runs away,
    And Pierrot still pursues?
Who knows but that we too shall play
    Our parts, and reign supreme
Upon the Stage of Silence, lass,
    Within the House of Dream?

PART IV

Poets of the American Scene

Horatio King

June 21, 1811 – May 20, 1897

Horatio King was a founding member of the Union Literary Society in DC in the 1840s. He hosted a popular salon in his house at 707 H Street NW (still standing, now a restaurant in the Chinatown neighborhood), which convened on Saturday evenings throughout the 1860s and 1870s and was nicknamed "King's Reunions." His salon evenings included readings and discussion of poetry and essays, which led to the founding of the Washington Literary Society in 1874. The *Washington Evening Times* credited his popular salons with contributing "to a great extent to elevate the literary tone of the city."

At the age of eighteen, King joined the staff of the *Jeffersonian,* a newspaper in Maine; in 1831 he became co-owner with Hannibal Hamlin. He discontinued the paper in 1838 and moved to DC in 1839 for an appointment as clerk in the Post Office Department. He served in progressively more responsible jobs for the next two decades, until retiring as postmaster general during the Civil War.

Although a Democrat, King supported abolitionist causes and was on the committee to determine rates of compensated emancipation for DC's slaves, who were the first freed in the United States. He was active in the Monument Society, which ensured the completion of the Washington Monument, serving as secretary of the organization. After his retirement from the Post Office Department, he remained in DC for the rest of his life, working as an attorney and journalist. King published *An Oration before the Union Literary Society of Washington* (1841), *Sketches of Travel, or Twelve Months in Europe* (1878), and *Turning on the Light: A Dispassionate Survey of President Buchanan's Administration* (1895). He is buried in Congressional Cemetery.

"All's Well"

List to the sound of bells,
As on the air it swells,

And in the darkness tells
   The hour of night;
Then hear the watchman's cry—
   On lookout to espy
All dangers far and nigh—
   That all is right.

The cheering words, "All's well,"
All nervous fears dispel;
And to our senses tell
   That safety reigns;
Then sink we into rest,
Lulled by the foamy crest
Upon the ocean's breast
   In somnous strains.

Now when life's end is near,
And all seems dark and drear,
We breathless list to hear
   The last hour bell;
O, may the joyful word
In silver tones be heard—
   All's well.

Anne Lynch Botta

November 11, 1815–March 23, 1891

Anne Lynch Botta lived in DC from 1850 to 1853, while serving as personal secretary to Senator Henry Clay. Grace Greenwood, another writer and a friend, reports that Senator Clay felt "not only the admiration he always felt for a clever, witty woman, but profound respect for her scholarly attainments, her rare good sense, and, above all, her purity of character."

Botta is the author of *Poems* (1849) and *A Handbook of Universal Literature* (1860, once a widely used textbook), and editor of an anthology, *The Rhode Island Book* (1841). Edgar Allan Poe, reviewing her *Poems*, wrote: "In modulation and vigor of rhythm, in dignity and elevation of sentiment, in metaphorical appositeness and accuracy, and in energy of expression, I really do not know where to point out anything American superior to them."

Born in 1815, Botta was educated at the Albany Female Academy and taught briefly in Albany, New York, and Providence, Rhode Island. After her sojourn in DC, she settled in New York, teaching at the Brooklyn Girls' Academy, writing freelance articles for magazines, and hosting a renowned Saturday-evening salon in her home, frequented by some of the most famous writers of the time, including William Cullen Bryant, Edgar Allan Poe, Helen Hunt Jackson, Margaret Fuller, Ralph Waldo Emerson, Horace Greeley, and Fanny Kemble.

After the death of family members, she raised two boys, a nephew and a grand-nephew. In addition to writing, she was a painter and sculptor. In middle age, she married a Dante Alighieri scholar who taught at New York University. After her death in 1891, her husband compiled her unpublished poems, along with letters and tributes, and published the posthumous *Memoirs of Anne C. L. Botta: Written by Her Friends* (1893).

Webster

"When I and all those that hear me shall have gone to our last home, and when the mould may have gathered on our memories, as it will on our tombs . . ."
> —*Daniel Webster's Speech in the Senate, July, 1850*

The mould upon thy memory!—No,
Not while one note is rung,
Of those divine, immortal songs
Milton and Shakespeare sung;—
Not till the night of years enshrouds
The Anglo-Saxon tongue.

No! let the flood of Time roll on,
And men and empires die;—
Genius enthroned on lofty heights
Can its dread course defy,
And here on earth, can claim the gift
Of immortality:

Can save from that Lethean tide
That sweeps so dark along,
A people's name;—a people's fame
To future time prolong,
As Troy still lives and only lives
In Homer's deathless song.

What though to buried Nineveh
The traveller may come,
And roll away the stone that hides
That long forgotten tomb;—
He questions its mute past in vain,
Its oracles are dumb.

What though he stand where Balbec stood
Gigantic in its pride;
No voice comes o'er that silent waste,
Lone, desolate and wide;—
They had no bard, no orator,
No statesman,—and they died.

They lived their little span of life,
They lived and died in vain;—
They sank ingloriously beneath
Oblivion's silent reign,
As sank beneath the Dead Sea wave
The Cities of the Plain.

But for those famed, immortal lands,
Greece and imperial Rome,
Where Genius left its shining mark,
And found its chosen home,
All eloquent with mind they speak,
Wood, wave and crumbling dome.

The honeyed words of Plato still
Float on the echoing air,
The thunders of Demosthenes
Aegean waters bear,

And the pilgrim to the Forum hears
The voice of Tully there.

And thus thy memory shall live,
And thus thy fame resound,
While far-off future ages roll
Their solemn cycles round,
And make this wide, this fair New World
An ancient, classic ground.

Then with our Country's glorious name
Thine own shall be entwined;
Within the Senate's pillared hall
Thine image shall be shrined;
And on the nation's Law shall gleam
Light from thy giant mind.

Our proudest monuments no more
May rise to meet the sky,
The stately Capitol o'erthrown,
Low in the dust may lie;
But mind, sublime above the wreck,
Immortal—cannot die.

The Bee

The honey-bee that wanders all day long,
The field, the woodland, and the garden o'er,
To gather in his fragrant winter store,
Humming in calm content his quiet song,
Seeks not alone the rose's glowing breast,
The lily's dainty cup, the violet's lips,—
But from all rank and noxious weeds he sips
The single drop of sweetness closely press'd
Within the poison chalice. Thus, if we
Seek only to draw forth the hidden sweet,
In all the varied human flowers we meet,
In the wide garden of humanity,
And like the bee, if home the spoil we bear,
Hived in our hearts it turns to nectar there.

To an Astronomer

Upon the Professor we'll waste not a glance,
    Since he has no eyes for us poor terrestrials;
With his heart can we have any possible chance,
    When he gives us for rivals a host of celestials?
What cares he for eyes, whether hazel or blue,
    Or for any slight charms such as we share between us,—
When, his glass in his hand, he can sit the night through,
    And ogle at leisure Diana and Venus.

In the Library

Speak low, tread softly through these halls;
Here genius lives enshrined,
Here reign, in silent majesty,
The monarchs of the mind.

A mighty spirit-host they come
From every age and clime;
Above the buried wrecks of years
They breast the tide of Time.

And in their presence-chamber here
They hold their regal state,
And round them throng a noble train,
The gifted and the great.

O child of earth, when round thy path
The storms of life arise,
And when thy brothers pass thee by
With stern, unloving eyes—

Here shall the Poets chant for thee
Their sweetest, loftiest lays;
And Prophets wait to guide thy steps
In wisdom's pleasant ways.

Come, with these God-anointed kings,
By thou companion here,
And in the mighty realm of mind
Thou shalt go forth a peer.

Donn Piatt

June 29, 1819 – November 12, 1891

Donn Piatt was an attorney and judge in Ohio until he joined the dip-
lomatic corps under President Franklin Pierce, serving as secretary
of the legation at Paris from 1853 to 1855. When the Civil War began,
Piatt volunteered as a private and was promoted to captain, then ad-
jutant general and judge advocate. After the war, he was a member of
the Ohio House of Representatives (from 1865 to 1866), then turned
to journalism, serving as Washington correspondent for the *Cincin-
nati Commercial* for three years, and in 1891 founding a weekly journal,
Washington Capitol, with George Alfred Townsend (who also wrote un-
der the pen name Gath). This journal was renowned for its criticism
of the U.S. Congress and the administration of Ulysses S. Grant. Upon
his retirement in 1880, Piatt returned to his native Ohio, where he and
his brother Abram built adjoining stone castles.

Piatt published several books, including *Memories of the Men Who
Saved the Union* (1887), *The Lone Grave of the Shenandoah, and Other
Tales* (1888), *The Reverend Malancthon Poundex, a Novel* (1893), *Sunday
Meditations and Prose Sketches* (1893), and *Poems and Plays* (1893). Piatt
was the cousin of another DC poet, John James Piatt.

We Parted at the Omnibus

We parted at the omnibus, I never can forget,
Your eyes, my dove, like stars above, with dew were heavy wet,
Your luggage, love, I handed up, as the driver 'round did pull,
I could not speak, for, oh! my heart, like the omnibus, was full.

Your slender hand's six-buttoned glove lay nestling soft in mine,
Those tender eyes upon me shone in sadness so divine;
"Through life, my love, I got with you," I boldly had begun,
When spoke a German passenger: "Dere's only zeats vor vun."

Your miniature I had, my sweet, all painted warm and bland,
My photograph I handed you, as the agent gave his hand.
"You'll write to me, I know you will, this aching heart to ease,
And every line from you will be"—"Miss, ten cents, if you please."

I placed you in a corner, dear, to take that dreary ride,
I saw a pair of checkered pants close sitting at your side;

With gun and hound from out the town to hunt 'twas going down;
I heard a suit of rusty black call pants a Mister Brown.

With wooden damn the stage door slammed and shut you from my
    sight,
I felt, indeed, that all was wrong, when the driver called "all right."
Off rolled the yellow misery that took of mine no heed;
For spanned hatracks prancing, a racker in the lead.

The war came on, and I went off—what patriot heart could lag?
I seized a musket in my zeal and rallied round the flag;
I left two fingers on the field where gallant Hooker led,
And lost a leg at Shiloh, where Sherman lost his head.

I fought and marched, and starved, alas! the toughest of our set;
A captain in the line, my girl, a gen'ral by brevet.
Of checkered pants I got a view, resplendent in the blue,
As sutler bold, he rallied too where profits did accrue.

When peace her downy pinions spread o'er all our land and sea,
I stumped my home, a veteran, with war's sad legacy;
I sought you, love, to find, alas! no footing left to me,
For General Brown was to the front, a millionaire was he.

'Twas at a grand reunion, given in honor of our cause,
The banners waved, the champagne popped, I got some wild
    applause;
I saw you enter, sweet and fair, the General led you down,
You leaned to him with loving trust, he called you Mrs. Brown.

Jeremiah Eames Rankin

January 2, 1828–November 28, 1904

Jeremiah Eames Rankin was the sixth president of Howard University,
serving from 1890 to 1903; the Rankin Chapel on the campus was
named for him. A white abolitionist and advocate for the temperance
movement, Rankin was a minister of the First Congregational Church
in DC (from 1869 to 1884) and author of numerous hymns.

Born in New Hampshire, Rankin was proud of his Scottish heritage. Prior to moving to DC, he led Presbyterian and Congregational churches in New York, Vermont, Massachusetts, and New Jersey. At First Congregational, he ministered to numerous well-known congregants of color, including Frederick Douglass, John Mercer Langston, and Senator Blanche Kelso Bruce. His published sermons were said to be favored reading by President Woodrow Wilson.

Rankin edited numerous hymnals, including *The Gospel Temperance Hymnal* (1878) and *Gospel Bells* (1880), and edited the anthology *German-English Lyrics, Sacred and Secular* (1897). He wrote one novel, *Esther Burr's Journal* (1903), and an advice book, *Gems for the Bridal Ring: A Gift for the Plighted and the Wedded* (1867). Other nonfiction titles include *Freedom and Citizenship* (1883), *The Function of Great Men* (1881), and *Moses and Joshua: A Discourse on the Death of Abraham Lincoln* (1865). Many of Rankin's poems were written in a Scottish dialect, under the influence of Robert Burns, including *Ingleside Rhaims* (1887), *The Auld Scotch Mither and Other Poems* (1873), and *Oor Kirk Fair and Ither Verses of That Ilk* (1881). Many of his poems addressed religious and sentimental themes and have not aged well, although they were popular in their day. His book-length poem *Broken Cadences* (1889), from which this selection comes, is notable for its rhymed iambic lines of differing lengths; it was divided into "The Cadences of Nature," "The Cadences of Life," and "The Cadences of Art."

From Broken Cadences: An Ode in Three Parts

I walked a city's rounds alone,—
A hamlet to a city grown,—
Where I had once in boyhood played.
The tiny brook revisited,
Where many an hour in sport had sped;
The pool where I was wont to wade,
Where I had headlong dared the shelving brim,
And learned the art to swim.
I could not find a spot
To answer to my early thought;
Proportions all were lost,
My every recollections crossed;
Leaning awhile,

Against the moss-grown stile,
Which oft in glee I'd climbed,
When childhood-limbed,
With eyelids dim,
I back to mem'ry brought
Many a lad and little maid,
Who tripped with me the everglade,
As once we sought
The Mayflower and forget-me-not.
Though still the same
Earth's outward look,
To outward eye
The hill, the sky,
The purling brook,
The sweet briar's breath;
I catalogued name after name,
That had been starred by death—
I stood at length, beneath the statue in the park,
And there my first companion came to mark:
The man who shook the Senate in debate,
Who saved the state!
The rest were dead and gone,
The man in bronze lived on.
His form had walked through furnace-flame
To be eternally the same.
To me
More real he,
Than all the dead, than all the living small and great.

Charles G. Halpine (Miles O'Reilly)

November 20, 1829–August 3, 1868

Born in Ireland, Charles G. Halpine immigrated to the United States in 1851, working in Boston as assistant editor of the *Boston Post* and in Washington as correspondent to the *New York Times*. While living in DC, he published a book of poems, *Lyrics by the Letter H*, in 1854. He enlisted in the army at the beginning of the Civil War, rising in the ranks to brigadier-general.

Writing under the pseudonym Miles O'Reilly, he wrote poems and articles from the point of view of a private that were published in the *New York Herald* and later collected into two volumes: *Life and Adventures, Songs, Services, and Speeches of Private Miles O'Reilly, 47th Regiment New York Volunteers* (1864), and *Baked Meats of the Funeral, a Collection of Essays, Poems, Speeches, and Banquets, by Private Miles O'Reilly, late of the 47th Regiment New York Volunteer Infantry, 10th Army Corps* (1866).

After the war, O'Reilly settled in New York, editing and then owning the *Citizen* newspaper. He died of an accidental overdose of chloroform, which he was taking to counter insomnia.

Webster

Gone! And the world may never hear again
    The grand old music of thy wondrous speech.
Striking far deeper than the mind can reach
    Into the hearts and purposes of men.

Gone! And the helm that in thy Roman hand
    Drove the stout vessel through the blinding storm,
Scarce to a feebler guidance will conform
    When waves beat high, and ropes break strand by strand.

Gone! We are like old men whose infant eyes
    Familiar grew with some vast pyramid;
Even as we gaze, earth yawns, and it is hid—
    A long, wide desert mocks the empty skies.

Eliza Woodworth

1831?–August 9, 1906

Eliza Woodworth was born in Perry, New York, and educated largely in the private library of her father, a minister. She never married and had a disability, or perhaps some long-term health problems; she described her body, in an article published in the *Ladies' Repository* in 1874, "Journeyings of an Invalid," as "the feeble tabernacle of the flesh in which I suffer." She argued that despite this impediment, her "spirit may wander over all the interesting places that are scattered through the wide, beautiful world." In that article, Woodworth described her varied reading habits, arguing that books will widen a reader's heart "in sympathy with far-off human creatures, living in different conditions from your own, but not aliens."

Woodworth edited the anthology *Selections from the British Poets* (1956) and published articles and poems in journals. It is unclear when she moved to Washington, DC, but she was living here in 1895 and was included in the anthology *The Poets and Poetry of Washington* edited by Ina Russelle Warren. Her house at 100 Eighth Street NE is still standing.

Asleep upon the Grass

Upon the warm and fragrant grass I lay;
    Above me towered the whispering maple tree
    (Whose voice, when storms march past, is like the sea),
And round me was the throng of summer day:
Thin gnats, and dusk ephemera, at play;
    Tossed yellow butterfly and banded bee,
    The large-eyed robins came and looked at me,
Then briskly hopped, content, about the brae
Wee, swinging spiders slid down mist-threads, nigh;
    Grim, hurried ants across my palm would pass,
The shortest way, and lady-bugs, unshy;
    Beetles came close, with backs like hammered brass,
For fear had left the elves that walk or fly—
    Then said, She is asleep upon the grass.

On the Beach

How the sea-flowers thrive on the grassy crag,
Uptossing in sun-winds each delicate head!
Do they watch the gulls that hasten or lag?
Do they watch the dawn and the evening red?

And the beach-bird skims round the shifting dune
With a plaintive and ever-recurring cry;
Does it grieve to the musky and steaming lagoon?
Does it mourn to the sea, and the splendid sky?

Long the tern has dropped all her nestless eggs
On the dry-drift-grass by the gray salt marsh;
She catches her fish in the shallow's dregs,
And rejoices with pipings loud and harsh.

Out on the bar the shearwater feeds—
Wide-winged he runs on the wave's green rims;
And the otter is fishing beyond the reeds,
Raising a welt like a snake as he swims.

Does the beach-bird mourn as he flits? Not he.
Do the flowers despair in the golden weather?
They woo the wind, while the somber bee
And gay butterflies flit, and toss up together.

Is the marsh tern shamed for her rusty voice?
Not she; 'tis a tern's and the best on earth;
It is rare, it is sweet, it is wholly her choice,
As she feeds with her friends, in clamorous mirth.

Well the shearwater knows that his tinted bill
Lures the limpid and curious fry at the bar;
And the otter's curved nails their purpose fulfill,
Deep-hooked in the slippery mullet and gar.

Oh, the marvelous gifts of Life in these!
And in man, in the lichen, the palm-tree and oak;
With strengths of the lands, and the sounding seas,
Strengths of the winds, and the lightning's stroke.

Edward Robert Bulwer-Lytton (Owen Meredith)

November 8, 1831–November 24, 1891

Edward Robert Bulwer-Lytton, also known as Owen Meredith, was a British diplomat who served as viceroy of India during the British Raj. His publications include *Pelham, or The Adventures of a Gentleman* (1828), *The Last Days of Pompeii* (1834), *Clytemnestra and Other Poems* (1855), *The Wanderers* (1859), *Lucile* (1860), *The Ring of Ainasis* (1863), *Fables in Song* (1874), *Glenaveril* (1885), and *After Paradise, or Legends of Exile* (1887). Early in his career, he lived in Washington with his uncle Henry Lytton Bulwer, also a British diplomat (to whom he served as personal secretary), and their house at 1525 H Street NW still stands; the former British ambassador's house is now the St. John's Church Parish House, facing Lafayette Square and the White House.

Historian Constance Green writes in *Reveille in Washington:* "In the winter of 1849–1850 . . . Bulwer Lytton, then aide to his uncle, the British minister, composed the romantic poem which, when published in 1860, led countless readers to name their daughters *Lucile.* Not until later did Washington hostesses learn that 'Owen Meredith' was one and the same as the attractive young Englishman who had secretly written poetry in the brownstone house looking out over Lafayette Square when he was not drinking and dancing with the belles of the capital."

His best-selling novels have not aged well. A modern contest sponsored by San Jose State University, the Bulwer-Lytton Fiction Contest, awards the most terrible opening lines to "the worst of all possible novels" and is inspired by the first sentence of his book *Paul Clifford* (1830), which reads: "It was a dark and stormy night; the rain fell in torrents—except at occasional intervals, when it was checked by a violent gust of wind which swept up the streets (for it is in London that our scene lies), rattling along the housetops, and fiercely agitating the scanty flame of the lamps that struggled against the darkness."

The Cloud
With shape to shape, all day,
And change to change, by foreland, firth, and bay,
The cloud comes down from wandering with the wind,
Through gloom and gleam across the green waste seas;
And, leaving the white cliff and lone tower bare
To empty air,
Slips down the windless west and grows defined
In splendor by degrees.

And, blown by every wind
Of wonder through all regions of the mind,
From hope to fear, from doubt to sweet despite
Changing all shapes, and mingling snow with fire,
The thought of her descends, sleeps o'er the bounds
Of passion, grows, and rounds
Its golden outlines in a gradual light
Of still desire.

John James Piatt

March 1, 1835 – February 16, 1917

John James Piatt was born in Indiana and apprenticed in the printer's trade as a young boy in Ohio. He had other poets in his immediate family: he was the cousin of Donn Piatt and married Sarah Morgan Bryan Piatt in June 1861. He was appointed a clerk in the U.S. Treasury Department later that same year, and he and his wife, both already well published, were a respected literary couple in Washington; they remained in DC for six years (after which time his federal employment ended and he returned to Ohio).

Piatt returned to DC in 1870, when he was hired as an enrolling clerk in the U.S. House of Representatives, and in 1871 he became the House librarian. After another return to Ohio, in 1882, he was appointed to the prestigious position of U.S. consul to Ireland and served overseas through 1893.

Piatt published three collaborative works: *Poems of Two Friends* with William Dean Howells (1860); and *The Nests of Washington and Other Poems* (1864) and *The Children Out-of-Doors: A Book of Verses by Two in One House* (1884), with his wife, Sarah. On his own, he published *Poems in Sunshine and Firelight* (1866), *Western Windows and Other Poems* (1869), *Landmarks and Other Poems* (1871), *Poems of House and Home* (1878), *Idyls and Lyrics of Ohio Valley* (1884), and *At the Holy Well: A Handful of New Verses* (1887).

In May 1903, the *Washington Evening Star* praised Piatt as one of the two top Ohio literary men, along with William Dean Howells, stating, "His verses are full of grace and feeling, and sing of the soil."

Taking the Night-Train

A tremulous word, a lingering hand, the burning
Of restless passion smoldering—so we part;
Ah, slowly from the dark the world is turning
When midnight stars shine in a heavy heart.

The streets are lighted, and the myriad faces
Move through the gaslight, and the homesick feet
Pass by me, homeless; sweet and close embraces
Charm many a threshold—laughs and kisses sweet.

From great hotels the stranger throng is streaming,
The hurrying wheels in many a street are loud;
Within the depot, in the gaslight gleaming,
A glare of faces, stands the waiting crowd.

The whistle screams; the wheels are fumbling slowly,
The path before us glides into the light:
Behind, the city sinks in silence wholly;
The panting engine leaps into the night.

I seem to see each street a mystery growing,
In mist of dreamland—vague, forgotten air:
Does no sweet soul, awakened, feel me going?
Loves no dear heart, in dreams, to keep me there?

To Walt Whitman, the Man
Homeward, last midnight, in the car we met,
While the long street streamed by us in the dark
With scattered lights in blurs of misty rain;
Then, while you spoke to me of hospitals
That know your visits, and of wounded men
(From those dread battles yonder in the South)
Who keep the memory of your form and feel
A light forerun your face where'er it comes,
In places hushed with fever, thrilled with pain,
I thought of Charity, and self-communed:
"Not only a slight girl, as poets dream,
With gentle footsteps stealing forth alone,
Veiling her hand from her soft timid eyes
Lest they should see her self-forgetful alms,
Or moving, lamp in hand, through glimmering wards
With her nun's coif or nurse's sacred garb:
Not only this,—but oft a sunburnt man,
Grey-garmented, grey-bearded, gigantesque,
Walking the highway with a cheerful stride,
And, like that Good Samaritan (rather say
This Good American!), forgetting not

To lift the hurt one as a little child
And make the weakest strong with manly cheer,
On Red-Cross errands of Good-Comradeship."

Harriet Prescott Spofford

April 3, 1835–August 14, 1921

Born in Maine, Harriet Prescott Spofford lived for most of her life in Massachusetts but resided in DC from 1865 to 1874 and set one of her novels, *Old Washington* (1906), in the city. Spofford published novels and collections of short fiction, including detective stories and gothic romances, as well as poems, essays, and plays. Much of her work first appeared in the *Atlantic Monthly, Harper's Bazaar, Scribner's, Century,* and other periodicals. Her books include *Sir Rohan's Ghost* (1860), *The Amber Gods and Other Stories* (1863), *New England Legends* (1871), *Poems* (1882), *A Scarlet Poppy* (1894), *In Titian's Garden* (1897), *Old Madame and Other Tragedies* (1900), *The Fairy Changeling* (1910), and *The Elder's People* (1920).

Spofford began writing in the 1850s, when her parents became sick and she needed to earn money to support her family. She married in 1865 to a lawyer; their only child, a son, died in infancy.

Thomas Wentworth Higginson championed Spofford as "a wonderful genius." In an 1859 letter (later published in his *Letters and Journals*), he wrote that Spofford "sent to the *Atlantic* a story, under an assumed name, which is so brilliant and shows such an extraordinary intimacy with European life that the editors seriously suspected it of being a translation from some first class Frenchman, a Balzac or Dumas, and I had to be called in to satisfy them that a demure little Yankee girl could have written it. Which, as you may imagine, delighted me much."

Evanescence

What's the brightness of a brow?
What's a mouth of pearls and corals?
Beauty vanishes like a vapor,
Preach the men of musty morals!

Should the crowd, then, ages since,
Have shut their ears to singing Homer,
Because the music fled as soon
As fleets the violets' aroma?

Ah, for me, I thrill to see
The bloom a velvet cheek discloses,
Made of dust—I well believe it!
So are lilies, so are roses!

Reprieve

Over the brink of the place I bent,
    And glanced in the darkling pool below—
Darkling with heavy hemlock shadows,
    And the gloom where sunbeams never go.

And a low, slow wind stirred the veiling branch
    With a ghastly twilight downward thrown,
And I saw a face, the face of a woman,
    A white dead-face I had thought my own!

A Weed

I am so small on this great scale
Of moons and suns and cosmic ways,
I am so poor in all that rears
The treasure of transcendent days,
I am so stained if any see
The shrinking soul in heaven's white blaze!

So small, alas, so poor, so stained,—
What glance that meets the idle soul
Can linger there with least delight
Nor spurn it with a beggar's dole?
Can heavenly help to feed it flow,
Can heavenly love about it roll?

And going sadly on my way
A little flower looks up at me,
A worthless weed beside the path,

That has no honey for the bee,
Nor any beauty that the eye,
The thrall of beauty, waits to see.

Because I am as worthless too,
I pluck the thing that has no use
Nor loveliness. Its fainting breath
Makes for a moment half excuse—
Lo, the precision of its lines
Star orbits to a leaf reduce!

Over its face the twilight tints
Are painted, evening skies less fair.
How lightly swept the master-hand
To make that petal melt in air!
What subtle thought was crowded here,
How exquisite the procreant care!

The golden eye of day is not
More golden than its heart set free!
What spent itself on this small flower?
What sends it brief felicity?
What lavish to a worthless weed
Shall not as lavish be to me!

Mary Toles Peet

January 16, 1836–March 5, 1901

Mary Toles Peet became deaf at age thirteen, following an illness described at the time as "brain fever." Although her parents were devastated by this loss, Peet felt (with some justification) that it actually provided her with educational opportunities she would not have gotten as a hearing woman.

She was educated at the New York Institution for the Deaf and Dumb and married one of her teachers a year after her graduation in 1854. While Isaac Lewis Peet continued to teach (and was later appointed principal), Mary Toles Peet raised their children (two sons and a daughter) and was active in campus life. She taught at the Institution from 1863 to 1867, and she and her husband were tireless advocates of the use of sign language in education rather than the oral method. The Peet family was socially prominent within the deaf community.

After her husband's death, Peet moved to Providence, Rhode Island, and Washington, DC, to join her daughter, Elizabeth. Peet lived in DC from 1900 through 1901, at the end of her life, when she invalided by a stroke. As her daughter was a professor and dean at Gallaudet University, Peet immediately found a warm supportive community and a full social life on another campus. Her funeral was held at the chapel of Gallaudet.

During her lifetime, Peet published poems regularly in *American Annals of the Deaf*. She privately published a biography of Gertrude Walter, *Gertrude, the Story of a Beautiful Life* (1899). Her daughter gathered her poems into a posthumous volume, *Verses* (1903).

Asked about the benefits of silence in 1853, Peet wrote the following, reported in the *Democratic Banner:* "By being deaf and dumb we are prevented from hearing many things which would make us unhappy, and speaking things which we should not; I have often thought that our reward in heaven would be even greater; for, will not the full tide of glorious melody sound even more beautiful to the ears which never wake to the discords of earth?"

Ethel's Letter

Wild winter was around me, dark and drear,
    And tenderest love was hid in frozen earth:
My heart would listen to no sound of mirth,
    Nor hope nor help could come from words of cheer.
I said: "Let silence still enshroud me here,
    All soothing sounds to me are little worth:
Not thus does solace come to this sad earth
    And sorrowing smile is brief as falling tear."
But when the budding spring smiled once again,
    I drew long breaths of life, all strange and sweet,
And June revived her soft and tender strain
    That sang in words my sorrow flew to meet.
So wake the blossoms of my hope again,
    When June unfolds her glory at my feet.

John Burroughs
April 3, 1837 – March 29, 1921

A naturalist and essayist, John Burroughs came to DC in 1864 to work as a clerk in the U.S. Treasury and remained into the 1880s. His nature essays and philosophical commentary were collected in thirty-two publications, including *Notes on Walt Whitman as Poet and Person* (1867), *Birds and Poets* (1877), *Camping and Tramping with Roosevelt* (1906), and *Under the Maples* (1921). His book *Wake Robin* (1871) was inspired in part by his hikes in Rock Creek Park. In addition to writing his own occasional poems, Burroughs edited an anthology, *Songs of Nature,* in 1901. Burroughs is remembered locally with a DC public elementary school in his name.

Burroughs had already read and admired Walt Whitman's *Leaves of Grass* when he happened upon him on the street in downtown DC one day in 1864. Burroughs was eighteen years younger than Whitman, and he quickly became a disciple of the older writer. He wrote: "One thing I plume myself upon in this world, and that is that I saw the greatness of the poet from the first. . . . That head, that presence, those words of love and wisdom convinced like Nature herself."

Burroughs would go on to become one of the most respected authors of his time. Many of his essays first appeared in popular magazines and were adopted by public school curricula across the United States. He is credited with developing a particularly American form of nature essay, combining close observation with philosophical analysis, and helping to define and develop the U.S. conservation movement.

In his essay "The Grist of Gods," Burroughs presciently wrote in 1908: "One cannot but reflect what a sucked orange the earth will be in the course of a few more centuries. Our civilization is terribly expensive to all its natural resources; one hundred years of modern life doubtless exhausts its stores more than a millennium of the life of antiquity."

The Bobolink
Daisies, clover, buttercup,
Redtop, trefoil, meadowsweet,
Ecstatic pinions, soaring up,
Then gliding down to grassy seat.

Sunshine, laughter, mad desires,
May day, June day, lucid skies,
All reckless moods that love inspires—
The gladdest bird that sings and flies.

Meadows, orchards, bending sprays,
Rushes, lilies, billowy wheat,
Song and frolic fill his days,
A feathered rondeau all complete.

Pink bloom, gold bloom, fleabane white,
Dewdrop, raindrop, cooling shade,
Bubbling throat and hovering flight,
And jocund heart as e'er was made.

Waiting

Serene, I fold my hands and wait
    Nor care for wind, or tide, or sea;
I rave no more 'gainst time or fate,
    For lo! my own shall come to me.

I stay my haste, I make delays,
    For what avails this eager pace?
I stand amid the eternal ways,
    And what is mine shall know my face.

Asleep, awake, by night or day,
    The friends I seek are seeking me;
No wind can drive my bark astray,
    Nor change the tide of destiny.

What matter if I stand alone?
    I wait with joy the coming years;
My heart shall reap where it has sown,
    And garner up its fruit of tears.

The waters know their own, and draw
    The brook that springs in yonder height;
So flows the good with equal law
    Unto the soul of pure delight.

The stars come nightly to the sky;
The tidal wave unto the sea;
Nor time, nor space, nor deep, nor high,
Can keep my own away from me.

Charlotte Forten Grimké
August 17, 1837–July 23, 1914

Charlotte Forten Grimké's poems were published during her lifetime in the *Liberator* and *Anglo African*, and her essays appeared in the *Atlantic Monthly* and *New England Magazine*. Grimké taught at Epes Grammar School in Salem, Massachusetts, in the late 1850s and taught slaves and former slaves in the South Carolina Sea Islands under the auspices of the Freedmen's Bureau during the Civil War. In the late 1860s until 1878, she worked as a clerk for the U.S. Treasury Department.

She was active in the Fifteenth Street Presbyterian Church, where her husband, Francis Grimké, was minister, and organized a women's missionary group. Beginning in 1887, she also opened her home for a weekly evening salon, the Art Club, where participants could discuss literature, music, and other subjects of intellectual interest, as well as issues of civil rights. Her journals were published posthumously. Her house, at 1608 R Street NW, still stands and is listed on the National Register of Historic Places. She is buried at National Harmony Memorial Park in Hyattsville, Maryland.

Although her poems were never gathered into a single-author book, Grimké was one of the best-known women poets of African descent of the nineteenth century.

Grimké's health was always delicate (as a child she was diagnosed with a recurring ailment then called "lung fever"), and she was older than her husband by thirteen years. After the early death of their only child, she was often invalided. In later life, Francis Grimké nursed her at home. Anna Julia Cooper, a friend of theirs, wrote: "The tender solicitude with which he cared for Mrs. Grimké and the fond cheerfulness with which he served her slightest wants was beautiful, and to my mind unparalleled among the sons of men."

In the obituary service he gave for her, her husband emphasized her delicacy and femininity. He wrote: "Mrs. Grimké had a lovely disposition, was sweet and gentle, and yet she was a woman of great strength of character. She was a lady in the best sense of that term—a woman of great refinement. There was not the slightest trace of coarseness about her in any shape or form. She had a bright sunny disposition. She never grew old in spirit—she was always young, as young as the youngest. She had a fine mind, carefully trained and cultivated by hard study and contact [with] the best literature and with cultured people. She had the keenest appreciation for all that was best in literature and art. She loved books and pictures and flowers and everything that was beautiful and soul-uplifting. She also had charming manners,—she was always thoughtful, always considerate for others, never allowing the thought of self to intrude or interfere with the comfort and happiness of others."

Her poem "The Gathering of the Grand Army" describes the two-day parade of Union troops down Pennsylvania Avenue at the end of the Civil War.

The Gathering of the Grand Army

Through all the city's streets there poured a flood,
A flood of human souls, eager, intent;
One thought, one purpose stirred the people's blood,
And through their veins its quickening current sent.

The flags waved gayly in the summer air,
O'er patient watchers 'neath the clouded skies;
Old age, and youth, and infancy were there,
The glad light shining in expectant eyes.

And when at last our county's saviors came,—
In proud procession down the crowded street,
Still brighter burned the patriotic flame,
And loud acclaims leaped forth their steps to greet.

And now the veterans scarred and maimed appear,
And now the tattered battle-flags uprise;
A silence deep one moment fills the air,
Then shout on shout ascends unto the skies.

Oh, brothers, ye have borne the battle strain,
And ye have felt it through the ling'ring years;

For all your valiant deeds, your hours of pain,
We can but give to you our grateful tears!

And now, with heads bowed low, and tear-filled eyes
We see a Silent Army passing slow;
For it no music swells, no shouts arise,
But silent blessings from our full hearts flow.

The dead, the living,—All,—a glorious host,
A "cloud of witnesses,"—around us press—
Shall we, like them, stand faithful at our post,
Or weakly yield, unequal to the stress?

Shall it be said the land they fought to save,
Ungrateful now, proves faithless to her trust?
Shall it be said the sons of sires so brave
Now trail her scarred banner in the dust?

Ah, no! again shall rise the people's voice
As once it rose in accents clear and high—
"Oh, outraged brother, lift your head, rejoice!
Justice shall reign,—Insult and Wrong shall die!"

So shall this day the joyous promise be
Of golden days for our fair land in store;
When Freedom's flag shall float above the free,
And Love and Peace prevail from shore to shore.

Charles Sumner

On seeing some pictures of the interior of his house, Washington, DC

Only the casket left, the jewel gone
Whose noble presence filled these stately rooms,
And made this spot a shrine where pilgrims came—
Stranger and friend—to bend in reverence
Before the great, pure soul that knew no guile;
To listen to the wise and gracious words
That fell from lips whose rare, exquisite smile
Gave tender beauty to the grand, grave face.

Upon these pictured walls we see thy peers,—
Poet, and saint, and sage, painter, and king,—
A glorious band;—they shine upon us still;
Still gleam in marble the enchanting forms
Whereupon thy artist eye delighted dwelt;
Thy favorite Psyche droops her matchless face,
Listening, methinks, for the beloved voice
Which nevermore on earth shall sound her praise.

All these remain,—the beautiful, the brave,
The gifted, silent ones; but thou art gone!
Fair is the world that smiles upon us now;
Blue are the skies of June, balmy the air
That soothes with touches soft the weary brow;
And perfect days glide into perfect nights,—
Moonlit and calm; but still our grateful hearts
Are sad, and faint with fear,—for thou art gone!

Oh friend beloved, with longing, tear-filled eyes
We look up, up to the unclouded blue,
And seek in vain some answering sign from thee.
Look down upon us, guide and cheer us still
From the serene height where thou dwellest now;
Dark is the way without the beacon light
Which long and steadfastly thy hand upheld.
Oh, nerve with courage new the stricken hearts
Whose dearest hopes seem lost in losing thee.

Wordsworth

Poet of the serene and thoughtful lay!
In youth's fair dawn, when the soul, still untried,
Longs for life's conflict, and seeks restlessly
Food for its cravings in the stirring songs,
The thrilling strains of more impassioned bards;
Or, eager for fresh joys, culls with delight
The flowers that bloom in fancy's fairy realm—
We may not prize the mild and steadfast ray
That streams from thy pure soul in tranquil song

But, in our riper years, when through the heat
And burden of the day we struggle on,
Breasting the stream upon whose shores we dreamed,
Weary of all the turmoil and the din
Which drowns the finer voices of the soul;
We turn to thee, true priest of Nature's fane,
And find the rest our fainting spirits need,—
The calm, more ardent singers cannot give;
As in the glare intense of tropic days,
Gladly we turn from the sun's radiant beams,
And grateful hail fair Luna's tender light.

At Newport

A quiet nook 'neath the o'erhanging cliffs:
The grim old giants frown upon us, but
Deny us not rest in their grateful shade.
Oh, deep delight to watch the gladsome waves
Exultant leap upon the rugged rocks;
Ever repulsed, yet ever rushing on—
Filled with a life that will not know defeat;
To see the glorious hues of sky and sea.
The distant snowy sails, glide spirit like,
Into an unknown world, to feel the sweet
Enchantment of the sea thrill all the soul,
Clearing the clouded brain, making the heart
Leap joyous as its own bright, singing waves!
"Ah, perfect day," cry happy voices—yet,
For me, beloved, the joy is incomplete—
Thou art not here!

A Parting Hymn

When Winter's royal robes of white
    From hill and vale are gone,
And the glad voices of the spring
    Upon the air are borne,
Friends, who have met with us before,
Within these walls shall meet no more.

Forth to a noble work they go:
    O, may their hearts keep pure,
And hopeful zeal and strength be theirs
    To labor and endure,
That they an earnest faith may prove
By words of truth and deeds of love.

May those, whose holy task it is
    To guide impulsive youth,
Fail not to cherish in their souls
    A reverence for truth;
For teachings which the lips impart
Must have their source within the heart.

May all who suffer share their love—
    The poor and the oppressed;
So shall the blessing of our God
    Upon their labors rest.
And may we meet again where all
Are blest and freed from every thrall.

Cincinnatus Heine Miller (Joaquin Miller)

September 8, 1837–February 17, 1913

Cincinnatus Heine Miller, who published under the pen name Joaquin Miller, was known as the "Poet of the Sierras" and built his modest rustic log cabin atop Meridian Hill in the late 1860s, now the site of Malcolm X Park in Washington. The National Park Service moved the cabin to a location in Rock Creek Park in 1912, where it still stands at Picnic Grove #6, just north of the intersection of Military Road and Beach Drive, a rare example of vernacular architecture, and the only log cabin in the city. A local press, the Word Works, has named its annual summer reading series after him.

Miller published essays and more than twenty books of poems, including *Specimens* (1869), *Songs of the Sierras* (1871), *Songs of the Soul* (1896), and *49: The Gold Seekers of the Sierras* (1910). He worked at various times as a mining-camp cook, lawyer, journalist, Pony Express rider, and was once jailed as a horse thief.

Miller lived in DC from 1883 to 1885, cutting an exotic figure with his long, flowing hair and buckskin clothing. While in Washington, Miller published *Memorie and Time* (1884) and permanently separated from his wife, Abbie. After just a couple of years' residence, he moved to Oakland, California, where he would live the rest of his life.

An obituary in the *Washington Evening Star* in 1913 described Miller as "a man of many peculiarities, but his urbanity of manner and the geniality he exhibited to his friends was never disturbed."

By the Pacific Ocean

Here room and kingly silence keep
Companionship in state austere;
The dignity of death is here,
The large, lone vastness of the deep;
Here toil has pitched his camp to rest:
The west is banked against the west.

Above yon gleaming skies of gold
One lone imperial peak is seen;
While gathered at his feet in green
Ten thousand foresters are told:
And all so still! so still the air
That duty drops the web of care.

Beneath the sunset's golden sheaves
The awful deep walks with the deep,
Where silent sea doves slip and sweep,
And commerce keeps her loom and weaves
The dead red men refuse to rest;
Their ghosts illume my lurid West.

Sea-Blown

Ah! there be souls none understand;
Like clouds, they cannot touch the land.
Unanchored ships, they blow and blow,
Sail to and fro, and then go down
In unknown seas that none shall know,
Without one ripple of renown.

Call these not fools, the test of worth
Is not the hold you have of earth.
Ay, there be gentlest souls sea-blown
That know not any harbor known.
Now it may be the reason is,
They touch on fairer shores than this.

Henry Adams

February 16, 1838 – March 27, 1918

Henry Adams was a historian and the grandson and great-grandson of U.S. Presidents John Adams and John Quincy Adams. He first lived in Washington with his parents at what is now the Arts Club of Washington, at 2017 I Street NW, during the winter of 1860–61. He wrote dispatches for a Boston newspaper and later published an essay, "The Great Secession Winter," which historian Garry Wills describes as "full of inside information" and still "repeatedly cited in treatments of the Civil War's onset." Adams then served as his father's personal secretary when Charles Francis Adams was appointed ambassador to the United Kingdom, after which Henry Adams was hired as a professor of history at Harvard University. He returned to DC in 1877, living on Lafayette Square from age thirty-nine until his death at age eighty. Neither of his later two houses still stand.

Adams married Marion Hooper, known to friends as Clover, in 1872. A talented amateur photographer, she was clever, outspoken, with a dazzling wit and a sharp tongue. Henry and Clover held a regular salon in their home for an elite group of intellectuals called the "Five of Hearts." Their friends were a powerful group that included politicians and some of the top artists in the United States at the time. But Clover also suffered from depression, and following the death of her father in 1883, she committed suicide in a particularly gruesome way: poisoning herself by drinking the chemicals she used to develop photographs. Adams commissioned a funerary monument for her in Rock Creek Cemetery, a masterpiece that has come to be called *Grief*, by sculptor Augustus Saint-Gaudens. The memorial is arguably the most important piece of figurative art in all of DC and one of the most important pieces of funerary art in the nation. The monument would, in turn, inspire a great deal of poetry. After his death, Adams was interred there as well, and, as he stipulated in his will, no names or dates accompany the sculpture.

Adams is best remembered as the author of two novels, *Democracy* (1880) and *Esther* (1884), and his masterful autobiography, *The Education of Henry Adams* (1918). He also wrote some poetry, biographies of Albert Gallatin and George Cabot Lodge, a critical study of Mont-Saint-Michel and Chartres, and the multivolume *History of the United States during the Administrations of Thomas Jefferson and James Madison* (1889–91). He is remembered locally with the Hay-Adams Hotel, built on the site of his last DC home and named for him and his best friend, John Hay.

Prayer to the Dynamo

Mysterious Power! Gentle Friend!
Despotic Master! Tireless Force!
You and We are near the End.
Either You or We must bend
To bear the martyrs' Cross.

We know ourselves, what we can bear
As men; our strength and weakness too;
Down to the fraction of a hair;
And know that we, with all our care
And knowledge, know not you.

You come in silence, Primal Force,
We know not whence, or when, or why;
You stay a moment in your course
To play; and, lo! you leap across
To Alpha Centauri!

We know not whether you are kind,
Or cruel in your fiercer mood;
But be you Matter, be you Mind,
We think we know that you are blind,
And we alone are good.

We know that prayer is thrown away,
For you are only force and light;
A shifting current; night and day;

We know this well, and yet we pray,
For prayer is infinite,

Like you! Within the finite sphere
That bounds the impotence of thought,
We search an outlet everywhere
But only find that we are here
And that you are—are not!

What are we then? the lords of space?
The master-mind whose tasks you do?
Jockey who rides you in the race?
Or are we atoms whirled apace,
Shaped and controlled by you?

Still silence! Still no end in sight!
No sound in answer to our cry!
Then, by the God we now hold tight,
Though we destroy soul, life and light,
Answer you shall—or die!

We are no beggars! What care we
For hopes or terrors, love or hate?
What for the universe? We see
Only our certain destiny
And the last word of Fate.

Seize, then, the Atom! rack his joints!
Tear out of him his secret spring!
Grind him to nothing!—though he points
To us, and his life-blood anoints
Me—the dead Atom-King!

The Capitol by Moonlight

Infinite Peace! The calm of moon and midnight! Where
The marble terrace gleams in silvery light,
Peace broods. Drugged by the brooding night
The crowded tree-tops sleep in passionless air.
Look up, where like a God, strong, serene, fair,
The pale dome soars and slumbers, shadowy, white,

Endymion, dreaming still that on his Latmian height
He feels Selene's breath warm on his eyes and hair.
Infinite Peace! Yet, bending from the West,
Flash out the fierceness and the fire of Mars,
While there beneath, straining to touch the stars
The obelisk mocks us with its sweet unrest,
And even this soft air of the terrace throbs
With some low moan—sigh of a heart that sobs.

John Hay

October 8, 1838–July 1, 1905

John Hay moved to DC to serve as one of two personal secretaries to President Abraham Lincoln, living in the White House beginning at age twenty-two, sharing a second-floor bedroom in the northeast corner of the residence with John G. Nicolay. Hay trained as a lawyer, and other than six years as a journalist for the *New York Tribune,* he spent his career in government.

Hay is the author of a novel, *The Bread-Winners* (1883); a travel memoir, *Castilian Days* (1875); and two books of poems, *Pike County Ballads* (1871) and *Poems* (1890). He coauthored with Nicolay the biography *Abraham Lincoln: A History* (1890).

Hay was always very modest about his literary achievements. In a letter to William Dean Howells in 1890, he wrote: "I have had the impudence to collect all my verses, new and stale, into one volume which Houghton & Mifflin have printed. But I have at the same time printed a little edition of them for my friends and lovers, of which I send you a copy. You will not suspect me of taking them too seriously in thus dressing them up. On the contrary, it is only the conscious amateur who does such things."

Hay held diplomatic posts in France, Spain, Austria, and the United Kingdom. He was secretary of state under Presidents William McKinley and Theodore Roosevelt. Hay was one of the first seven people elected to the American Academy of Arts and Sciences in 1904. None of his former homes, other than the White House, still stand. His grand mansion on Lafayette Square, built on the same property as the home of his best friend, Henry Adams, is now the site of the Hay-Adams Hotel.

The Crows at Washington

Slow flapping to the setting sun
    By twos and threes, in wavering rows,
As twilight shadows dimly close,
The crows fly over Washington.

Under the crimson sunset sky
Virginian woodlands leafless lie,
    In wintry torpor bleak and dun.
Through the rich vault of heaven, which shines
    Like a warmed opal in the sun,
With wide advance in broken lines
The crows fly over Washington.

Over the Capitol's white dome,
    Across the obelisk soaring bare
To prick the clouds, they travel home,
Content and weary, winnowing
    With dusky vans the golden air,
Which hints the coming of the spring,
Though winter whitens Washington.

The dim, deep air, the level ray
Of dying sunlight on their plumes,
    Give them a beauty not their own;
Their hoarse notes fail and faint away;
    A rustling murmur floating down
Blends sweetly with the thickening glooms;
They touch with grace the fading day,
    Slow flying over Washington.

I stand and watch with clouded eyes
    These dim battalions move along;
Out of the distance memory cries
    Of days when life and hope were strong,
When love was prompt and wit was gay;
Even then, at evening, as today,
    I watched, while twilight hovered dim
    Over Potomac's curving rim,
This selfsame flight of homing crows

Blotting the sunset's fading rose,
    Above the roofs of Washington.

Two on the Terrace
Warm waves of lavish moonlight
The Capitol enfold,
As if a richer noon light
Bathed its white walls with gold.
The great bronze Freedom shining,
Her crest in ether shrining,
Peers eastward as divining
The new day from the old.

Mark the mild planet pouring
Her splendor o'er the ground;
See the white obelisk soaring
To pierce the blue profound.
Beneath the still heavens beaming,
The lighted town lies gleaming,
In guarded slumber dreaming—
A world without a sound.

No laughter and no sobbing
From those dim roofs arise,
The myriad pulses throbbing
Are silent as the skies.
To us their peace is given,
The mead of spirits shriven;
I see the wide, pure heaven
Reflected in your eyes.

Ah love! a thousand eons
Shall range their trooping years;
The morning stars their paeans
Shall sing to countless ears.
These married States may sever,
Strong Time this dome may shiver,
But love shall last forever
And lovers' hopes and fears.

So let us send our greeting,
A wish for trust and bliss,
To future lovers meeting
On far-off nights like this,
Who, in these walls' undoing
Perforce of Time's rough wooing,
Amid the crumbling ruin
Shall meet, clasp hands, and kiss.

Esmerelda Boyle

September 29, 1840–April 18, 1928

Esmerelda Boyle was born in Washington, DC, the daughter of Commodore Junius I. Boyle of the U.S. Navy. She was one of three cofounders of the Washington Literary Society in 1874, and early meetings of the society were held in her mother's parlor in Foggy Bottom (at 723 Twenty-First Street NW, now razed). Membership was originally limited to thirty men and women, later raised to forty, and fortnightly meetings consisted of a short program (a reading of a paper, poems, or a musical selection) followed by conversation. Members included librarians, educators, historians, and clergy; all were Caucasians of high social standing.

Boyle's books include *Thistledown* (1871), *The Story of Felice* (1872), *Songs of Land and Sea* (1875), *The Image Breaker* (1875), *Father John McElroy, the Irish Priest* (1878), and *Saint Cecilia's Gates* (1890), although she is best remembered for her *Biographical Sketches of Distinguished Marylanders* (1877).

For the last fifteen years of her life, Boyle resided in Grand Island, Nebraska, where she had relatives nearby. She conducted private classes in French and Spanish until her health deteriorated. The *Grand Island Independent* reported after her death in 1928: "Possessed of a keen intellect, a charming and gentle manner, she soon won for herself many warm personal friends, who took a kindly interest in her. Of southern birth and in her earlier years surrounded by an atmosphere of wealth and culture, she accepted life's vicissitudes which later beset her with an innate combination of pride and independence, and was wont to discourage the many kindly ministrations of relatives and friends."

Love Me Little, Love Me Long

Love me little, love me long,
Through the springtime rain and sun,
Through the might of Right and Wrong,
When the days of youth are done.

In the noon-tide's glorious glow,
When the evening mounteth high
On her throne of gleaming snow,
In her pageant robes to die.

With pink flushes on her cheek,
With gold arrows in her hand,
Pointing upward to each peak
Where her marshaled armies stand;

When the rose has lost its bloom,
When the leaves are dropping down,
In the Autumn's purple gloom,
On the grasses sear and brown;

When the bird shall fold its wings,
And in silence hold its song,
With that peace the twilight brings,
Love me little, love me long.

George Alfred Townsend (Gath)

January 30, 1841–April 15, 1914

George Alfred Townsend wrote under the pen name Gath. He was a journalist for the *Philadelphia Enquirer, New York Herald, New York World, Chicago Tribune,* and *New York Graphic,* and cofounder of the *Capital* with Donn Piatt. Gath was best known as a Washington correspondent who covered the Civil War and the assassination of Abraham Lincoln.

Gath published nonfiction, including *The Life, Crime, and Capture of John Wilkes Booth* (1865), *The New World Compared to the Old* (1871), and *The Swamp Outlaws: or the North Carolina Bandits* (1872); a memoir, *Campaigns of a Non-Combatant* (1866); novels, including *The En-*

tailed Hat (1884), *Katy of Catoctin* (1887), and *Columbus in Love* (1893); short fiction, including *Tales of the Chesapeake* (1880) and *Bohemian Days: Three American Tales* (1880); a guidebook, *Washington, Outside and Inside* (1873); and poetry, including *Poetical Addresses of George Alfred Townsend* (1881) and *Poems of Men and Events* (1899).

The estate Townsend built in the Catoctin Mountains of Maryland is now Gathland State Park, and one of the original buildings, Gathland Hall, now serves as the park headquarters.

Cloture

The Senate sloths sit up tonight—
    Dear Kitty come with me!
The crowded Capitol was bright,
    Dark was our gallery;
They crowded me and Kitty so,
    Her courage to assure
My arm around her waist I throw:
    "The subject is *Cloture.*"

"How mad they get," said Kitty soon,
    "On matters so demure!
They rush upon each other close,
    Is that not like *Cloture?*"
"No, *This* more like that thing occult"—
    She cuddled up demure:
"I hope we'll come to some result
    And early pass *Cloture.*"

Nought did we hear that blessed night
    Yet sat in perfect bliss;
When noise and wrath were at their height
    Cloture concealed a kiss:
"Are you in favor of repeal!
    I think 'tis quite obscure."
"Light up the subject with your lips!—
    Dear Kitty, press *Cloture!*"

"Why do we need so much Reserve?
    I'm sure we are secure.

I think more faith would give them nerve,—
    And therefore more *Cloture.*"
"Kitty, our circulation's high,
    This panic may endure,
And Legal Tender's in my eye
    If you but say *Cloture?*"

At panic prices we drove back,—
    That Herdic tilted sure;
Kitty came sliding down the hack
    And all went on cloture:
"I've changed my mind; 'tis nice to wait,—
    Engagements can endure.
But never let them close debate
    While we can have *Cloture.*"

Julia Von Stosch Schayer

January 7, 1842 – March 29, 1928

Julia Von Stosch Schayer is the author of *Tiger Lily and Other Stories* (1883). She published short fiction and poetry in such journals as the *Atlantic Monthly, Scribner's Monthly,* and the *Century.* One of her stories, "The Major's Appointment," was adapted into a play, and another, "Story of Two Lives," was adapted for an episode of the television show *Your Favorite Story.*

Schayer was married twice; her second husband was appointed deputy recorder of deeds in Washington, which brought her to the city. Two of her children also became writers: Richard Schayer was a screenwriter of more than one hundred films, and Leonora Speyer (also included in this volume) won the 1927 Pulitzer Prize for poetry. The home they shared when the children were young still stands, at 1318 Thirtieth Street NW in Georgetown. Schayer is buried in Glenwood Cemetery.

The Moon-Flower

The sun has burned his way across the sky,
And sunk in sultry splendor; now the earth
Lies spent and gray, wrapped in the grateful dusk;

Stars tremble into sight, and in the west
The curved moon glows faintly. 'Tis the hour!
See! Flower on flower the buds unfold, until
The air is filled with odors exquisite
And amorous sighs, and all the verdurous gloom
Is starred with silvery disks.
                                    Oh, Flower of Dreams!—
Of lover's dreams, where bliss and anguish meet;
Dreams of dead joys, and joys that ne'er have been;
Keenest of all, the joys that ne'er shall be!

Ambrose Bierce

June 24, 1842–1914?

Ambrose Bierce lived in DC from 1899 through 1913, renting at four different addresses, all of which still stand: the Olympia Apartments, 1368 Euclid Street NW in the Columbia Heights neighborhood; 18 Logan Circle NW; 1825 Nineteenth Street NW in Dupont Circle; and the El Dorado Apartments at 1321 Fairmont Street NW in Columbia Heights. While in Washington, Bierce completed his satirical *Devil's Dictionary* (1911) and his word-usage compendium *Write It Right* (1909). Some of his other publications include *The Fiend's Delight* (1873), *Cobwebs from an Empty Skull* (1874), *Tales of Soldiers and Civilians* (1891), *Black Beetles in Amber* (1892), *Fantastic Fables* (1899), *Shapes of Clay* (1903), and *The Cynic's Word Book* (1906).

Bierce served in the Union army during the Civil War, then began his career as a journalist. He is best remembered for his short story "An Occurrence at Owl Creek Bridge." He published twelve books during his lifetime, a combination of fiction, poetry, and nonfiction. In October 1913, he left DC for a tour of his old Civil War battlefields, then traveled to Mexico to observe Pancho Villa's army during the Mexican Revolution. He was never heard from or seen again, and the exact circumstances and date of his death remain a mystery.

In *The Devil's Dictionary*, he defined a "Washingtonian" as "A Potomac tribesman who exchanged the privilege of governing himself for the advantage of good government. In justice to him it should be said that he did not want to."

The Statesmen

How blest the land that counts among
    Her sons so many good and wise,
To execute great feats of tongue
    When troubles rise.

Behold them mounting every stump,
    By speech our liberty to guard.
Observe their courage—see them jump,
    And come down hard!

"Walk up, walk up!" each cries aloud,
    "And learn from me what you must do
To turn aside the thunder cloud,
    The earthquake too.

"Beware the wiles of yonder quack
    Who stuffs the ears of all that pass.
I—I alone can show that black
    Is white as grass."

They shout through all the day and break
    The silence of the night as well.
They'd make—I wish they'd *go* and make—
    Of Heaven a Hell.

A advocates free silver, B
Free trade and C free banking laws.
Free board, clothes, lodging would from me
Win warm applause.

Lo, D lifts up his voice: "You see
    The single tax on land would fall
On all alike." More evenly
    No tax at all.

"With paper money," bellows E,
    "We'll all be rich as lords." No doubt—
And richest of the lot will be
    The chap without.

As many "cures" as addle-wits
    Who know not what the ailment is!
Meanwhile the patient foams and spits
    Like a gin fizz.

Alas, poor Body Politic,
    Your fate is all too clearly read:
To be not altogether quick,
    Nor very dead.

You take your exercise in squirms,
    Your rest in fainting fits between.
'Tis plain that your disorder's worms—
    Worms fat and lean.

Worm Capital, Worm Labor dwell
    Within your maw and muscle's scope.
Their quarrels make your life a Hell,
    Your death a hope.

God send you find not such an end
    To ills however sharp and huge!
God send you convalesce! God send
    You vermifuge.

The New Decalogue
Have but one God: thy knees were sore
If bent in prayer to three or four.

Adore no images save those
The coinage of thy country shows.

Take not the Name in vain. Direct
Thy swearing unto some effect.

Thy hand from Sunday work be held—
Work not at all unless compelled.

Honor thy parents, and perchance
Their wills thy fortunes may advance.

Kill not—death liberates thy foe
From persecution's constant woe.

Kiss not thy neighbor's wife. Of course
There's no objection to divorce.

To steal were folly, for 'tis plain
In cheating there is greater gain.

Bear not false witness. Shake your head
And say that you have "heard it said."

Who stays to covet ne'er will catch
An opportunity to snatch.

A Year's Casualties
Slain as they lay by the secret, slow,
Pitiless hand of an unseen foe,
Two score thousand old soldiers have crossed
The river to join the loved and lost.
In the space of a year their spirits fled,
Silent and white, to the camp of the dead.

One after one, they fall asleep
And the pension agents awake to weep,
And orphaned statesmen are loud in their wail
As the souls flit by on the evening gale.
O Father of Battles, pray give us release
From the horrors of peace, the horrors of peace!

Alfred Islay Walden

1843–January 1884

Born enslaved, Alfred Islay Walden traveled from North Carolina to
DC by foot in the winter of 1867, determined to study for the ministry.
He was awarded a scholarship to Howard University and earned his
degree in 1876. During his time in DC, he earned his living by doing
manual labor and selling his political ballads on the street. He also or-
ganized Sabbath schools for African American children.

He subsequently moved to New Jersey, where he became one of
the first African American graduates of New Brunswick Theological
Seminary. Ordained in 1879, Walden returned to North Carolina and
led a congregation until his death. He published two books of poems:

Walden's Miscellaneous Poems (1873) and *Walden's Sacred Poems, with a Sketch of His Life* (1877).

Dedicated to a Young Lady Representing the Indian Race at Howard University

While sitting in my room kind Miss,
I thought I'd sing a praise,
But now I think I'll write a word,
To light up thy days.

It's true I often write on Queens,
And those of noble fame;
But now I seek to write a line
Upon thy honored name.

What's in thy name moves me to write,
This little verse on thee?
Perhaps it is thy pleasant ways
And cheering looks to me.

How oft I think of thee kind Miss,
And oft admire thy grace,
Because I know that thou art of
Another noble race!

When by the bells to meals we're called
Or round the table meet,
With anxious eye I look to see
If thou art in thy seat.

And then I cast my eyes around,
Through hall, through long and wide,
And then I quickly look to see
Thy tea-mate by thy side.

But first of all the bell is rung,
And each within his place,
In silence each one bows his head,
'Till some one asks the grace.

Then each in seat with upturned plates,
And scarce a word is said,
Until we have a full supply
Of meats and baker's bread.

And dishes, too, are passing round
About from you and me;
And Clara she looks up and asks—
Pray, sir, what can it be?

It's pork of course, or else it's beef;
Perchance it may be ham—
Except the baker cooked a goose,
And passed it off for lamb.

And if he has a cut will tell,
If round about its swallow,
For surely it is not so dead,
That it would fail to halloo.

While all of this is going on,
There're other things in view;
For oft I catch myself, dear Miss,
Exchanging looks with you.

But soon we're through, the bell does ring,
We're called by duty's 'larms;
Nor can I longer sit and look
Upon thy brilliant charms.

I'd speak of all my table mates
Had I another pen,
For surely we're as happy guests
As here have ever been.

The Nation's Friend

This nation has a faithful friend,
In whom she may confide;
Whose influence is like a sea,
Flowing both deep and wide.

Let us behold the sea, how calm—
What ships her billows float,
Come let us hasten to the shore,
And get on freedom's boat.

Upon her deck the nations meet;
The white and colored there,
Where no first place nor second known,
No difference in the fare.

I saw her raise her banner high,
And cast it to the breeze,
While tempests raged and billows rolled
She sailed through gulfs and seas.

Through smoke and fog she onward went
This nation to defend,
When Dixie cried, "Take her last son,
And her last dollar spend."

When hissing shot around her fell,
From rebel cannon's mouth,
She stood the storm, the rain, the hail,
And now can stand the drouth.

I heard her cry, while sailing on—
And Justice is her name—
Grant equal rights to every man,
And amnesty the same.

She soon will land her noble crew
Within a city bright,
Where nations in one brotherhood
Drink national delight.

Where we may have our public schools,
With open doors displayed;
Where all may drink at wisdom's fount
With none to make afraid.

Young friends, I know you will be there
Bright, shining, as the sun;

With equal rights secured for all,
When Sumner's work is done.

The nation's friend! still firm he stands,
With neither sleep nor slumber,
Come every Freedman in this land
And hail the name of Sumner.

Charles Warren Stoddard
August 7, 1843–April 23, 1909

Charles Warren Stoddard lived at 300 N Street NW in the Truxton Circle neighborhood from 1889 to 1892, while head of the English Department at the Catholic University of America. His house still stands. He published a novel, *For the Pleasure of His Company* (1903); a volume of poetry, *Poems* (1867); and at least thirteen nonfiction travel books, including *South Sea Idyls* (1873), *Mashallah!: A Flight into Egypt* (1881), *The Lepers of Molokai* (1885), and *Over the Rocky Mountains to Alaska* (1899). Stoddard also wrote a memoir about his conversion to Catholicism, *A Troubled Heart and How It Was Comforted* (1885). In addition, Stoddard wrote journalism, as a correspondent for the *San Francisco Chronicle*, and as coeditor of the *Overland Monthly*.

Stoddard credited Walt Whitman's "Calamus" poems as an inspiration for much of his homoerotic writing about the natives of the South Seas. He developed lifelong literary friendships with Ambrose Bierce, Henry Adams, and Joaquin Miller, among others.

The First Rain
Between the ranks of thistle, down the road,
The phantom flocks of sunbeams hastily,
With gilded feathers of the butterfly,
Disperse away; anon a weary load
Of grain, wild scented, being freshly mowed,
Comes smoking on; as from the brooding sky
There fall deliberate, still showers of shy,
Big rain-drops all around. The teamsters goad
The swaying oxen, steaming, to a shed
For covering. The brown and dusty trees
Are whispering, as eagerly they spread

Their branches in the rain, and stand at ease,
And listen, yonder in the clover bed
The happy buzzing of ten thousand bees!

Emily Thornton Charles (Emily Hawthorn)
March 21, 1845 – April 25, 1895

Emily Thornton Charles, who published under the pen name Emily
Hawthorn, is the author of two books of poems: *Hawthorn Blossoms*
(1876) and *Lyrical Poems* (1886). She worked as a journalist; her pro-
fessional positions included managing editor of *Washington World* and
editor of the *National Veteran*. She was also a professional elocutionist,
giving speeches on women's suffrage. Hawthorn served on the execu-
tive committee of the National Woman's Press Association and as chair
of the Washington Society of American Authors. Her life was marked
by loss: both her father and a brother died in the Civil War. She mar-
ried Daniel B. Charles but was widowed by age twenty-four in 1874
and raised their two young sons on her own.

Two of her former houses still stand: 1516 Q Street NW in the
Logan Circle neighborhood, and 1231 W Street NW in the Cardozo
neighborhood. She is buried in Rock Creek Cemetery. An obituary in
the *Washington Evening Star* stated she "had been prominent for many
years in Washington as a woman of high attainments in scholarship
and a writer of verse of a high order of merit."

Rondeau
Let us love
While we may.
Land above,
Land of clay,
Do unite
Fair and bright;
Do meet
And complete,
In unions,
Communions—
Something sweet

Which we greet;
For its form,
Mid life's storm
Gives us hope,
Lifts us up
On its wings,
Joy it brings,
And with wiles
Care beguiles.
Thus our song,
Loud and long,
E'er the same,
Bears the name
Of this dove.
Call it "Love" —
Thrills our heart,
Every part—
May it come
To its home,
Builds its nest
In our breast,
We are blest—
Love possessed.

William Henry Babcock

January 19, 1849 – July 20, 1922

William Henry Babcock was born in St. Louis and practiced law in DC at the U.S. Patent Office and privately. His books include *The Brides of the Tiger: Tales of Adventure When These Colonies Were New* (1892); *Cian of the Chariots: A Romance of the Days of Arthur* (1898), credited as the first Arthurian historical novel published in the United States; and *The Tower of Wye* (1901). A number of his books were set in Washington, including *Cypress Beach* (1884), *An Invention of the Enemy* (1889), and *Kent Fort Manor* (1903). He published three books of poems, *Lord Stirling's Stand, And Other Poems* (1880), *Lays from over the Sea* (1882), and *Legends of the New World* (1919), with subjects ranging from admired authors to travels in Cuba. His essays appeared in *American Anthropologist,* the *Journal of American Folklore, Folk-Lore Journal,* and *Geographical Review.* His scholarly publications include *Recent History and Present Status of the Vinland Problem* (1921), *The Two Lost Centuries of Britain* (1890), *Legendary Islands of the Atlantic: A Study in Medieval Geography* (1922), and *Early Norse Visits to North America* (1913).

Babcock and his wife, Gertrude Lee Babcock, raised a large family of seven children. The house where he lived in the 1800s, at 1113 Independence Avenue SE on Capitol Hill, and a later residence at 303 E Street NE, still stand.

Walt Whitman

Athlete of Paumanok, whose strenuous line
Has clasped a continent with stained arm,
Thou art not of today nor years that shine
With the soul's promise and the spirit's charm.
The rosy white-limbed pagan days were thine
When men found godhead in the gracious form;
And, garlanded, came dancing round the shrine,
Or led the bounding choir in nudity divine.
Restored in thee the very soul we scan
Of that blithe-blooded rare boy-bather's land:
The glad fond kinship with all nature's plan;
Keen eyes, free breath, the comrade-clasping hand,
And the strong sympathy with man as man,
Whole-hearted and invincible and grand.

Edgar Poe's Grave

Chill the nook beside the barren street,
Walled from man but open to the sky.
O'er the stone the cloudy shadows fleet;
Clings the mist, a pallid winding sheet;
    Death and life have met eternally.
Still the pageant troops before his eye,
    Who abode in starlit mystery.
Wayward spirit of the haunted glen,
Tuneful wanderer of the midnight blast,
Doomed awhile to dwell with mortal men

Singing phantom kindred as they passed,
Airy harp with notes beyond our ken,
Subtle, pure, our one unearthly pen,
    Come what may the foremost and the last!

Grace Denio Litchfield

November 19, 1849–December 4, 1944

Grace Denio Litchfield was the author of seventeen books of poems, fiction, and nonfiction. After a childhood spent mostly in Europe, she lived for more than fifty years in DC, beginning in 1888. She published individual stories in popular magazines such as *Harper's* and the *Atlantic*. Some of her books include *Only an Incident* (1883), *Mimosa Leaves: Poems* (1895), a first-person account of an earthquake on the French Riviera called *In the Crucible* (1897), *Vita: A Drama* (1904), *The Song of the Sirens* (1917), and *As a Man Sows and Other Stories* (1926).

An article in the *Washington Evening Star* on March 14, 1920, called her residence (at 2010 Massachusetts Avenue NW, now razed) "one of the revered literary shrines of the capital. . . . Miss Litchfield's home and very presence recall the golden age of letters in Washington. . . . All about her quaint drawing room, where treasures of old mahogany, bric-a-brac and paintings appear, are autographed copies of the famous authors of Washington and of the nation at large."

The Setting Sun
One radiant outflash of surpassing splendor,
And with the perfect peace of self-surrender,
    Without a tear,
    Without a fear,
Like some high spirit summoned from our sight,
The sun steps down into the unknown night.

Good Bye
We say it for an hour or for years;
We say it smiling, say it choked with tears;
We say it coldly, say it with a kiss;
And yet we have no other word than this—
    "Good bye,"

We have no dearer word for our heart's friend,
For him who journeys to the world's far end,
And scars our soul with going; but we say,
As unto him that steps but o'er the way,
                    "Good bye."

Alike to those we love and those we hate
We say no more in parting. At life's gate,
To him who passes out beyond earth's sight,
We cry, as to the wanderer for a night—
                    "Good bye."

Robert Underwood Johnson
January 12, 1853 – October 14, 1937

A native of DC, Robert Underwood Johnson began his writing career as an editor for the *Century Magazine* and *Scribner's Monthly*. Among other accomplishments, he was one of the driving forces behind the creation of Yosemite National Park in California, pushed for international copyright laws as secretary of the American Copyright League, worked to preserve as a museum the rooms in Rome where John Keats died, and served as a secretary of the American Academy of Arts and Letters.

Johnson is perhaps best remembered as the U.S. ambassador to Italy in the early 1920s, where he helped coordinate Italy's recovery from World War I. He wrote seven books of poems, including *The Winter Hour* (1892), *Songs of Liberty* (1897), *Poems of War and Peace* (1916), and *Italian Rhapsody* (1917). His memoir, *Remembered Yesterdays*, was published in 1923.

In Tesla's Laboratory
Here in the dark what ghostly figures press!—
No phantom of the Past, or grim or sad;
No wailing spirit of woe, no specter, clad
In white and wandering cloud, whose dumb distress
Is that its crime it never may confess;
No shape from the strewn sea; nor they that add
The link of Life and Death,—the tearless mad,
That live nor die in dreary nothingness:

But blessed spirits waiting to be born
Thoughts to unlock the fettering chains of Things;
The Better Time; the Universal Good.
Their smile is like the joyous break of morn;
How fair, how near, how wistfully they brood!
Listen! that murmur is of angels' wings.

On Nearing Washington

City of homes and in my heart my home!
    (Though other streets exact a grudging fee):
    How leap my pulses when afar I see
    The dawn creep whitening down thy solemn dome!
For now my care-restricted steps may roam
    Thy urban groves—a forest soon to be—
    Where, like thy shining river, placid, free,
Contentment dwells and beckons me to come.

Ah, city dear to lovers!—that dost keep
    For their delight what Mays and what Novembers!—
    Kindling the flame, and if it ever sleep,
New-lighting it within the breathing embers;
    Dear even in their sorrow! for when they weep
    'Tis for rare joys, scarce known till Love remembers.

William Temple Hornaday

December 1, 1854–March 6, 1937

William Temple Hornaday was a zoologist and the author of fifteen books of nonfiction, as well as poems and songs. His books include *Two Years in the Jungle* (1885), *The Extermination of the American Bison* (1887), *American Natural History* (1904), *Campfires in the Canadian Rockies* (1906), and *Our Vanishing Wild Life* (1913).

Hornaday was chief taxidermist of the U.S. National Museum from 1882 to 1890, where he revolutionized museum exhibits by displaying wildlife in their natural settings. He is one of the founders of the Smithsonian Institution's National Zoological Park. He later served as director of the Bronx Zoo for thirty years and was cofounder (with Theodore Roosevelt) and president of the American Bison Society. Hornaday is credited with discovering the American crocodile, saving the American bison and the Alaskan fur seal from extinction, and founding the American conservation movement.

While director at the Bronx Zoo, Hornaday displayed a human being in the monkey house. The exhibition of Ota Benga, a native of the Congo, was a great scandal in the African American press, but New York mayor George McClellan refused to meet with a delegation of African American clergy, and Hornaday never apologized, justifying the exhibit as "ethnological," although he closed it after two days.

His house, at 404 U Street NW in the LeDroit Park neighborhood, still stands.

The Whispering Pine

Half way down the side of the Sunset Divide
    In view of the valley of Peace,
There's a sturdy young pine that's exclusively mine,
    And beneath it my striving will cease.
When I rest in its shade and its branches are swayed
    By the breezes that waft from the West,
That evergreen tree softly whispers to me
    Of the memories locked in my breast.

When I pillow my head on its pine-needle bed
    Wireless messages come to my tree,
And its branches are stirred by the tender things heard
    And transmitted in whispers to me.
My Ship, far at sea, sends a message to me,
    And I hear it once more, with a sigh,
"Oh be of good cheer, for your Fortune is here,
    And I'm coming to port,—by and by!"

There are times when I hear with a sigh and a tear
    Sweet voices like wind-harps in tune,
That softly implore from a far-distance shore,
    "Oh Comrade! Come hitherward soon!"
Then I see my young bride as she stood by my side
    In the little white church on the hill.
She was queenly and sweet; all her charms were complete,
    And bless her! she's young to me still!

When my days are far spent, and my bow is unbent,
    I will go to my evergreen tree,
And within its sweet shade my last bed shall be made,
    With my loved ones in close touch with me.
As the years come and go those who miss me will know
    How their souls may hold converse with mine;
For each message of love will be caught from above,
    And sent down by my whispering pine.

Anne Kelledy Gilbert

1859–November 6, 1944

Anne Kelledy Gilbert was born in Port Gibson, Mississippi, and educated in Mississippi and Baltimore. A longtime DC resident, she authored a book of poems, *The Angel of the Battlefield* (1928). Gilbert contributed to such periodicals as the *Washington Post*, *New York Times*, and *Literary Digest*. She also was included in the anthologies *Home and Holiday Verse* (1939) and *District of Columbia Poets: An Anthology of 32 Contemporaries* (1932).

In the introduction to the latter, editor Edith Mirick praises her as a "true prophet of her native city," stating that "Mrs. Gilbert has devoted her art deliberately to celebrating her city, and her book is one of the few which have kept this purpose in mind."

Grief

Adams Memorial, Rock Creek Cemetery

Dry cones of yesteryear hang from the pine,
    As bronzed and retrospective as is she,
    The still, bronze woman who keeps pensively
Her tireless vigil in this bosky shrine.
The juniper's jade prisms softly shine
    Against the incense-gloom; a vested bee
    Drones through the sacred stillness reverently,
Where rhododendron-lamps incarnadine.

The Spring is dying with the dying day.
    How many a season, pondering here alone,

While breathed the rose or sighed the motley leaf,
Have you watched wending its appointed way?
  Men call you Peace ... because they hear no moan ...
  The Peace of God ... distilled from conquered grief.

Arlington

(A Military Burial)

How reverently the sunlight falls
    On Arlington near close of day,
Veiling its marble-studded slopes
    In revery.

From where the pillared mansion, throned,
    Envisages the peaceful scene,
The grassy vales, the towering trees
    With graves between,

The soul takes flight with yonder plane,
    Hovering lonely against the sky
Among lesser birds that twitteringly
    Homeward fly.

Hark! The sob of mournful strains;
    The heavy scrape of marching feet;
The mounted guard with clanging sword;
    The gun's repeat!

The gate stands wide: a veteran comes.
    The flag he served enwraps him now;
Flanked by the comrades of his youth
    He keeps his vow.

His vigorous mount, in mourning draped,
    Follows slowly, awed and meek;
With toes reversed the dangling boots
    The stirrups seek.

The big guns boom his rank on earth;
    The surplice priest intones a prayer,

The volley clangs! The bugle sounds!
    We leave him there.

The air is still. Broad darkness falls.
    The birds are mute beneath the leaves
Save distantly a whippoorwill
    Grieves . . . grieves.

Snow

Snow-fields flash in prismatic light
    where wheat-tents bivouacked, row on row,
    a scant month ago . . .

Where wheat-heads nodded crowns, sun-bright,
    above the wealth of pumpkin-gold
    mined from summer's mould . . .

Where wheat grains pushed, on an April night,
    through the strength of restraining sod,
    demolished clod by clod . . .

Where a dream-hope, nourished by nine moons' light,
    fragile and mute was shrouded so
    under impassive snow.

Cecil Arthur Spring-Rice
February 27, 1859 – February 14, 1918

Cecil Arthur Spring-Rice was the British ambassador to the United States from 1914 to 1918. He was also stationed in DC earlier in his diplomatic career, from 1886 to 1888, and from 1889 to 1891. He was a close personal friend to Henry and Clover Adams, living near them on Lafayette Square, and wrote this poem about Clover's gravesite after her suicide.

Rice's other diplomatic postings included Tehran, Cairo, St. Petersburg, Persia, and Sweden. He was married in 1904 and fathered two children. He was knighted in 1906. His book, *Poems,* was published posthumously in 1920.

While posted to DC, Spring-Rice lived at the British legation, at

1525 H Street NW. That house still stands and is now the St. John's Church Parish House.

The St. Gaudens Monument at Rock Creek Cemetery

Note by Author: It is told of the founder of one of the Sufi sects in Western Asia that, hearing of the great beauty of a certain lady, he sought her in marriage and promised her parents to build a beautiful house for her. The request was granted and the house built. The bride was brought into it veiled, according to custom. When the veil was removed, the bridegroom saw before him, not the bride, but the angel Azrael. He fell at the angel's feet, crying 'Have mercy!' And the angel answered, 'I am mercy.'

'Son of man, behold, I take from thee the desire of thine eyes at a stroke— yet shalt thou neither mourn nor weep—neither shall thy tears run down.' So spake I unto the people in the morning; and in the evening my wife died.
    —EZEKIEL, XXIV, 16.

I.
I built my love a temple and a shrine,
And every stone of it, a loving thought:
And far and wide, and high and low I sought
For sweetest fancies on the walls to twine
And deeds of gold and words that purest shine
And strength of marble faithfulness enwrought
With love's enchantments.—Lady, dearly bought
Nor lightly fashioned was that house of thine.
Who came to dwell within it? Not the face
I dreamed of—not the dear familiar eyes,
The kind, the soft, the intimately sweet.
Dread presence—great and merciful and wise—
All humbly I draw near thy dwelling place
And lay the vacant crown before thy feet.

II.
O steadfast, deep, inexorable eyes,
Set look inscrutable, nor smile nor frown!
O tranquil eyes that look so calmly down
Upon a world of passion and of lies!

For not with our poor wisdom are you wise,
Nor are you moved with passion such as ours,
Who, face to face with those immortal powers
That move and reign above the stainless skies
As friend with friend, have held communion—
Yet have you known the stress of human years,
O calm, unchanging eyes! And once have shone
With these our fitful fires, that burn and cease,
With light of human passion, human tears,
And know that, after all, the end is peace.

Carrie Williams Clifford

September 14, 1862–November 10, 1934

Carrie Williams Clifford is the author of two books of poems, *Race Rhymes* (1911) and *The Widening Light* (1922). In addition, her short fiction, articles, and poems were published in the top African American journals *Opportunity* and the *Crisis*. Her poems are notable for her mastery of traditional verse forms, particularly the sonnet.

She and her husband, William Clifford, a lawyer, moved from Cleveland to DC around 1910, after the birth of their two sons. She hosted a Sunday-evening salon in her home for artists and intellectuals of color (such as Mary Church Terrell, Alain Locke, William L. Hunt, Amanda Hilyer, Harry T. Burleigh, Will Marion Cook, and Georgia Douglas Johnson) and was active in groups advocating for civil rights and women's rights, including the National Association of Colored Women, the National Federation of Colored Women's Clubs, the Bethel Literary and Historical Association, and the NAACP. Her house, at 939 S Street NW, is still standing.

An article in the *Colored American* in 1902 states: "Mrs. Clifford has always shown a marked taste for literature. From early childhood she learned and recited extracts from the standard authors; and although she has never professionally gone on the stage, wherever she has appeared she has elicited nothing but praise."

In her preface to *The Widening Light*, published in 1922, Clifford wrote: "The author makes no claim to unusual poetic excellence or literary brilliance. She is seeking to call attention to a condition, which she, at least, considers serious. Knowing that this may often be done more impressively through rhyme than in an elegant prose, she has taken this method to accomplish this end. . . . The theme of the group here presented—the uplift of humanity—is the loftiest that can animate the heart and pen of man: the treatment, she trusts, is not wholly unworthy. . . . [S]he sends these lines forth with the prayer that they may change some heart, or right some wrong."

To Howard University

Upon the Semi-Centennial Celebration

The pall of battle scarce had passed away,
Hearts yet were hot with hate and hard with greed,
When some love-kindled spirit hid the seed,
Whose spreading branches shelter us today;
Beloved Mother, you for whom we pray,
Be fortified to meet our every need,
At your full breasts the hungry children feed,
Nor turn a single thirsting soul away!
What hath God wrought in fifty years! we've crossed
The Valley-of-Humiliation: then
Advancing up the Hill-of-Progress, tossed
A Challenge to the world of other men.
And reaching out for all that's manhood's due
Our thanks go winging up to God and You!

Peril

As, when some filthy sore grows menacing,
Polluting all the currents of pure air,
Dispersing its vile atoms everywhere
While with death-poisoned tentacles they cling,
To our hearts' treasuries, devouring,
And laying waste the temples of our care,
The surgeon with blade kind but firm lays bare
And cuts away the flesh, foul, festering:
So must the learned doctors of the State
Relentlessly cut the leprous sore

Of prejudice! else will they find too late,
Its rank corruption eating thro' the core
Of human brotherhood! Grim germs of Hate,
Razing our kingdom with titanic roar!

Tercentenary of the Landing of Slaves at Jamestown

Upon the slaver's deck, a motley band
Of blacks looked out upon the boundless main,
Knowing with anguished hearts that ne'er again
Their feet, with pride, would press their native land;
Theirs thenceforth to obey the rude command
Of masters, wielding cruel lash and chain,
Wringing three centuries of toil and pain
From helpless slaves! Then waved war's magic wand,
And, at the sign, up rose twelve million men
A brave, patriotic host, of great power,
To serve America in her crucial hour;
Titanic power, to bless or curse; for when
Pent wrong, injustice and oppression break,
Vesuvius-like, the heart of earth they shake!

Egyptian Sphinx

Inscrutable and awe-inspiring Sphinx,
Inimitable and immortal, whose
Majestic head of massed and matted kinks
Constrains alike the savant and the muse
To marvel at thy muted mystery!
What age-long memories thy face betrays!
What moving visions thou hast seen, dost see!
Thou art the symbol that, to present days,
The ancient years indubitably links!
Wherever men their righteous voices raise
Such deeds of grandeur to extol and praise,
The Sons of Africa, who builded thee,
Through us shall swell the song of jubilee:
And matchless thou shalt stand, imperial Sphinx.

Lincoln

Upon the dedication of the Lincoln Memorial at Washington, May 30, 1922

Son of the people, softly, sweetly rest!
Thy universal heart felt all the woes
Of mankind! They only were thy foes
Who hated right—who loved the evil best:
How hard man's cruelty upon thee pressed,
Thy deeply-lined and tragic visage shows!
Thy great soul-agony, only God knows,
When this great Union's fate was put to test!
But trusting in Jehovah's power to guide,
Nor caring if the whole world should deride,
With granite will, thou stoodst the Right beside.
Thus from the lowly cabin thou didst climb
To hallow this memorial sublime,
And men shall love thee to the end of time.

Maud Andrews Ohl (Annulet Andrews)

December 29, 1863–1943

Maud Andrews Ohl, who also published under the pen name Annulet Andrews, was the first woman to write for the *Atlanta Constitution*. She moved to DC with her husband, Josiah K. Ohl, also a journalist, when he was named Washington correspondent for the *Atlanta Constitution*, and she remained until his death in 1920, when she returned to Georgia. Her DC address still stands: the Envoy Apartments, 2400 Sixteenth Street NW, in the Columbia Heights neighborhood.

Ohl's journalism included society sketches, drama criticism, and essays advocating social reform. She was a charter member of the Georgia Women's Press Club. Her books include a biography of James McNeill Whistler, *Cousin Butterfly* (1904); two novels, *The Wife of Narcissus* (1908) and *Melissa Starke* (1935); and a collection of poems, *Songs of Day and Night* (undated). Her short fiction and essays appeared in journals such as the *Cosmopolitan*, *Harper's Magazine*, *Lippincott's*, and *Puck*.

Why Is It?
We spent the summer by the sea,
Together gaily swam and flirted;
Her lissome limbs, from toe to knee,
Were freely left to kick unskirted.
But, if her buttoned body slipped,
A glimpse of snow-white shoulders showing,
She'd quickly pin the place that ripped,
While blushes on her face were glowing.

To-night I take her to the ball.
She cometh down—a dream Elysian;
As bare as Eve's before the fall
Her shoulders are, a lovely vision.
Enchained, I gaze from head to foot.
Beneath her soft skirts' silky laces
There peeps a dainty little boot;
She draws it back—how red her face is.

Richard Hovey
May 4, 1864–February 24, 1900

Richard Hovey was born in Normal, Illinois, and grew up in North Amherst, Massachusetts, and Washington, DC. He attended Dartmouth College and penned the school's alma mater, "Men of Dartmouth." He then attended General Theological Seminary in New York and taught English literature at Barnard College and Columbia University.

Hovey collaborated with the Canadian poet Bliss Carman on three books of "gypsy" poems, the *Songs of Vagabondia* series (1893, 1896, 1900), and published three verse plays on the subject of Launcelot and Guinevere (1891, 1895, 1900). Other books include *Seaward* (1893), *Taliesin: A Masque* (1896), and *Along the Trail* (1898).

Hovey died on the operating table at age thirty-five, while undergoing what was considered a minor operation of the abdomen. Newspapers of the time reported his cause of death as "apoplexy." An obituary in the *Washington Evening Star* expressed "genuine grief and a feeling of personal loss. . . . Mr. Hovey was a poet of undoubted ability, and was well known in literary circles of the capital city. His work had attracted wide attention during the past few years, and his reputation gave promise of becoming much more extensive."

A cargo ship was named in his honor in 1943 but was sunk during World War II by a Japanese submarine in the Arabian Sea, killing eight U.S. Marines.

An Off-Shore Villanelle
Over the dun depths where the white shark swims,
Waiting his fated prey with hungry eyes,
Swiftly the light skiff skims.

The laughing skipper trims
Seaward his course. What recks he that it lies
Over the dun depths where the white shark swims?

He shouts for glee in the mad wind's teeth. Fast dims
The land to a low long cloud-line in the skies.
Swiftly the light skiff skims,

Brushing the foaming brims
Of the wave-breakers as in mirth it flies
Over the dun depths where the white shark swims.

What brings the white girl there, about whose limbs
The wet skirts cling, as stormward, petrel-wise,
Swiftly the light skiff skims?

The strong sea-devils wreak their cruel whims
In vain. Who heeds the hatred of their cries?
Swiftly the light skiff skims
Over the sun depths where the white shark swims.

Evening on the Potomac
The fervid breath of our flushed Southern May
Is sweet upon the city's throat and lips,
As a lover's whose tired arm slips
Listlessly over the shoulder of a queen.

Far away
The river melts in the unseen.
Oh, beautiful Girl-City, how she dips

Her feet in the stream
With a touch that is half a kiss and half a dream!
Her face is very fair,
With flowers for smiles and sunlight in her hair.

My westland flower-town, how serene she is!
Here on this hill from which I look at her,
All is still as if a worshipper
Left at some shrine his offering.

Soft winds kiss
My cheek with a slow lingering.
A luring whisper where the laurels stir
Wiles my heart back to woodland-ward again.

But lo,
Across the sky the sunset couriers run,
And I remain
To watch the imperial pageant of the Sun
Mock me, an impotent Cortez here below,
With splendors of its vaster Mexico.

O Eldorado of the templed clouds!
O golden city of the western sky!
Not like the Spaniard would I storm thy gates;
Not like the babe stretch chubby hands and cry
To have thee for a toy; but far from crowds,
Like my faun brother in the ferny glen,
Peer from the wood's edge while thy glory waits,
And in the darkening thickets plunge again.

John Claggett Proctor

November 15, 1867 – April 19, 1956

John Claggett Proctor lived his entire life in Washington; two of his addresses still stand at 1605 Jonquil Street NW and 1233 Madison Street NW. He began working at age fifteen as a printer, then earned a law degree from the National University Law School and was admitted to the bar in 1894.

Proctor was active in several DC organizations, including the Masons, the Society of Natives, the Association of the Oldest Inhabitants, Sons of Union Veterans of the Civil War, the Columbia Historical Society, and the DC Federation of Citizen's Associations. He wrote articles for the *Sunday Star* newspaper from 1928 until the early 1950s, which were collected in the 1949 volume *Proctor's Washington and Environs*. In 1950, he self-published his volume of collected poems, *Proctor's Poems*. He is buried in a large family mausoleum in Rock Creek Cemetery.

This poem was first published in a periodical, the *Come-Back*, on June 18, 1919. Walter Reed Hospital opened in 1909 with 80 beds and expanded in World War I to 2,500 beds. The facility closed in 2011. The lower part of Georgia Avenue was first paved in 1916, just three years before this poem was written, but upper Georgia Avenue remained unpaved until after the war.

Georgia Avenue

Oh, what a road to Walter Reed!
A rocky road is it indeed!
The ditches in the thoroughfare
Make angels weep and preachers swear.

The wounded in the ambulance
Imagine they are still in France
As over hump and bump they go
To where they hardly ever know.

A ride upon a camel's back
Is pleasant to the reel and rack
Endured as your auto hits
The gulleys and the open pits.

And should you take a trolley car
You'll find it worse, indeed, by far,
For crooked track and flattened wheel
May make you lose your latest meal.

Of all the streets of Washington
This one will surely take the bun;
It is the most unusual street
That you, perhaps, in life will meet.

They call it Georgia Avenue—
But what on earth did Georgia do
To merit such a big disgrace?
(A slap, it seems, right in the face.)

For Georgia is a good old State
Where everything is up to date,
And if I represented it
I'd start right in and do my bit.

I'd tack right to the District bill
An item which they could not kill:
I'd make the delegation aid
And soon I'd have asphaltum laid.

Helen Hay Whitney

March 11, 1875–September 24, 1944

Helen Hay Whitney published children's literature and poetry; her twelve books of poems include *Some Verses* (1898) *The Rose of Dawn* (1901), *Sonnets and Songs* (1905), *Gypsy Verses* (1907), and *Herbs and Apples* (1910).

The daughter of John Hay, she was raised in DC during the years he served as secretary of state. She came from considerable wealth and married into more wealth, becoming known as a prominent socialite in New York City and one of the wealthiest women in the country.

She married Payne Whitney in 1902. After her husband's death in 1927, she became an owner and breeder of racehorses, managing two stables of thoroughbreds. Horses Whitney owned won multiple awards in the American Grand National steeplechase, the Kentucky Derby, and the Belmont Stakes. She was also a notable philanthropist, bequeathing funds to Yale University, and the Metropolitan Museum of Art in New York. At the end of her life, she created the Helen Hay Whitney Foundation with her daughter Joan (the owner of the New York Mets baseball team), to support postdoctoral research by young biomedical scientists.

In *An American Anthology*, editor Edmund Clarence Stedman praised her poetry "for its artistic perfection, impassioned lyrical expression, and suggestion of reserved dramatic force."

Alone

I only wanted room to be alone.
    I saw the days like little silver moons
      Cool and restrained shine forth; there were no noons
To make me glad with glory, to atone.
I dreamed of solitude. When one has known
    Ardent and eager verity, the tunes
      Of semi-truths are sweet, as subtle runes
Attest the bud more dear than flower full blown.

To be alone, to watch the dusk and weep
    For beauty's face that is so veiled, to know
      How exquisite the earth breaths come and go,
To feel my life a silent, empty room
Where lovely thoughts might take new shape and bloom—
That is the dream that is more dear than sleep.

Sapphics

Leave the Vine, Ah Love, and the wreath of myrtle,
Leave the song, to die, on the lips of laughter,
Come, for love is faint with the choric measure,
    Weary of waiting.

Down the sky in lines of pellucid amber
Blows the hair of her whom the gods have treasured,
Fair, more fair is mine in the ring of maidens,
    Mine for the taking.

The Seal

The document of day is folded down,
Night, the great lawyer, takes the waiting sheet,
And o'er the murky shadows of the town
Sets his red seal, to make the deed complete.

❖ PART V ❖

The Rise of the Personal

Paul Claudel

August 6, 1868 – February 23, 1955

Paul Claudel was a French poet, dramatist, and diplomat, and the younger brother of the sculptor Camille Claudel. He was nominated six times for a Nobel Prize in literature, although his right-wing political views made him a controversial figure. Most famous for his devoutly Catholic verse dramas, he was the author of three memoirs, twenty-three plays, fourteen volumes of poetry, and twenty volumes of essays. His best-known plays include *Le partage de midi/The Break of Noon* (1906), *L'annonce faite a Marie/The Tidings Brought to Mary* (1910), and *Le soulier de satin/The Satin Slipper* (1931). He wrote the text for *Jeanne d'Arc au bûcher/Joan of Arc at the Stake* (1939), an "opera-oratorio" with music by Arthur Honegger. Many of his plays were set to music by Darius Milhaud.

Claudel was an avid correspondent, and seventeen volumes of his letters have been published, including volumes dedicated to Jean-Louis Barrault, Gaston Gallimard, Andre Gide, Francis Jammes, Darius Milhaud, Lugné-Poe, Jacques Rivière, and André Suarès. Claudel was elected to the Académie Française and received the Grand Cross of the French Legion of Honour.

A member of the French diplomatic corps from 1893 to 1936, he lived in a house at 2460 Sixteenth Street NW in Adams Morgan, now the Council for Professional Recognition, while French ambassador to the United States.

Sieste

Deux heures après diner
Il est temps de se reposer

Ni mouvement aucun bruit
Deux heures après midi

Un chien prudent vient inspecter
La terrasse du café

Tout est fermé à la Mairie
Item à la gendarmerie

Dans le vide de l'église
Le crucifix agonise

Le jet d'eau chez le notaire
Suit son rêve protocolaire

Mais la chambre silencieuse
Dégage une odeur ombreuse

De feuillage et de lilas
De cire et de chocolat.

Dans la corbeille à ouvrage
Le livre abandonné surnage

Et l'œil sous le long cil éteint
Tenant sa main avec sa main

Insensible à travers le store
Au rayon qui la colore

Sommeille dans le demi-soleil
Une jeune fille vermeille.

Nap
Two hours after dining,
It's time to rest

No movement, no noise
Two hours after noon

A cautious dog inspects
The café terrace

The town hall is closed,
So is the police station

In the empty church
The crucifix writhes in its death throes

The fountain of the notary
Pursues his dream of perfect protocol

But the empty bedroom
Emits a faint odor

Of old leaves and lilac,
Wax and chocolate.

In her work basket
An abandoned book floats

Her eye's long lashes close
On its lower lashes, as if hand in hand

Unaware behind the blinds
To the rays that spotlight her skin,

Drowsing in the sunshine:
A young girl the color of cinnabar.

Alice Archer Sewall James

August 23, 1870 – September 20, 1955

Alice Archer Sewall James was a painter in oils and pastels who exhibited works at the Paris Salon, and a poet who published works for children and adults, including *An Ode to Girlhood and Other Poems* (1899), *The Ballad of the Prince* (1900), *The Torch: A Pageant* (1922), and *The Morning Moon* (1941).

Born in Urbana, Ohio, her father, a Swedenborgian minister, encouraged her creativity from an early age, and she spent much of her teenage years traveling in Europe. James, known to friends as "Archie," moved to DC and married John H. James Jr., a Civil War veteran and inheritor of a fortune his father amassed as a banker and railroad builder. The marriage was strained, partly due to her poor health, and for many years she gave up writing and painting. In later years, James reemerged to teach studio art and art history at Urbana University.

There Is a Veil
There is a veil o'er everything.
And so we muffled walk till death,
Unless some heart shall sob or sing
And lift it with a sudden breath.

Then do we see in vision plain
The radiance desired and clear.
And when the veil has dropped again,
We walk but absent-minded here.

The Greek Bath
Behold him fresh-sprung from the tepid bath,
Light-poised, refulgent; from his polished limbs
The vapors warm drip to the rosy heels
That kiss the pavement; to his cheek and neck
The ruddy curls beaded with moisture cling.
The breast, superb, with delicate desires
Pants after life indefinite; alert
In his own glory rests he. Hail, all hail,
Thou passing instant of the Perfect, hail.
For with the act which wakes and which destroys,
Lo, how he swift has turned upon his thigh
With movement slight, and glances to his heel.

James Weldon Johnson
June 17, 1871–June 26, 1938

James Weldon Johnson is remembered best for his leadership in the National Association for the Advancement of Colored People (NAACP), as well as for his writing, which includes novels, poems, and collections of folklore.

Johnson's books of poems include *To a Friend* (1892), *Lift Every Voice and Sing* (1899), *O Black and Unknown Bards* (1908), *Fifty Years* (1917), and *God's Trombones* (1927). He is also the author of the remarkable novel *The Autobiography of an Ex-Colored Man* (1912), and he edited *The Book of American Negro Poetry* (1922) and *The Book of American Negro Spirituals* (1925).

He lived at 1333 R Street NW while working for the NAACP (a house that still stands). Other jobs Johnson held include U.S. consul to Venezuela (1906–8) and U.S. consul to Nicaragua (1909–13), and chair of creative literature at Fisk University. Howard University conferred an honorary degree to Johnson in 1923.

Mother Night

Eternities before the first-born day,
Or ere the first sun fledged his wings of flame,
Calm Night, the everlasting and the same,
A brooding mother over chaos lay.
And whirling suns shall blaze and then decay,
Shall run their fiery courses and then claim
The haven of the darkness whence they came;
Back to Nirvanic peace shall grope their way.

So when my feeble sun of life burns out,
And sounded is the hour for my long sleep,
I shall, full weary of the feverish light,
Welcome the darkness without fear or doubt,
And heavy-lidded, I shall softly creep
Into the quiet bosom of the Night.

To America

How would you have us, as we are?
Or sinking 'neath the load we bear?
Our eyes fixed forward on a star?
Or gazing empty at despair?

Rising or falling? Men or things?
With dragging pace or footsteps fleet?
Strong, willing sinews in your wings?
Or tightening chains about your feet?

O Black and Unknown Bards

O black and unknown bards of long ago,
How came your lips to touch the sacred fire?
How, in your darkness, did you come to know
The power and beauty of the minstrel's lyre?

Who first from midst his bonds lifted his eyes?
Who first from out the still watch, lone and long,
Feeling the ancient faith of prophets rise
Within his dark-kept soul, burst into song?

Heart of what slave poured out such melody
As "Steal away to Jesus"? On its strains
His spirit must have nightly floated free,
Though still about his hands he felt his chains.
Who heard great "Jordan roll"? Whose starward eye
Saw chariot "swing low"? And who was he
That breathed that comforting, melodic sigh,
"Nobody knows de trouble I see"?

What merely living clod, what captive thing,
Could up toward God through all its darkness grope,
And find within its deadened heart to sing
These songs of sorrow, love and faith, and hope?
How did it catch that subtle undertone,
That note in music heard not with the ears?
How sound the elusive reed so seldom blown,
Which stirs the soul or melts the heart to tears.

Not that great German master in his dream
Of harmonies that thundered amongst the stars
At the creation, ever heard a theme
Nobler than "Go down, Moses." Mark its bars
How like a mighty trumpet-call they stir
The blood. Such are the notes that men have sung
Going to valorous deeds; such tones there were
That helped make history when Time was young.

There is a wide, wide wonder in it all,
That from degraded rest and servile toil
The fiery spirit of the seer should call
These simple children of the sun and soil.
O black slave singers, gone, forgot, unfamed,
You—you alone, of all the long, long line
Of those who've sung untaught, unknown, unnamed,
Have stretched out upward, seeking the divine.

You sang not deeds of heroes or of kings;
No chant of bloody war, no exulting paean
Of arms-won triumphs; but your humble strings
You touched in chord with music empyrean.
You sing far better than you knew; the songs
That for your listeners' hungry hearts sufficed
Still live,—but more than this to you belongs:
You sang a race from wood and stone to Christ.

Paul Laurence Dunbar
June 27, 1872–February 9, 1906

Paul Laurence Dunbar was the first African American poet to become nationally known and celebrated by both readers of color and a mainstream white audience. His books of poems include *Oak and Ivy* (1892), *Majors and Minors* (1895), *Lyrics of a Lowly Life* (1896), *Poems of Cabin and Field* (1899), *When Malindy Sings* (1903), and *Lyrics of Sunshine and Shadow* (1905). His works of fiction include *The Uncalled* (1898), *Folks from Dixie* (1898), *The Strength of Gideon* (1900), and *The Sport of the Gods* (1902). He also wrote the lyrics for *In Dahomey*, the first musical written and performed entirely by African Americans to appear on Broadway.

Dunbar moved to Washington in 1897 to take a job at the Library of Congress. He hated the job and left it after less than a year. In 1898 he married another writer, Alice Moore Dunbar-Nelson, and they lived with Paul's mother in two locations in the LeDroit Park neighborhood of DC. One of those houses, a rowhouse at 1934 Fourth Street NW, still stands.

In 1900, diagnosed with tuberculosis and alcoholic, he left the area to try to regain his health. He returned to DC briefly, then Dunbar moved to his mother's home in Dayton, Ohio, where he died in 1906 at the age of thirty-three. He is remembered locally with a DC public high school named in his honor.

According to his wife, Alice Dunbar-Nelson, writing after Dunbar's death, the poem "Lover's Lane" was inspired by walks the two made down Spruce Street (now U Street NW), their first address in the LeDroit Park neighborhood. Dunbar-Nelson wrote, "The white arc light of the corner lamp, filtering through the arches of the maples on Spruce street, make for the tender suggestion in 'Lover's Lane,' where the lovers walk side by side under the "shadder-mekin' trees."

Dunbar's "dialect poems" were widely praised by mainstream white audiences during his lifetime and have often been controversial among people of color, but they have recently generated new interest among scholars. Dunbar was seeking new ways to express what made African American experience distinct. Although some readers have argued that the use of dialect furthers negative racial stereotypes, used sensitively, dialect draws on the rich folk traditions of the rural South to elevate vernacular speech and African American cultural identity.

Lover's Lane

Summah night an' sighin' breeze,
'Long de lovah's lane;
Frien'ly, shadder-mekin' trees,
'Long de lovah's lane.
White folks' wo'k all done up gran' —
Me an' 'Mandy han'-in-han'
Struttin' lak we owned de lan',
'Long de lovah's lane.

Owl a-settin' 'side de road,
Long de lovah's lane,
Lookin' at us lak he knowed
Dis uz lovah's lane.
Go on, hoot yo' mou'nful tune,
You ain' nevah loved in June,
An' come hidin' f'om de moon
Down in lovah's lane.

Bush it ben' an' nod an' sway,
Down in lovah's lane,
Try'n' to hyeah me whut I say
'Long de lovah's lane.
But I whispahs low lak dis,
An' my 'Mandy smile huh bliss —
Mistah Bush he shek his fis',
Down in lovah's lane.

Whut I keer ef day is long,
Down in lovah's lane.
I kin allus sing a song
'Long de lovah's lane.
An' de wo'ds I hyeah an' say
Meks up fu' de weary day
W'en I's strollin' by de way,
Down in lovah's lane.

An' dis t'ought will allus rise
Down in lovah's lane;
Wondah whethah in de skies
Dey's a lovah's lane.
Ef dey ain't, I tell you true,
'Ligion do look mighty blue,
'Cause I do' know whut I'd do
'Dout a lovah's lane.

Slow through the Dark

Slow moves the pageant of a climbing race;
Their footsteps drag far, far below the height,
And, unprevailing by their utmost might,
Seem faltering downward from each hard won place.
No strange, swift-sprung exception we; we trace
A devious way thro' dim, uncertain light,—
Our hope, through the long vistaed years, a sight
Of that our Captain's soul sees face to face.
Who, faithless, faltering that the road is steep,
Now raiseth up his drear insistent cry?
Who stoppeth here to spend a while in sleep
Or curseth that the storm obscures the sky?
Heed not the darkness round you, dull and deep;
The clouds grow thickest when the summit's nigh.

Douglass

Ah, Douglass, we have fall'n on evil days,
Such days as thou, not even thou didst know,
When thee, the eyes of that harsh long ago

Saw, salient, at the cross of devious ways,
And all the country heard thee with amaze.
Not ended then, the passionate ebb and flow,
The awful tide that battled to and fro;
We ride amid a tempest of dispraise.

Now, when the waves of swift dissension swarm,
And Honour, the strong pilot, lieth stark,
Oh, for thy voice high-sounding o'er the storm,
For thy strong arm to guide the shivering bark,
The blast-defying power of thy form,
To give us comfort through the lonely dark.

We Wear the Mask

We wear the mask that grins and lies,
It hides our cheeks and shades our eyes,—
This debt we pay to human guile;
With torn and bleeding hearts we smile,
And mouth with myriad subtleties.

Why should the world be over-wise,
In counting all our tears and sighs?
Nay, let them only see us, while
    We wear the mask.

We smile, but, O great Christ, our cries
To thee from tortured souls arise.
We sing, but oh the clay is vile
Beneath our feet, and long the mile;
But let the world dream otherwise,
    We wear the mask!

Leonora Speyer

November 7, 1872–February 10, 1956

Leonora Speyer, the daughter of another writer, Julia Von Stosch Schayer, was born in DC and educated in the DC public schools and the Brussels Conservatory of Music. Speyer began her career as a concert violinist, performing with the Boston Symphony Orchestra and the New York Philharmonic, as well as orchestras in France, England, and Germany. After living abroad for most of her adult life, she returned to the United States with her second husband at the start of World War I.

Speyer won the Pulitzer Prize for poetry for her second book, *Fiddler's Farewell* (1926). Her other books are *Slow Wall* (1939), *Naked Heel* (1931), and *A Canopic Jar* (1921). Speyer also translated poetry and libretti from German and French, and several of her poems were set to music. A childhood home of hers in the Georgetown neighborhood of DC still stands, at 1318 Thirtieth Street NW.

The Saint-Gaudens Statue in Rock Creek Cemetery, Washington

Are there no tears for other hearts to shed?
Those heavy eyes have drained the world of grief,
And yet no solace found, no drear relief,
Such as my heart would seek, and find, I know,
Had I been given the weight of that vast woe,
And wept through pain to peace! But you, instead,
Have drowned all healing in a shoreless sea
Of unforgiven wrong, whose every breath
Lifts windy clamor through the soul's hushed space,
Fanning to greater grief, to swifter glow,
The flame that smolders still in that bronze face,
Sadder than life, and sadder far than death,
Because of love renounced and joy to be,
And faith and hope and immortality.

Suddenly

Suddenly flickered a flame,
Suddenly fluttered a wing:
What, can a dead bird sing?
Somebody spoke your name.

Suddenly fluttered a wing,
Sounded a voice, the same,
Somebody spoke your name:
Oh, the remembering!

Sounded a voice, the same,
Song of the heart's green spring,
Oh, the remembering:
Which of us was to blame?

Song of the heart's green spring,
Wings that still flutter, lame,
Which of us was to blame?—
God, the slow withering!

Ascent

Mountains take too much time.
Start at the top and climb.

Measure Me, Sky

Measure me, sky!
Tell me I reach by a song.
Nearer the stars;
I have been little so long.

Weigh me, high wind!
What will your wild scales record?
Profit of pain,
Joy by the weight of a word.

Horizon, reach out,
Catch at my hands, stretch me taut.
Rim of the world,
Widen my eyes by a thought.

Sky, be my depth,
Wind be my width and my height,
World, my heart's span;
Loveliness, wings for flight.

Mary Berri Chapman Hansbrough

December 1872–June 5, 1951

Mary Berri Chapman Hansbrough was born and educated in DC, where both her parents worked as examiners in the U.S. Patent Office. She began writing stories at age nine. A painter in watercolors and oils as well as a poet, Hansbrough published *Lyrics of Love and Nature* (1895), which also included her illustrations. Individual poems appeared in such publications as *Harper's Magazine* and the *Century*.

Hansbrough married Senator Henry Clay Hansbrough in 1897, after a whirlwind courtship of only seven weeks, which was widely covered in the society sections of newspapers. The *Midland Monthly Magazine* reported it as "a genuinely romantic love match" when the senator "at first sight fell in love with her. His wooing was an ardent one," said the *Roanoke Times*, noting that Hansbrough was "a young woman of 22" and the senator, a widower, was forty-nine, and that she was "distinguished in Washington society circles not only for her beauty, but for her talents." They lived in a large house at 2023 Florida Avenue NW in the Dupont Circle neighborhood.

Despite his support of her creative career, the couple separated after only a few years. The senator brought a chancery suit against his wife, to gain control of her inheritance, claiming she was mentally incompetent. In 1909, Hansbrough was admitted to St. Elizabeths Hospital for treatment of mental illness, and she remained confined there over forty years until her death at age seventy-nine. She is buried at Rock Creek Cemetery.

Debonair

Smile once again,
Seek other men,—
They are abundant;
Waste no regret,
Don't even fret,—
Tears are redundant;
For to coquette
Is to forget,—
Tears are redundant;
Smile once again,
Seek other men,—
They are abundant.

After Grief

Oh, dread to muse too much, for memory
Casts up past sadness, as the sighing sea
In reaching out, along the golden sand,

Drags dank and slimy things upon the strand
Which have no sympathy with sunny land,
And but recall the storm's past potency.

Alice Moore Dunbar-Nelson

July 19, 1875–September 18, 1935

Alice Moore Dunbar-Nelson is the author of two books of short fiction, *Violets and Other Tales* (1895) and *The Goodness of St. Rocque* (1899). She edited two anthologies, *Masterpieces of Negro Eloquence* (1914) and *The Dunbar Speaker and Entertainer* (1920). Dunbar-Nelson was a regular columnist for the *Pittsburgh Courier* and the *Washington Eagle* and coeditor of the *A.M.E. Review*. She also served as a Mid-Atlantic field organizer for women's suffrage, a representative for the Woman's Committee on the Council of Defense, and was a popular speaker to a wide range of groups. She cofounded the Industrial School for Colored Girls in Marshalltown, Delaware.

Dunbar-Nelson married Paul Laurence Dunbar in 1898 and moved to DC. One of their houses, at 1934 Fourth Street NW, still stands in the LeDroit Park neighborhood. The marriage was not a happy one; Dunbar was physically abusive, and the pair separated in 1902 (although never divorced), and Dunbar died of tuberculosis and alcoholism in 1906.

Dunbar-Nelson subsequently moved to Maryland and Delaware. She married two more times but always retained her eminent first husband's last name (and split his royalty payments with her mother-in-law). Her third marriage, to Robert J. Nelson, a journalist, was her happiest. Her diary, *Give Us Each Day: The Diary of Alice Dunbar-Nelson*, edited by Gloria T. Hull, was published posthumously in 1984, and *The Works of Alice Dunbar-Nelson*, also edited by Hull, was published in three volumes as part of the Schomburg Library of Nineteenth-Century Black Women Writers in 1988.

I Sit and Sew

I sit and sew—a useless task it seems,
My hands grown tired, my head weighed down with dreams—
The panoply of war, the martial tread of men,

Grim-faced, stern-eyed, gazing beyond the ken
Of lesser souls, whose eyes have not seen Death
Nor learned to hold their lives but as a breath—
But—I must sit and sew.

I sit and sew—my heart aches with desire—
That pageant terrible, that fiercely pouring fire
On wasted fields, and writhing grotesque things
Once men. My soul in pity flings
Appealing cries, yearning only to go
There in that holocaust of hell, those fields of woe—
But—I must sit and sew.

The little useless seam, the idle patch:
Why dream I here beneath my homely thatch,
When there they lie in sodden mud and rain,
Pitifully calling me, the quick ones and the slain?
You need me, Christ! It is no roseate dream
That beckons me—this pretty futile seam,
It stifles me—God, must I sit and sew?

The Lights at Carney's Point
O white little lights at Carney's Point,
    You shine so clear o'er the Delaware;
When the moon rides high in the silver sky,
    Then you gleam, white gems on the Delaware.
Diamond circlet on a full white throat,
    You laugh your rays on a questing boat;
Is it peace you dream in your flashing gleam,
    O'er the quiet flow of the Delaware?
And the lights grew dim at the water's brim,
    For the smoke of the mills shredded slow between;
And the smoke was red, as is new bloodshed,
    And the lights went lurid 'neath the livid screen.
O red little lights at Carney's Point,
    You glower so grim o'er the Delaware;
When the moon hides low sombrous clouds below,
    Then you glow like coals o'er the Delaware.

Blood red rubies on a throat of fire,
 You flash through the dusk of a funeral pyre;
Are there hearth fires red whom you fear and dread
 O'er the turgid flow of the Delaware?
And the lights gleamed gold o'er the river cold,
 For the murk of the furnace shed a copper veil;
And the veil was grim at the great cloud's brim
 And the lights went molten, now hot, now pale.
O gold little lights at Carney's Point,
 You gleam so proud o'er the Delaware;
When the moon grows wan in the eastering dawn,
 Then you sparkle gold points o'er the Delaware.
Aureate filigree on a Croesus' brow,
 You hasten the dawn on a gray ship's prow.
Light you streams of gold in the grim ship's hold
 O'er the sullen flow of the Delaware?
And the lights went gray in the ash of day,
 For a quiet Aurora brought a halcyon balm;
And the sun laughed high in the infinite sky,
 And the lights were forgot in the sweet, sane calm.

Sonnet

I had not thought of violets of late,
The wild, shy kind that spring beneath your feet
In wistful April days, when lovers mate
And wander through the fields in raptures sweet.
The thought of violets meant florists' shops,
And cabarets and soaps, and deadening wines.
So far from sweet real things my thoughts had strayed,
I had forgot wide fields; and clear brown streams;
The perfect loveliness that God has made,—
Wild violets shy and Heaven-mounting dreams.
And now—unwittingly, you've made me dream
Of violets, and my soul's forgotten gleam.

To the Negro Farmers of the United States

God washes clean the souls and hearts of you,
His favored ones, whose backs bend o'er the soil,

Which grudging gives to them requite for toil
In sober graces and in vision true.
God places in your hands the pow'r to do
A service sweet. Your gift supreme to foil
The bare-fanged wolves of hunger in the moil
Of Life's activities. Yet all too few
Your glorious band, clean sprung from Nature's heart;
The hope of hungry thousands, in whose breast
Dwells fear that you should fail. God placed no dart
Of war within your hands, but pow'r to start
Tears, praise, love, joy, enwoven in a crest
To crown you glorious, brave ones of the soil.

Gertrude Simmons Bonnin (Zitkala-Ša)

February 22, 1876–January 26, 1938

Zitkala-Ša, who was also given the name Gertrude Simmons by missionaries and used both names professionally, is famous for being the author of one of the first American Indian autobiographies written in English that was not filtered through an editor or translator. Born on a Yankton Sioux Indian Reservation in South Dakota in the same year as the Battle of Little Big Horn (also known as the Battle of the Greasy Grass), Zitkala-Ša was the daughter of a white trader and a Yankton mother. She was sent at age eight to White's Manual Labor Institute in Wabash, Indiana, where she was subjected to the assimilative practices of most Indian boarding schools: forbidden to speak the Sioux language, forced to attend Christian worship, dressed in "white" clothes, and her long hair cut short (which she considered a particularly acute humiliation). Although she excelled in her studies, especially reading and writing, she felt the trauma of being stripped of her heritage. She graduated in 1895 and attended Earlham College for two years (1895–97). In college, she developed prize-winning skills in oratory and music (piano, violin, and voice), and she went on to study at the New England Conservatory of Music.

Zitkala-Ša began publishing autobiographical articles in 1900 in such journals as the *Atlantic Monthly, Harper's Magazine,* and *Everybody's Magazine,* which were collected as *American Indian Stories* in

1921. She also compiled a collection of Sioux myths, *Old Indian Legends* (1901). In addition, Zitkala-Ša published poems and wrote the first opera authored by an American Indian, *The Sun Dance Opera* (1913). She also coauthored the nonfiction book *Oklahoma's Poor Rich Indians* (1924), which exposed the theft of Indian lands by the oil industry.

Zitkala-Ša taught briefly at the Carlisle Industrial Training School in Pennsylvania. After her marriage to Raymond Telephause Bonnin (also Yankton), she moved to the Uintah Ouray Ute Reservation in Utah, where her husband was employed by the Bureau of Indian Affairs, and gave birth to a son, her only child, Raymond Ohiya. On the Ute Reservation, Zitkala-Ša worked for the Society of American Indians (SAI), a nonprofit pan-Indian political group. In 1916, when she was elected secretary of the SAI, the Bonnins moved to the DC area. They settled in a neighborhood in Arlington, Virginia, Lyon Park, which had restrictive covenants at the time, but those covenants only specified that African Americans and Jews were banned from buying property, so by this loophole the laws did not affect them.

Zitkala-Ša edited the SAI publication *American Indian Magazine*, taking up such causes as the recognition of World War I Indian soldiers, Indian land rights, and the push to grant U.S. citizenship to Indians. She later worked for the General Federation of Women's Clubs to form an Indian Welfare Committee, and for the Indian Rights Association and the American Indian Defense Council. With her husband, she cofounded the National Council of American Indians to lobby Congress and the Bureau of Indian Affairs for individual land and financial claims, improved health care and education, cultural recognition, and voting rights for American Indians.

Zitkala-Ša died in Washington in 1938, and her husband died in 1942. They are buried together at Arlington National Cemetery.

Winona's Aria: The Magic of the Night

(from *The Sun Dance Opera*)

The magic of the Night of Nights beckons me
A wonder-world is sheltered 'neath the trees.
From grass and shrubs and willows low
Come mystic voices, sighs enchanting breeze.

The pallid lake lies quiet now
Beneath yon mountain's somber breath.
The moonlight flickers—branches bow
But I? My lover comes! He comes to me!

Oh Night of Nights!
He comes—in his serenade!
Before the coyote's call at morn,
Or bird awakes its mate at dawn,
While mystic voices sing their song
He comes—my lover comes—I know 'tis he!

Ohiya, yes Ohiya brave—in his serenade.
I pass into the nightworld unafraid.
He comes to chant ecstasy
He comes to chant his serenade.

Natalie Clifford Barney

October 31, 1876–February 2, 1972

Natalie Clifford Barney was an American expatriate feminist poet whose Paris salons, which she hosted for more than sixty years, were famous for drawing modernist artists. Barney spent early years, beginning at age ten, in a house at 2306 Massachusetts Avenue NW on Sheridan Circle with her mother, the painter Alice Pike Barney. That house still stands; it is now the embassy of Latvia.

In 1900, Barney published *Quelques portraits-sonnets de femmes/ Some Portrait-Sonnets of Women*, becoming the first woman poet to write openly about lesbian love since Sappho. Over the course of her life, she wrote seven books of poems and plays (in English and French), as well as a novel, two memoirs, and two books of epigrams. Barney wrote, "If I had one ambition it was to make my life itself into a poem."

More Night!

Moon-love, star-love, the love of silver water,
The weeping face of love touched in the dark,
And murdered joy, lost souls of joy that caught her
    A glow-worm's warmth and spark.

Birds of prey, invisible, now hover
About her midnights hammocked in unrest—
A moving shadow, faithless as a lover,
    Is all her arms have pressed—

Too luminous the dreaming of the sleeper
Whose tears are prophecies and second-sight.
Has death no under-sea, no darkness deeper,
    In which to satiate our need of night?

A Sonnet to My Lady with the Jaundice

Was not Titania golden? See these flowers
Are they for being yellowish less fair?
Apollo and the Goddesses all share
In this most glorious hue. The jealous bowers
Of Kings are coloured thus, their reed of powers,
Their rings, their chains, the crowns that they must wear
Golden their mistress and their minion's hair
Golden the bannered sun above their towers!
Reflecting butter-cups amuses Puck
But flower-rubbed eye-lids, and complexions mend
So fear not broken crystals long ill-luck
But look in this new mirror, lovely friend.
Both gods and fairies wait on lovers' wills.
That jaundices be changed to daffodils!

How Write the Beat of Love

How write the beat of love, the very throb,
The rhythm of our veins' deep eloquence?
How fix that darkness-rending final sob,
That perfect swoon of each united sense.

The full-sailed rising of your body's sweep
—Adrift and safe on joy's last tidal wave—
Will toss you on the silver sands of sleep,
Forgetful of the ecstasy you gave.

Your breath ebbs restful as the falling tide:
A sea becalmed! . . . Lay me in valleyed part

Of breasts whose undulating crests subside—
Ah how they marked the high beats of your heart!

Georgia Douglas Johnson
September 10, 1877?–May 14, 1966

Georgia Douglas Johnson was the author of four books of poems, six plays, and thirty-two song lyrics, making her one of the best-published women authors of the Harlem Renaissance period. One of her song lyrics, "Hail to Fair Washington," was set to music by Madame Lillian Evanti, the first professional opera singer of African descent. The two women hoped it would be adopted by the city as an anthem, but their efforts were not successful. That song includes the lines: "I love to stroll through Congress halls / where all the laws are made / then pause by the Potomac / where weeping willows shade."

After her husband's death in 1925, Johnson became the family's primary wage earner, working at a series of government jobs, including for the DC Public Schools and the U.S. Department of Labor, and selling articles to newspapers, earning enough to send her two sons to college and graduate school.

Johnson began publishing actively in 1916, prior to the start of the Harlem Renaissance, and her first book, *The Heart of a Woman*, came out in 1918, followed by *Bronze: A Book of Verse* in 1922, and *An Autumn Love Cycle* in 1928. A final book of poems, *Share My World*, was self-published in 1962 near the end of her life. Her newspaper column, "Homely Philosophy," was syndicated to twenty newspapers between 1926 and 1932.

In the introduction to her second book, *Bronze*, Johnson wrote this credo: "This book is the child of a bitter earth-wound. I sit on the earth and sing—sing out, and of, my sorrow. Yet, fully conscious of the potent agencies that silently work in their healing ministries, I know that God's sun shall one day shine upon a perfected and unhampered people."

A gifted organizer, a generous friend, a mentor to many, Johnson hosted weekly salons in her home at 1461 S Street NW from 1921 to approximately 1928; she continued hosting gatherings more sporadically through the Great Depression and into the early 1940s. She wrote that she named her house "Half-Way House" because "I'm half way between everybody and everything, and I bring them together." The house still stands, although a large addition has been added to the rear. It is marked by a historic plaque.

The Heart of a Woman

The heart of a woman goes forth with the dawn,
As a lone bird, soft winging, so restlessly on,
Afar o'er life's turrets and vales does it roam
In the wake of those echoes the heart calls home.

The heart of a woman falls back with the night,
And enters some alien cage in its plight,
And tries to forget it has dreamed of the stars,
While it breaks, breaks, breaks on the sheltering bars.

Little Son

The very acme of my woe,
The pivot of my pride,
My consolation, and my hope
Deferred, but not denied.
The substance of my every dream,
The riddle of my plight,
The very world epitomized
In turmoil and delight.

Prejudice

These fell miasmic rings of mist with ghoulish menace bound,
Like noose-horizons tightening my little world around.
They still the souring will to wing, to dance, to speed away,
And fling the soul insurgent back into its shell of clay.
Beneath incrusted silences, a seething Etna lies,
The fire of whose furnaces may sleep, but never dies!

Common Dust

And who shall separate the dust
What later we shall be:
Whose keen discerning eye will scan
And solve the mystery?

The high, the low, the rich, the poor,
The black, the white, the red,
And all the chromatique between,
Of whom shall it be said:

Here lies the dust of Africa;
Here are the sons of Rome;
Here lies the one unlabeled,
The world at large his home!

Can one then separate the dust?
Will mankind lie apart,
When life has settled back again
The same as from the start?

To John Brown
We lift a song to you across the day
Which bears through travailing the seed you spread
In terror's morning, flung with fingers red
In blood of tyrants, who debarred the way
To Freedom's dawning. Hearken to the lay
Chanted by dusky millions, soft and mellow-keyed,
In minor measure, Martyr of the Freed,
A song of memory across the day.

Truth cannot perish though the earth erase
The royal signals, leaving not a trace,
And time still burgeoneth the fertile seed,
Though he is crucified who wrought the deed:
O Alleghenies, fold him to your breast
Until the judgment! Sentinel his rest!

Pledge
With kisses I'll awake you love
So tenderly at morn,
The pledges of my fealty
Diurnally reborn.

We'll thread life's way together love,
And when the fading light

Dips softly over western hills
I'll kiss your eyes goodnight.

Eloise Bibb Thompson

June 29, 1878–January 8, 1928

Eloise Bibb Thompson was born in New Orleans and published one book (under her maiden name), *Poems*, in 1895 at age seventeen. "Tribute," reprinted from that book, honors Alice Moore Dunbar-Nelson, whose book *Violets and Other Tales* was published that same year (and by the same publisher, Monthly Review Press in Boston).

Bibb attended Oberlin College, worked as a teacher in the New Orleans Public Schools, then moved to DC in 1903 to attend Howard University's Teacher's College. She graduated in 1908 and was hired by Howard as head resident of the Colored Social Settlement House, where she remained through 1911, when she married and moved with her husband, Noah Davis Thompson, to Los Angeles, and later to New York City. Her articles and poems appeared in the *Los Angeles Tribune*, *Out West*, the *Tidings*, and *Morning Sun*; she also wrote plays and short fiction, gave public lectures, and was active in the Catholic Church.

Tribute

(To the sweet bard of the Woman's Club, Miss Alice Ruth Moore)

I peer adown a shining group,
Where sages grace the throng,
And see the bard of Wheatley Club
Proclaimed the Queen of Song.

I see her reach the portico,
Where muses smiling now,
Adorn with the green laurel wreath,
Her broad and thoughtful brow.

Fair Alice! shed thy radiance more,
And charm us with thy verse;
So dulcet, so harmonious,
So graceful, sweet, and terse.

After Reading Bryant's Lines to a Waterfowl
No forward soul, ambition stung,
And sunk in carnal bliss,
E'er dreamed a dream so fraught with heav'n
And gave us verse like this.

No lute attuned for flattery's ear,
Or stuck by greed for gain,
E'er woke such cadences so sweet
Or played so rare a strain.

Not men, but Angels sing like this,
Lit with celestial fire,
And sweep the strings with airy touch
Of an immortal lyre.

Don Marquis

July 29, 1878 – December 29, 1937

Born in Walnut, Illinois, Don Marquis was the author of more than thirty-five books. His columns, illustrations, and essays were published in various magazines including *Saturday Evening Post, Collier's, Harper's, Scribner's, Golden Book,* and *Cosmopolitan*. He is remembered best for creating the characters Archy and Mehitabel, a cockroach and an alley cat, supposed authors of humorous verse. In 1943, the United States Navy christened a Liberty ship, the USS *Don Marquis,* in his memory.

Marquis lived in a house at 1224 Thirteenth Street NW in the Thomas Circle neighborhood at the start of his journalistic career while working at the *Washington Post*. This structure's continued survival in the midst of high-rises is a delightful surprise.

His works include the plays *The Dark Hours* (1924), *Out of the Sea* (1927), *Master of the Revels* (1934), and *Everything's Jake* (produced posthumously in 1978) and the books *The Awakening* (1924), *Pandora Lifts the Lid* (1924), *archy and mehitabel* (1927), *Love Sonnets of a Cave Man* (1928), *archys life of mehitabel* (1933), and *archy does his part* (1935).

E. B. White provided an introduction to *The Lives and Times of Archy and Mehitabel* in 1950, writing: "He was the sort of poet who does not create easily; he was left unsatisfied and gloomy by what he produced; day and night he felt the juices squeezed out of him by the merciless demands of daily newspaper work; he was never quite certified by intellectuals and serious critics of belles lettres. He ended in an exhausted condition—his money gone, his strength gone. . . . In his domestic life he suffered one tragedy after another—the death of a young son, the death of his first wife, the death of his daughter, finally the death of his second wife. Then sickness and poverty. All these things happened in the space of a few years. He was never a robust man—usually had a puffy, overweight look and a gray complexion. He loved to drink, and was told by doctors that he mustn't." Yet White concludes that Marquis's poems will remain popular with readers because they are funny, wise, tender, and tough.

The Prude's Alphabet

A is for Tarsus. The current short skirts
Do not conceal it, which pleases the flirts.

B is the letter for Gentleman Cow—
Some persons throw them. I cannot see how.

C for a Cow's little child that drinks milk;
There's another kind, too, that is covered with silk.

D is for—Dash! It is so like a curse
That nothing could make me employ it in verse!

E is for *Embonpoint*,—much nicer word
Than some of the synonyms which I have heard.

F is for Falstaff, a naughty old man;
Avoid his example as much as you can.

G for a substance that's made into strings
For fiddles; 'tis taken from kitties and things.

H for a word that means . . . well, embrace.
The rhyme for it, "rug." It may lead to disgrace!

I is a painful dermal disease
That keeps people scratching. Don't mention it please!

J is for Jackal, a terrible beast
Whose dinner demeanor's not nice in the least.

K is the joint midway of the limb;
It moves when we walk, it moves when we swim.

L for the members producing the gait—
The iniquitous Octopus really has eight!

M is for Modest. Sincerely I trust
That you'll always be modest. Be Modest or . . . bust.

N for a kind of an orange; the kind
That is simple and sweet and has a thin rind.

O for obnoxious! It grieves me to find
So much that is so in my delicate mind.

P for a word that sounds very like dimple;
Cosmetics produce them on gentle or simple.

Q is for Questionable persons and things—
If people are married they ought to have rings.

R is for Roué; for decency's sake
Avoid such grosser locutions as rake.

S is for Polecat, so pretty and cute;
Don't make him a pet, he's a treacherous brute.

T is for Tongue. O, pray, keep it clean,
And never say bluntly the things that you mean!

U for the garments worn next to the skin;
In winter they're thick and in summer they's thin.

V is for Vampire—I don't mean the ladies
That movie films show sending persons to Hades.

W is for Weather, the safest of topics—
But even so, children, don't dwell in the tropics!

X, Y and Z are Equations Unknown,
So a prudent young person will let them alone.

A Politician

Leader no more, be judged of us!
Hailed Chief, and loved, of yore—
Youth and the faith of youth, cry out:
"Leader and Chief no more!"

We dreamed a Prophet, flushed with faith,
Content to toil in pain
If that his sacrifice might be,
Somehow, his people's gain.

We saw a vision, and our blood
Beat red and hot and strong:
"Lead us" (we cried) "to war against
Some foul, embattled wrong!"

We dreamed a Warrior whose sword
Was edged for sham and shame;
We dreamed a Statesman far above
The vulgar lust for fame.

We were not cynics, and we dreamed
A Man who made no truce
With lies nor ancient privilege
Nor old, entrenched abuse.

We dreamed . . . we dreamed . . . Youth dreamed
a dream! And even you forgot
Yourself, one moment, and dreamed, too—
Struck, while your mood was hot!

Struck three or four good blows . . . and then
Turned back to easier things:
The cheap applause, the blatant mob,
The praise of underlings!

Praise . . . praise . . . was ever man so filled,
So avid still, of praise?
So hungry for the crowd's acclaim,
The sycophantic phrase?

O you whom Greatness beckoned to . . .
O swollen Littleness
Who turned from Immortality
To fawn upon Success!

O blind with love of self, who led
Youth's vision to defeat,
Bawling and brawling for rewards,
Loud, in the common street!

O you who were so quick to judge—
Leader, and loved, of yore—
Hear now the judgment of our youth:
"Leader and Chief no more!"

Angelina Weld Grimké

February 27, 1880–June 10, 1958

Angelina Weld Grimké was born in Boston to a biracial family. Not long after Grimké's birth, her parents separated, and her mother later committed suicide. Grimké was sent to live in DC with her aunt and uncle, Charlotte Forten Grimké (also included in this volume) and Reverend Francis Grimké, from age fourteen to eighteen, while her father served as U.S. consul to the Dominican Republic. After graduating from college in Cambridge, Massachusetts, her father, Archibald Grimké, a lawyer and diplomat, relocated to DC with his daughter.

From 1902 to 1916, Grimké taught at Armstrong Manual Training School, and from 1916 until her retirement in 1926, she taught at Dunbar High School, both DC Public Schools. Grimké's essays, short fiction, and stories were published in journals (such as the *Crisis* and *Opportunity*) and anthologies (*The New Negro, Caroling Dusk, Negro Poets and Their Poems*). Her play *Rachel* was produced in 1916 and published in 1920, making her one of the earliest published African American playwrights.

A recurring theme of Grimké's poems is thwarted longing; many unpublished poems (and her diaries) are more explicitly lesbian. Many critics feel that she was forced by her father to choose him over romantic attachments, and that choice was made as she continued to live with him as an adult, caring for him for the two years of his final illness. After her father's death, Grimké moved to Brooklyn and maintained a quiet, semi-reclusive life.

A Winter Twilight

A silence slipping around like death,
Yet chased by a whisper, a sigh, a breath;
One group of trees, lean, naked and cold,
Inking their crests 'gainst a sky green-gold;
One path that knows where the corn flowers were;
Lonely, apart, unyielding, one fir;
And over it softly leaning down,
One star that I loved ere the fields went brown.

The Want of You

A hint of gold where the moon will be;
Through the flocking clouds just a star or two;
Leaf sounds, soft and wet and hushed,
And oh! The crying want of you.

Dawn

Grey trees, grey skies, and not a star;
    Grey mist, grey hush;
And then, frail, exquisite, afar,
    A hermit-thrush.

To the Dunbar High School: A Sonnet

And she shall be the friend of youth for aye:
Of quick'ning youth whose eyes have seen the gleam;
Of youth between whose tears and laughter stream:
Bright bows of hope; of youth, audacious, gay,
Who dares to know himself a Caesar, say,
A Shakespeare or a Galahad. The dream
To him is real; and things are as they seem,
For beauty veils from him the feet of clay.
How holy and how wonderful her trust—
Youth's friend, and yes, how blest. For down the west
Each day shall go the sun, and time in time

Shall die, the unborn shall again be dust;
But she with youth eternal on her breast,
Immortal, too, shall sit serene, sublime.

To Keep the Memory of Charlotte Forten Grimké

Still are there wonders of the dark and day;
The muted shrilling of shy things at night,
So small beneath the stars and moon;
The peace, dream-frail, but perfect while the light
Lies softly on the leaves at noon.
These are, and these will be
    Until eternity;
But she who loved them well has gone away.

Each dawn, while yet the east is veil'd grey,
The birds about her window wake and sing;
And far away, each day, some lark
I know is singing where the grasses swing;
Some robin calls and calls at dark.
These are, and these will be
    Until eternity;
But she who loved them well has gone away.

The wild flowers that she loved down green ways stray;
Her roses lift their wistful buds at dawn,
But not for eyes that loved them best;
Only her little pansies are all gone,
Some lying softly on her breast.
And flowers will bud and be
    Until eternity;
But she who loved them well has gone away.

Where has she gone? And who is there to say?
But this we know: her gentle spirit moves
And is where beauty never wanes,
Perchance by other streams, 'mid other groves:
And to us here, ah! she remains. A lovely memory
    Until eternity;
She came, she loved, and then she went away.

Juan Ramón Jiménez

December 24, 1881–May 29, 1958

Juan Ramón Jiménez was a Spanish poet, editor, and critic. Among his better-known works are *Sonetos espirituales 1914–1916/Spiritual Sonnets* (1916), *Piedra y cielo/Stones and Sky* (1919), *Poesía, en verso, 1917–1923* (1923), *Poesía en prosa y verso/Poetry in Prose and Verse* (1932), *Voces de mi copla/Voices of My Song* (1945), and *Animal de fondo/Animal at Bottom* (1947).

At the outbreak of the Spanish Civil War, Jiménez and his wife, Zenobia Camprubí Aymar, also a writer, went into exile in Cuba and the United States. He was a professor of Spanish language and literature at the University of Maryland from 1943 to 1951 and was awarded the Nobel Prize in literature in 1956. Jiménez is remembered locally with an academic hall on the University of Maryland campus named in his honor. A plaque at the entrance features a translation of one of Jiménez's poems. A former home, the Dorchester Apartments at 2480 Sixteenth Street NW in Adams Morgan, still stands.

El mar

Le soy desconocido,
Pasa, como un idiota,
ante mí; cual un loco, que llegase
al cielo con la frente
y al que llegara el agua a la rodilla,
la mano inmensa chorreando
sobre la borda.

Si le toco un dedo,
alza la mano, ola violenta,
y con informe grito mareante,
que nos abisma,
dice cosas borrachas, y se ríe,
y llora, ye se va . . .

A veces, las dos manos
el la borda, hunde el barco
hasta su vientre enorme
y avanza su cabeza, susto frío,
hasta nuestro minuscule descuido.

Y se encoge
de hombros y sepulta
su risottada roja en las espumas
verdes y blancas . . .
            Por doquiera
asoma y nos espanta; a cada instante
se hace el mar casi humano para odiarme.

            . . . Le soy desconocido.

The Sea

        To him I am unknown,
He passes like an idiot,
in front of me, a madman
whose forehead reaches heaven
while standing in water up to his knees,
his immense and weeping hand
defining the shore.
        If I reach in with my finger
he raises his hand in a violent wave
and screams himself dizzy
into the abyss,
then stumbles like a drunk
and laughs
then cries, then departs . . .
        Sometimes with both hands
on shore, he swallows boats,
taking us whole into his huge belly
and his head emerges, cold with fright,
to see our haphazard insignificance.
        Then, shrugging
his shoulders, he buries
his red lips among the foam
glowing green and white . . .
        He looms
and terrifies us, and any moment
his hate can turn almost human.

        . . . To him I am unknown.

Jessie Redmon Fauset

April 27, 1882 – April 30, 1961

Jessie Redmon Fauset is the author of four novels: *There Is Confusion* (1924), *Plum Bun* (1928), *The Chinaberry Tree* (1931), and *Comedy, American Style* (1933). She also wrote poems and essays and worked as an educator and editor.

Fauset was born in New Jersey and raised in Philadelphia. In grade school, she was frequently the only African American student in her classes. She graduated Phi Beta Kappa from Cornell University; then, while teaching full-time in the DC Public Schools, she earned a master's degree from the University of Pennsylvania.

Fauset taught French and Latin at M Street High School from 1907 through 1919. Two houses where Fauset rented rooms are still standing: 1812 Thirteenth Street NW and 1716 Seventeenth Street NW. She rented in a total of five locations while teaching for the DC Public Schools.

Fauset subsequently moved to New York to become literary editor of the *Crisis*, the official publication of the NAACP. In that position, from 1919 through 1926, she mentored several younger writers, such as Claude McKay, Countee Cullen, Arna Bontemps, Nella Larsen, and Langston Hughes, and influenced top African American leaders to support the important role the arts could play in what was then called "racial uplift." Fauset was a guiding spirit for the Harlem Renaissance and for literary modernism in general.

Langston Hughes wrote: "Jessie Fauset at the *Crisis*, Charles Johnson at *Opportunity*, and Alain Locke in Washington, were the three people who midwifed the so-called New Negro Literature into being. Kind and critical—but not too critical for the young—they nursed us along until our books were born."

Fauset returned to teaching in 1926 and married Herbert Harris, an insurance broker, in middle age. She lived in New Jersey and Philadelphia in later years and died of heart disease at age seventy-nine.

Oriflamme

I can remember when I was a little, young girl, how my old mammy would sit out of doors in the evenings and look up at the stars and groan, and I

would say, 'Mammy, what makes you groan so?' And she would say, 'I am
groaning to think of my poor children; they do not know where I be and
I don't know where they be. I look up at the stars and they look up at the
stars!'

—SOJOURNER TRUTH

I think I see her sitting, bowed and black,
    Stricken and seared with slavery's mortal scars,
Reft of her children, lonely, anguished, yet
    Still looking at the stars.

Symbolic mother, we thy myriad sons,
    Pounding our stubborn hearts on Freedom's bars,
Clutching our birthright, fight with faces set,
    Still visioning the stars!

Dead Fires

If this is peace, this dead and leaden thing,
    Then better far the hateful fret, the sting.
Better the wound forever seeking balm
    Than this gray calm!
Is this pain's surcease? Better far the ache,
    The long-drawn dreary day the night's white wake,
Better the choking sigh, the sobbing breath
    Than passion's death!

Rondeau

When April's here and meadows wide
Once more with spring's sweet growths are pied
    I close each book, drop each pursuit,
    And past the brook, no longer mute,
I joyous roam the countryside.

Look, here the violets shy abide
And there the mating robins hide—
    How keen my sense, how acute,
        When April's here!

And list! down where the shimmering tide
Hard by that farthest hill doth glide,

Rise faint strains from shepherd's flute,
Pan's pipes and Berecyntian lute.
Each sight, each sound fresh joys provide
When April's here.

La vie c'est la vie
On summer afternoons I sit
Quiescent by you in the park
And idly watch the sunbeams gild
And tint the ash-trees' bark.

Or else I watch the squirrels frisk
And chaffer in the grassy lane;
And all the while I mark your voice
Breaking with love and pain.

I know a woman who would give
Her chance of heaven to take my place;
To see the love-light in your eyes,
The love-glow on your face!

And there's a man whose lightest word
Can set my chilly blood afire;
Fulfillment of his least behest
Defines my life's desire.

But he will none of me, nor I
Of you. Nor you of her. 'Tis said
The world is full of jests like these.—
I wish that I were dead.

Edith B. Mirick
November 16, 1883 – February 11, 1972

Edith Brown Mirick attended Columbian College, the forerunner to George Washington University, and published her poems in prominent journals such as *Poetry, Voices, Hound & Horn,* and *Palms.* She published three books of poems: *5 Poets* (1929, a chapbook-sized selection of poems, presented along with four others), *Flower and Weed* (1930), and *These Twinkling Acres* (1935). She also edited two anthologies: *Tanka and Hokku*, the first-known anthology of tanka written in English (1931), and *District of Columbia Poets: An Anthology of 32 Contemporaries* (1932). Mirick lived at 3314 Newark Street NW in the Cleveland Park neighborhood and is buried along with her husband, Lieutenant Carlos B. Mirick, at Arlington National Cemetery.

Turn of Tide

We know this for a transient interlude,
The sunny afternoon that idles by,
We saw too well how tyrannously rude
The breakers were this morning where we lie.
Now we may write our names upon the sand—
The tide has ebbed and left it smooth as stone—
Erect our castles with a cupping hand;
Then walk away and leave the place alone.

There is so little left to mark the spot,
The house we built looked taller as we lay,
That dwindles now to what a child might do.
Why will it need so dark a tide to blot
The castle out, and doom the poor display
Of fragile footprints, lying two and two?

Walter Everette Hawkins

November 17, 1883–?

Walter Everette Hawkins is the author of two books of poems: *Chords and Discords* (1909) and *Petals from the Poppies* (1936). A native of North Carolina, he was the thirteenth child of parents born into slavery. He graduated from Kittrell College and Howard University School of Law (1915) and worked for the U.S. Post Office in DC, before moving to Brooklyn.

Hawkins published regularly in journals, including the socialist journal the *Messenger*, where he served at one time as editor of "The Poet's Corner" column. According to critic Lorenzo Thomas, Hawkins's poem "Where Air of Freedom Is," first published in the *Messenger*, prompted J. Edgar Hoover to report evidence of "radicalism and sedition among Negroes as reflected in their publications" in 1918. Other journals where Hawkins's writing appeared include the *African Times and Orient Review, American Atheist,* and the *Crisis.*

A Spade Is Just a Spade

As I talk with learned people,
One remark they often make
Quite beyond my comprehension,
But I yield for conscience sake;
That 'tis best not be too modest
Whatsoever thing is said:
Give to everything its color,
Always call a spade a *spade.*

Now I am not versed in Logic,
Nor these high-flown classic things,
And am not adept in solving
Flighty aphoristic slings;
So this proverb seems to baffle
All the efforts I have made —
Now what else is there to call it,
When a spade is *just a spade?*

Where Air of Freedom Is

Where air of freedom is,
I will not yield to men, —
To narrow caste of men
Whose hearts are steeped in sin.
I'd rather sell the king
And let his goods be stole,
Than yield to base control
Of vile and godless men.
Where air of freedom is,
I will not yield to men.
I'd rather choose to die
Than be a living lie, —

A lie in all I teach,
A lie in all I preach,
While truth within my heart
Its burning fires dart
To burn my mask of sin.
I'd rather victory win
Thru martyr's death than grin
At wrongs of godless men.
Where air of freedom is,
I will not yield to men.
I spurn the alms of men,
The livery of kings,
I own far nobler things.
I'd rather choose to own
The pauper's garb and bone,
The eagle's eye of truth,
The lion's strength of youth,
The liberty of thought,
A free man's right, unbought,
A conscience and a soul
Beyond the king's control
Than be the lord of slaves
Of quaking, aching slaves,
Of senseless, soulless knaves,
Or seek to revel in
His ill-got wealth and fame,
His world-wide name of shame,
His liberty to sin,—
I will not yield to men!

Child of the Night

Child of the Night am I,—
    Night's sable son;
When the elf-children came,
    Lo! I was one.
Darkness was over me when I was born,
I court the night-spirits and scoff at the morn;

Rainbows of midnight my features adorn.
  At the great forge of Time,
  Making men's souls sublime,
  I stood arrayed in Night
   Ere light was born.

  Poised on the Wings of Night,
   Upward I glide;
  Floating the flings of light,
   Proudly I ride.
I rest on the pillows of thunderous clouds,
Arrayed in the billows on wondrous shrouds,
I whip up the lightnings and mock the pale crowds.
  Making men's souls sublime,
  I stood arrayed in Night
   Ere light was born.

  Blessing the sable sons,
   Lifting their shroud;
  Pressing less able ones,
   Purging the proud.
I daub them with ebony, smother their pride,
I swab them with smoke and their vanity chide,
Is the soul of a man in the hue of his hide?
  Making men's souls sublime,
  I stood arrayed in Night
   Ere light was born.

  Child of the dusky veil,
   Kissed by the Sun,
  Girded in trusty mail,
   Truth bids me on;
Cloud me in battle smoke, night-shrouds attend me,
The beginning was blackness and so will the end be;
Black gods and black angels, surround and defend me!
  Making men's souls sublime,
  I stood arrayed in Night
   Ere light was born.

Louise Kidder Sparrow

January 1, 1884–July 9, 1979

Louise Kidder Sparrow was born in Massachusetts and moved to DC in 1909 to further her studies in sculpture. She was awarded an honorary degree from the Paris Colonial Exposition in 1931 and a bronze medal from the Society of Washington Artists in 1930. Her portrait busts are in the collections of the U.S. Capitol, Howard University, the U.S. Military Academy, the Montana State Capitol, and the U.S. Naval Observatory. She was a member of the Society of Washington Artists and the Arts Club of Washington, and a Fellow of the Royal Society of the Arts in London. Injuries sustained as a result of a car crash in 1934 forced Sparrow to give up sculpture.

Sparrow wrote several books of poetry, including *Lyrics and Translations* (1904), *Narrative Poems, From a Journal in Verse* (1970), and *Spiced Herbs and Rose Petals from the Old Blue Jar* (1971), as well as nonfiction, including *The Last Cruise* (1924) and *Virginia Byways* (1946). She also translated poetry from French and Italian into English. Her first husband was a captain in the U.S. Navy; she is buried alongside him at Arlington National Cemetery.

Hokkus in Sequence

Dreams of love and you—
While timorous bird-voices
Flush the throat of dawn.

I hear the singing
Of the scythe, and muse on Time's
Implacable flight.

Under the dark side
Of the wings, there nestles Life's
Little sister, Death.

Elinor Wylie

September 7, 1885–December 16, 1928

Elinor Wylie is the author of five books of poems, including *Nets to Catch the Wind* (1921) and *Angels and Earthly Creatures* (1928), and four novels, including *Jennifer Lorn* (1923) and *The Orphan Angel* (1926). Her *Collected Poems* (1932) and *Collected Prose* (1933) were published posthumously.

Wylie was born into a socially prominent family, and she scandalized the society world with her multiple marriages and affairs. Her first husband, Philip Simmons Hichborn, was mentally unstable and abusive. Wylie had one son with him, but she abandoned both husband and son to live with another married man, Horace Wylie, a DC lawyer. When her affair was widely reported in society columns of newspapers, she was ostracized by her family, and the couple moved to England and lived under an assumed name. After Wylie's first husband committed suicide, and Horace attained a divorce, they returned to the United States and married. Wylie's third husband was another poet, William Rose Benét, but this marriage, too, was short-lived.

Wylie became part of the literary community centered in Greenwich Village in New York. She worked as poetry editor for *Vanity Fair* (1923–25) and as a contributing editor of the *New Republic* (1926–28).

Two of her DC houses still stand. The first, at 1707 N Street NW, is where Wylie lived with her first husband, from 1906 to 1910. A second address at 2153 Florida Avenue NW is the location where Wylie lived briefly after separating from her second husband, from 1920 to 1921.

Wild Peaches

1

When the world turns completely upside down
You say we'll emigrate to the Eastern Shore
Aboard a river-boat from Baltimore;
We'll live among wild peach trees, miles from town,
You'll wear a coonskin cap, and I a gown
Homespun, dyed butternut's dark gold colour.
Lost, like your lotus-eating ancestor,
We'll swim in milk and honey till we drown.
The winter will be short, the summer long,
The autumn amber-hued, sunny and hot,
Tasting of cider and of scuppernong;
All seasons sweet, but autumn best of all.
The squirrels in their silver fur will fall
Like falling leaves, like fruit, before your shot.

2

The autumn frosts will lie upon the grass
Like bloom on grapes of purple-brown and gold.
The misted early mornings will be cold;
The little puddles will be roofed with glass.
The sun, which burns from copper into brass,
Melts these at noon, and makes the boys unfold
Their knitted mufflers; full as they can hold
Fat pockets dribble chestnuts as they pass.
Peaches grow wild, and pigs can live in clover;
A barrel of salted herrings lasts a year;
The spring begins before the winter's over.
By February you may find the skins
Of garter snakes and water moccasins
Dwindled and harsh, dead-white and cloudy-clear.

3

When April pours the colours of a shell
Upon the hills, when every little creek
Is shot with silver from the Chesapeake
In shoals new-minted by the ocean swell,
When strawberries go begging, and the sleek
Blue plums lie open to the blackbird's beak,
We shall live well—we shall live very well.
The months between the cherries and the peaches
Are brimming cornucopias which spill
Fruits red and purple, sombre-bloomed and black;
Then, down rich fields and frosty river beaches
We'll trample bright persimmons, while you kill
Bronze partridge, speckled quail, and canvasback.

4

Down to the Puritan marrow of my bones
There's something in this richness that I hate.
I love the look, austere, immaculate,
Of landscapes drawn in pearly monotones.
There's something in my very blood that owns
Bare hills, cold silver on a sky of slate,
A thread of water, churned to milky spate

Streaming through slanted pastures fenced with stones.
I love those skies, thin blue or snowy gray,
Those fields sparse-planted, rendering meagre sheaves;
That spring, briefer than apple-blossom's breath,
Summer, so much too beautiful to stay,
Swift autumn, like a bonfire of leaves,
And sleepy winter, like the sleep of death.

Sonnet

You are the faintest freckles on the hide
Of fawn; the hoofprint stamped into the slope
Of slithering glaciers by the antelope;
The silk upon the mushroom's under side
Constricts you, and your eyelashes are wide
In pools uptilted on the hills; you grope
For swings of water twisted to a rope
Over a ledge where amber pebbles glide.

Shelley perceived you on the Caucasus;
Blake prisoned you in glassy grains of sand
And Keats in goblin jars from Samarcand;
Poor Coleridge found you in a poppy-seed;
But you escape the clutching most of us,
Shaped like a ghost, and imminent with speed.

Atavism

I was always afraid of Somes's Pond:
Not the little pond, by which the willow stands,
Where laughing boys catch alewives in their hands
In brown, bright shallows; but the one beyond.
There, when the frost makes all the birches burn
Yellow as cow-lilies, and the pale sky shines
Like a polished shell between black spruce and pines,
Some strange thing tracks us, turning where we turn.

You'll say I dream it, being the true daughter
Of those who in old times endured this dread.
Look! Where the lily-stems are showing red
A silent paddle moves below the water,

A sliding shape has stirred them like a breath;
Tall plumes surmount a painted mask of death.

Mariano Brull
February 24, 1891–June 8, 1956

Mariano Brull is considered one of the leading Cuban poets of the twentieth century. He spent part of his childhood in Spain before graduating in 1914 from the University of Havana with a doctor of law degree. After a few years of practicing law, Brull entered the diplomatic service. His first posts were in the United States, Peru, and Spain; he later served in Paris, Rome, and Brussels, where he worked with German Jews seeking visas to emigrate, and as commissioner for the repatriation of Cubans fleeing the Spanish Civil War. Seeing that war was imminent, he insisted on returning to Havana in 1939. The ship carrying all of Brull's effects was torpedoed by the Germans and sank. After the war, he served posts in Canada and Uruguay as Cuba's ambassador.

Brull published six books of poetry: *La casa del silencio/The House of Silence* (1916), *Poemas en menguante/Waning Poems* (1928), *Canto redondo/Round Song* (1934), *Solo de rosa/Rose Solo* (1941), *Temps en peine/Time in Sorrow* (1950), and *Rien que . . . /Nothing More Than . . .* (1954), as well as a Spanish translation of Paul Valéry's *Le cimetiére marin/The Graveyard by the Sea* and *La jeune parque/The Young Fate*.

A house where Brull lived from 1943 to 1945, during World War II, still stands at 2016 Hillyer Place NW.

Interior: Soneto V

Me encuentro mudo y solo en la estancia vacía
donde todas las cosas me hablan de su existencia:
parece que su cuerpo, donde habitar solía,
ha dejado una huella de espiritual esencia.

La luna del espejo en donde se veía
finge a cada momento reflejar su presencia.
Canta en la jaula el pájaro con más melancolía,
y la estancia la pueblan sordos ecos de ausencia.

Con los filos dorados, un libro de oraciones
abierto sobre un mueble, dice: "Las aflicciones
del mundo son pequeñas . . . Volver la vista a Dios . . ."

Los ojos vuelvo. Y pienso melancólicamente:
¡Quién hubiera podido saborear dulcemente
la exquisita tristeza de su postrer adiós!

Interior: Sonnet V
Silent and alone in the empty room
where all things explain her existence:
That the body where she used to live appears
as a trace of spiritual essence.

The mirror reflected in the moon
each moment casts back her presence.
The melancholy bird sings in its cage,
the room drowns in echoes of absence.

The gilt-edged pages of a prayer book
open on a desk read, "The afflictions
of the world are small . . . toward God turn your eyes . . ."

The look is returned. I think sadly:
Who could have tasted in such sweet despair
the exquisite sadness of her final goodbye!

Caresse Crosby
April 20, 1891–January 24, 1970

Caresse Crosby, born Mary Phelps Jacob, is the author of five books
of poems and one memoir and was editor of one of the earliest literary
journals based in DC, *Portfolio*. Crosby was also the inventor, at age
nineteen, of the first modern brassiere to receive a patent and gain
wide acceptance.

In 1925, she cofounded Black Sun Press in France with her second
husband, Harry Crosby, publishing such writers as James Joyce, Ernest
Hemingway, D. H. Lawrence, and T. S. Eliot. After her husband's sui-
cide, she founded Crosby Continental Editions, to publish inexpensive

paperback reprints of modern writers. In 1936 she left her expatriate life and bought Hampton Manor, a 486-acre estate in Bowling Green, Virginia, where she provided refuge to European artists during World War II.

Crosby lived in DC from 1937 to 1950 and opened a modern art gallery. One of her addresses, 1606 Twentieth Street NW in the Dupont Circle neighborhood, still stands. This was the second location of the Crosby Gallery of Modern Art (the first location was in Georgetown). The building had a printing press in the English basement, a second-floor art gallery with high ceilings and ample natural light, and her residence on the floors above. Crosby began publication of *Portfolio: An Intercontinental Review* while living in this house, publishing a total of six issues between 1945 and 1948, combining visual art and poetry.

A peace activist and promoter of international artistic exchange, Crosby also founded Women Against War and started an artist colony in a fifteenth-century castle in Rome, Castello di Rocca Siniblada, in the 1950s. Her poetry books are *Crosses of Gold* (1925), *Painted Shores* (1927), *The Stranger* (1927), *Impossible Melodies* (1928), and *Poems for Harry Crosby* (1930). Her autobiography is *The Passionate Years* (1953).

Coffin's Beach

A long curved beach of sunny sand,
Beyond a vast of ocean blue;
And on one hand the gorse and fern
Fringing brown dunes that blot the view.
Whilst overhead 'gainst azure sky
Soft dusted with a foam-like fleece,
The plaintive gulls in circles fly,
And crested wavelets kiss the beach.
Why should these beauties serve as shrouds,
Oppress my mind with somber dread,
Forewarn of storms behind the clouds,
And turn my thoughts upon things dead . . .
    Some drifting ghost disturbs my calm
    Upon the beach at Annisquam.

Nile-Boat

I.
Here where the weekly sky-line
made merry and the castles of
Ibrim nodded, a million Sungods danced.

II.
We looked back at the women all
black and maybe of consequence
guarding their flocks of unfolding
declensions and dark past
the doors of the Nile to command—
dark, dark and mnemonic—
fearing to shatter the ah of
an obelisk—fearing to laugh
lest the dust become
camphor and cardamom
steamboats and ivory—sunlight
for centuries—

Archibald MacLeish

May 7, 1892–April 20, 1982

Archibald MacLeish lived in DC from 1939 through 1949, serving as librarian of Congress, director of the War Department's Office of Facts and Figures, assistant director of the Office of War Information, and as assistant secretary of state for public affairs.

Prior to moving to DC, MacLeish was a practicing lawyer and an editor for the *New Republic* and *Fortune Magazine*. He also spent much of the 1920s as part of the expatriate arts community in Paris. After leaving DC, MacLeish taught at Harvard University and Amherst College.

Despite his lack of background in library science, at the Library of Congress, MacLeish was responsible for many notable successes, including raising salaries and restructuring staff, improving internal communication with division chiefs, improving the system of cataloging the collection, and increasing the Library's endowment. He also reconceptualized the office of U.S. poet laureate, brought a number of important foreign writers-in-exile to work at the Library, including Saint-John Perse, and was instrumental in gaining the release of Ezra Pound from his incarceration at St. Elizabeths Hospital.

MacLeish won the Pulitzer Prize for poetry twice, in 1933 and 1953, and the Pulitzer Prize for drama in 1959, for his verse play *J. B.* MacLeish is the author of more than twenty books of poems, including *Nobodaddy* (1926), *Conquistador* (1932), and *The Human Season* (1972). He also published history, correspondence, biography, and literary criticism, and seventeen plays and radio dramas.

Two of his homes in the area still stand: one at 1520 Thirty-Third Street NW in Georgetown, and the other, the Robert E. Lee Boyhood Home, at 607 Oronoco Street in Old Town Alexandria, Virginia.

Soul-Sight

Like moon-dark, like brown water you escape,
O laughing mouth, O sweet uplifted lips.
Within the peering brain old ghosts take shape;
You flame and wither as the white foam slips
Back from the broken wave: sometimes a start,
A gesture of the hands, a way you own
Of bending that smooth head above your heart,—
Then these are varied, then the dream is gone.

Oh, you are too much mine and flesh of me
To seal upon the brain, who in the blood
Are so intense a pulse, so swift a flood
Of beauty, such unceasing instancy.
Dear unimagined brow, unvisioned face,
All beauty has become your dwelling place.

Jean Toomer

December 26, 1894 – March 30, 1967

Jean Toomer is best known as the author of *Cane* (1923), a collection of fiction and poems set in Georgia and DC, widely acknowledged as one of the masterpieces of the Harlem Renaissance. He also published plays and essays. His volume *Collected Poems* was published posthumously in 1988.

Toomer was only twenty-eight when *Cane* was published to great critical acclaim. In an introduction to a later edition of the book, Darwin T. Turner writes: "Like a nova, Toomer's literary career exploded into brilliance with *Cane*, then faded from the view of all but the few who continuously scanned the literary galaxy. Although he published a few essays, poems, and stories during more than thirty years of subsequent effort, he never again sold a book to a commercial publisher. Time, however, has restored his reputation . . . and Jean Toomer is ranked among the finest artists in the history of Afro-American literature."

Toomer was born in DC and lived in New Rochelle, New York, as a child, returning to DC after his mother's death to live with his grandfather P. B. S. Pinchback, the first African American U.S. governor. A childhood home at 1422 Harvard Street NW, in the Columbia Heights neighborhood, still stands and is marked with a historic plaque. He attended segregated African American DC public schools, Garnet Elementary and Dunbar High School. Of mixed race, Toomer later renounced racial classification, identifying only as American. He married twice, both times to white women. He studied with the spiritual leader George Ivanovitch Gurdjieff in France, led Unitism communities in New York and Chicago, and later joined the Quakers.

Beehive
Within this black hive tonight
There swarm a million bees;
Bees passing in and out the moon,
Bees escaping out the moon,
Bees returning through the moon,
Silver bees intently buzzing,
Silver honey dripping from the swarm of bees
Earth is a waxen cell of the world comb,
And I, a drone,
Lying on my back,
Lipping honey,
Getting drunk with silver honey,
Wish that I might fly out past the moon
And curl forever in some far-off farmyard flower.

Seventh Street

Money burns the pocket, pocket hurts,
Bootleggers in silken shirts,
Ballooned, zooming Cadillacs,
Whizzing, whizzing down the street-car tracks.

Her Lips Are Copper Wire

whisper of yellow globes
gleaming on lamp-posts that sway
like bootleg licker drinkers in the fog

and let your breath be moist against me
like bright beads on yellow globes

telephone the power-house
that the main wires are insulate

(her words play softly up and down
dewy corridors of billboards)

then with your tongue remove the tape
and press your lips to mine
till they are incandescent

Reapers

Black reapers with the sound of steel on stones
Are sharpening scythes. I see them place the hones
In their hip-pockets as a thing that's done,
And start their silent swinging, one by one.
Black horses drive a mower through the weeds,
And there, a field rat, startled, squealing bleeds,
His belly close to ground. I see the blade,
Blood-stained, continue cutting weeds and shade.

Otto Leland Bohanan

(1895?–December 6, 1932)

Otto Leland Bohanan was born in Washington, DC, around 1895 and
attended DC Public Schools, Catholic University, and Howard University, where he earned a BA in 1914 and was active in the glee club

and editor of the *Howard University Journal*. He was also a member of the Alpha Chapter of Omega Psi Phi Fraternity and composed their song "Omega Men Draw Nigh" in 1917. Bohanan moved to New York to continue his studies at Columbia University, where he earned an MA from the Teachers College in 1928. Throughout his schooling, Bohanan studied both literature and music, and an article in the *Afro American* newspaper reported that he "possessed a voice of unusual range and quality and he sang in nine languages."

Bohanan's poems appeared in the *Crisis* and in the anthologies *The Book of American Negro Poetry* (1922), *Readings from Negro Authors: For Schools and Colleges* (1931), and *Negro Poets and Their Poems* (1935). At the time of his early death in 1932, Bohanan was a music teacher at DeWitt Clinton High School in New York and was just beginning to get professional concert bookings.

The Washer-Woman

A great swart cheek and the gleam of tears,
The flutter of hopes and the shadow of fears,
And all day long the rub and scrub
With only a breath betwixt tub and tub.
Fool! Thou hast toiled for fifty years
And what hast thou now but thy dusty tears?
In silence she rubbed . . . But her face I had seen,
Where the light of her soul fell shining and clean.

Muna Lee

January 29, 1895–April 3, 1965

Muna Lee was an advocate for women's suffrage and other feminist causes, and a leader of the Pan-American movement. She published one book of poetry, *Sea-Change* (1923), and coauthored five mystery novels with Maurice Guinness during the Great Depression. In addition, she translated books from Spanish to English by Rafael de Nogales, Jorge Carrera Andrade, and Rafael Altamira, and wrote a children's book, *Pioneers of Puerto Rico* (1944). Her translations of Latin American poets, published widely in anthologies and journals, introduced more than thirty Hispanic authors to English readers.

Lee married Luis Muñoz Marín in 1919, and they had two children, living alternately on the U.S. mainland and Puerto Rico. In the mid-1920s, they maintained a Sunday-night salon in their apartment on the West Side of New York City, gathering together writers and critics, as well as teachers, diplomats, polar explorers, and revolutionaries.

From 1930 to 1932, Lee lived at the Sewell-Belmont House, now a museum, located at 144 Constitution Avenue NE on Capitol Hill, and worked for the National Women's Party as director of national activities. After her return to Puerto Rico, she worked at the University of Puerto Rico and edited such journals as *Le democracia, Equal Rights,* and *Art in Review.* She separated from her husband and returned to DC in 1941, to work as a cultural affairs specialist in the U.S. State Department. She remained until her retirement in 1965 and died later that year of cancer in her home in Old San Juan.

"Melilot," the weed described in the final poem in this selection, is perhaps better known as sweet clover.

Methodist Revival

When the throbbing drums of the opening hymns were still,
The preacher shouted, "Brethren! let us pray!"
And ardently he pled that God that day
Might bend a hundred sinners to His will.
The prayer ended, he touched a lighter note—
Joked with the choir, and merrily mocked the Devil;
Then flung God's curse at the drunken nation's revel
With a voice that sobbed and fluted in his throat.

"Oh, my beloved . . . !" he launched his passionate pleas.
A woman stood. "Praise Jesus!" shrieked another,
A girl ran sobbing and knelt beside her mother.
At a sudden word, again the music swept
The tent with thunder. Quivering, one wept,
Wretched, and shamed, and groveling on one's knees.

Electors

The drugstore was a club, in whose talk took part—
Tall men, slouch-hatted, neither old nor young
Men who had failed elsewhere, and who had wrung

Stakes from scant capital for another start.
Not hopeless men: here was a junction which
Ensured a Harvey Eating House; next year
Congress would pass the Enabling Act; right here
Would be a metropolis: they would all be rich.

These consummations meanwhile they awaited
In the drugstore, talking politics till night.
Texans, farmers, and carpet-baggers they hated;
Feared the Negro—"This state should be lily-white,"
And arguments to damn whatever scheme
Were the epithets "Utopia" and "dream."

Melilot

Behind the house is the millet plot,
And past the millet, the stile;
And then a hill where melilot
Grows with wild chamomile.

There was a youth who bade me goodbye
Where the hill rises to meet the sky.
I think my heart broke; but I have forgot
All but the smell of the white melilot.

Herbert Gerhard Bruncken

September 21, 1896–January 15, 1956

Herbert Gerhard Bruncken is the author of several books of poems, including *Our Lady of the Night* (1915), *Hall Bedroom* (1936), *Last Parade* (1938), *The Long Night* (1939), *Hue and Cry* (1941), and *Noise in Time* (1949). He edited the *Minaret* from 1911 to 1926, a journal he founded in DC and later moved to New York.

Bruncken attended DC Public Schools and Columbia University and made a living for many years as a reporter before returning to the city of his birth and becoming a librarian in Milwaukee, Wisconsin. Poems of his appeared in such prominent periodicals as the *New Yorker, Poetry, Dial,* and *Commonweal.* In 1940, he won the Shelley Memorial Award from the Poetry Society of America.

To a Thrush at Evening

O I can hear you
    When the mist comes down
Like a proud pale lady
    With a rustling gown.

     And oh!
How my heart
    Like the mist is light,
When I hear you sing
    In the cool of night.

O brown little singer,
    You sing from the dawn,
Till the long dark shadows
    Cover up the lawn.

     And oh!
Then I listen
    When the mist comes down
Like a proud pale lady
    With a rustling gown.

When the swallows blot
    The sunset sky,
And the minstrel lark
    Has ceased his cry;

     Then oh!
Brown singer
    In the woodway aisles,
Your note is a prayer
    To the long tree files.

And my heart is gay
    When the mist comes down
Like a proud pale lady
    With a rustling gown.

Rondeau

O dark the day; grey mist descending,
The branches black with rain are bending;
    And snow-birds haunt the lonely air,
    Like silent ships on oceans bare,
No gentle home their souls befriending.

The day shall have no radiant ending;
No symphony of colors blending
    The red and gold of sunset fair.
      O dark the day!

The leaden air the sea is lending
Its mourning tones; and the attending
Rocks and cliffs her colors bear.
    The sea gulls voice the sea's despair,
Their lonely cries through mist ascending.
      O dark the day!

Esther Popel Shaw

July 16, 1896–January 28, 1958

Esther Popel was born in Harrisburg, Pennsylvania, and, in 1919, became the first African American woman to graduate from Dickinson College in Carlisle, Pennsylvania. After graduation, Popel moved to Baltimore, working for the War Risk Insurance Department and teaching for two years. She then moved to DC and taught in the DC Public Schools. She married William A. Shaw, was widowed in 1946, and raised their daughter, Patricia Shaw Iversen, on her own. One of her apartments, at 111 Columbia Road NW, is still standing.

Publishing under her maiden name, Popel was the review editor for the *Journal of Negro Education* and published poems, book reviews, and essays in *Opportunity*, the *Crisis*, the *Journal of Negro Life*, and the *Journal of the National Association of College Women*. Fluent in four languages (French, Spanish, Latin, and German), Popel taught foreign languages at two DC Public Schools: Shaw Junior High and Francis Junior High. Popel was an active member of the Saturday Nighters, a literary salon in the home of Georgia Douglas Johnson, and a member of the Lincoln Memorial Temple. She wrote six plays for junior high school students and was a popular public speaker for women's clubs in DC and New York. Her book, *A Forest Pool*, was privately printed as a "gift edition" in Washington, DC, in 1934. Toward the end of her life, Popel was a member of a writers' group led by Inez Boulton that also included such notable writers as Owen Dodson, Charles Sebree, Paul Lawson, and May Miller.

In an article, "Personal Adventures in Race Relations," written for public speaking engagements and published in 1946, she wrote: "At a time when all our energies are needed to meet and solve together the crucial problems of the postwar period, we find a large element of the population torn by resentment, suspicion and hatred. The constant and soul-searching humiliation that is the outgrowth of the dangerously reactionary policies of prejudice and biracialism serves to undermine the faith of the Negro, and other minorities, in the very foundation of the democracy they are asked to defend."

Flag Salute

"*I pledge allegiance to the flag*" —
They dragged him naked
Through the muddy streets,
A feeble-minded black boy!
And the charge? Supposed assault
Upon an aged woman!
"*Of the United States of America*"—
One mile they dragged him
Like a sack of meal,
A rope around his neck,
A bloody ear
Left dangling by the patriotic hand
Of Nordic youth! (A boy of seventeen!)
"*And to the Republic for which it stands*"—
And then they hanged his body to a tree,
Below the window of the county judge
Whose pleadings for that battered human flesh
Were stifled by the brutish, raucous howls
Of men, and boys, and women with their babes,

Brought out to see the bloody spectacle
Of murder in the style of '33!
(Three thousand strong, they were!)
"One Nation, Indivisible"—
To make the tale complete
They built a fire—
What matters that the stuff they burned
Was flesh—and bone—and hair—
And reeking gasoline!
"With Liberty—and Justice"—
They cut the rope in bits
And passed them out,
For souvenirs, among the men and boys!
The teeth no doubt, on golden chains
Will hang
About the favored necks of sweethearts, wives,
And daughters, mothers, sisters, babies, too!
"For ALL!"

Grant Me Strength

Give me the strength
Of verdant hills
Washed clean by summer rain;

Of purple hills
At peace when weary Day
Sinks quietly to rest
In Night's cool arms;

Of rugged, wind-whipped hills
That lift their heads
Above the petty, lowland, valley things,
And shake their shoulders free
Of bonds that hold
Them close to earth;

Of snow-capped hills
Sun-kissed by day, by night
Companioned by the stars;

Of grim volcanoes
Pregnant with the fires
Of molten fury!

Grant me strength,
Great God,
Like that of hills!

Theft

The moon
Was an old, old woman tonight,
Hurrying home;
Calling pitifully to her children,
The stars,
Begging them to go home with her
For she was afraid,
But they would not.
They only laughed
While she crept along
Huddling against the dark blue wall of the Night,
Stooping low,
Her old black hood wrapped close about her ears,
And only the pale curve of her yellow cheek,
With a tear in the hollow of it,
Showing through.
And the wind laughed too,
For he was teasing the old woman,
Pelting her with snowballs,
Filling her old eyes with flakes of them,
Making her cold.
She stumbled along, shivering,
And once she fell,
And the snow buried her;
And all her jewels
Slid from the old bag
Under her arm
And fell to earth,
And the tall trees seized them,

And hung them about their necks,
And filled their bony arms with them.
And their nakedness was covered by her jewels,
And they would not give them back to her.
The old moon-woman moaned piteously,
Hurrying home;
And the wild wind laughed at her
And her children laughed too,
And the tall trees taunted her
With their glittering plunder.

Ruth Muskrat Bronson

October 3, 1897–June 12, 1982

Ruth Muskrat Bronson was born on the Delaware County Indian Reservation, in what was then Indian Territory and is now the state of Oklahoma. She attended the University of Oklahoma and the University of Kansas, then transferred to Mount Holyoke College, graduating in 1925 with a BA in English.

Bronson served for twelve years as the head of the scholarship and loan program at the Bureau of Indian Affairs in Washington, DC (1930–44), and wrote a high school textbook, *Indians Are People, Too* (1944). She served as executive secretary of the National Congress of American Indians and created their legislative news service. She was a popular speaker at tribal meetings across the United States and a leader on issues such as native water rights along the Colorado River, native rights in the Territory of Alaska, and medical care for American Indians.

Bronson subsequently worked as a health education specialist for the Indian Health Service on the San Carlos Apache Indian Reservation in Arizona. She was awarded the 1937 Indian Achievement Medal of the Indian Council Fire, the 1962 Oveta Culp Hobby Service Award from the U.S. Department of Health, Education and Welfare, and a 1978 National Indian Child Conference Merit Award. She published poetry in journals and is the author of the nonfiction books *The Church in Indian Life* (1945) and *Shall We Repeat Indian History in Alaska?* (1947).

Sentenced: A Dirge

They have come, they have come,
Out of the unknown they have come;
Out of the great sea they have come;
Dazzling and conquering the white man has come
To make this land his home.

We must die, we must die,
The white man has sentenced that we must die,
Without great forests must we die,
Broken and conquered the red man must die,
He cannot claim his own.

They have gone, they have gone,
Our sky-blue waters, they have gone,
Our wild free prairies they have gone,
To be the white man's own.

They have won, they have won,
Through fraud and through warfare they have won,
Our council and burial grounds they have won,
Our birthright for pottage the white man has won,
And the red man must perish alone.

Songs of the Spavinaw

I am the river of Spavinaw,
    I am the river of pain;
Sadness and gladness must answer my law;
Measure for measure I give, and withdraw
Back through the hills of the Spavinaw,
    Hiding away from the plain.

I am the river of Spavinaw;
    I sing the songs of the world;
Dashing and whirling, swishing and swirling,
Delicate, mystical, silvery spray hurling,
    Sing I the songs of the world,
    The passionate songs of the world.

I sing of laughter and mirth,
  And I laugh in a gurgle of glee
As the myriad joys of the earth
  Trip through the light with me.
Gay shallows dimple, sparkle and ripple,
  Like songs that a lover would sing,
    Skipping in moonlight,
    Tripping in moonlight,
  Whispering echoes of spring.

And again
  I move with the slow sadness of pain.
In my dark blue deep, where the shadows creep,
  I catch up life's sorrows and mirror them back again.
And my song is a throbbing, pitiful sobbing,
  Choked by an agonized pain.

And then
  I move forth toward the beckoning north,
    And I sing of the power of men.
      As I dash down my falls,
      As I beat at my walls
Frantically fighting, running and righting,
All through the flood, through the snarling and biting,
  I sing of the power of men,
  Of the hurry and power of men.

    I am the river of Spavinaw,
    I am the giver of pain;
Sadness and gladness must answer my law;
Measure for measure I give, and withdraw
Back through the hills of the Spavinaw,
  Hiding away from the plain.

The Hunter's Wooing

Come roam the wild hills, my Cherokee Rose,
Come roam the wild hills with me.
We'll follow the path where the Spavinaw flows,

Dashing wild on its way to the sea,
On its wearisome way to the sea.
We'll chase the fleet deer from its lair in the woods;
We'll follow the wolf to his den.

When the sun hides his face, we'll rest in the woods;
Hid away from the worry of men.
Hid away from the bother of men.

And then we'll go home, my Cherokee Rose,
Where the Senecas live in the heart of the hills
By the rippling Cowskin, where the Saulchana grows,
We'll go home to the Coyauga hills,
To the sheltering Coyauga hills.

Joseph Auslander

October 11, 1897–June 22, 1965

Joseph Auslander was the first person to serve as poet consultant at the Library of Congress and the longest-serving (from 1937 to 1941). Auslander published six volumes of poems; his best known is *The Unconquerables* (1943), poems addressed to the war-torn, German-occupied countries of Europe.

His secretary at the Library of Congress was his second wife, Audrey Wurdemann, winner of the Pulitzer Prize for poetry in 1935 for her book *Bright Ambush*, and, at age twenty-four, the youngest winner of that award. Of the two, Wurdemann is the better poet. Together they collaborated on short stories and two novels, *My Uncle Jan* (1945) and *The Islanders* (1951).

Auslander attended Harvard University and the Sorbonne in Paris and taught at Columbia University and served as the poetry editor for the *North American Review* and the *Measure*. He translated poems from Italian and French. In his role as poet consultant for the Library of Congress, Auslander instituted the Library's reading series. His house at 3117 Thirty-Fifth Street NW, in the Cathedral Heights neighborhood, still stands.

Dawn at the Rain's Edge

The drowsy, friendly, comfortable creak
    Of axles arguing and wet spokes gleaming,
When old empty tumbrels blunder dreaming, too sleepy to speak,
    Blunder down the road in the rain dreaming.

And the house-lights rub at the shining dripping shadows
    Over the windows; through the drenched silver willows;
        everywhere:
In the sulphurous fluctuant marsh this side the steaming meadows
    Where black weeds trouble the moon's drowned hair.

There is a sudden fuss of draggled feathers and the swing
    Of winds in a hissing burst of raindrops; then a cry
Of color at the hill's rim; a strange bright glimmering
    And a lark talking madness in some corner of the sky.

Home-Bound

The moon is a wavering rim where one fish slips,
The water makes a quietness of sound;
Night is an anchoring of many ships
Home-bound.

There are stranger tunnelers in the dark, and whirs
Of wings that die, and hairy spiders spin
The silence into nets, and tenanters
Move softly in.

I step on shadows riding through the grass,
And feel the night lean cool against my face;
And challenged by the sentinel of space,
I pass.

Lewis Grandison Alexander

July 4, 1900–1945

Lewis Grandison Alexander was born in DC and educated in the DC
Public Schools and at Howard University and the University of Penn-

sylvania. He began writing poetry at age seventeen and had a particular affinity for Japanese traditional verse forms such as haiku (sometimes called hokku) and tanka. As he wrote in "Japanese Hokkus," an essay in the December 1923 issue of the *Crisis:* "Its real value is not in its physical directness but in its psychological indirectness . . . not in what is said but what is suggested . . . written in the spaces between the lines."

Alexander was a member of the Playwriters Circle, the Randall Community Center Players, and the Ira Aldridge Players, all based in DC, where he wrote plays, acted, and designed costumes. Alexander also starred in the original Broadway production of *Salome* in 1923.

His poems were published in a number of journals, including the *Crisis,* the *Messenger, Opportunity, Palms, Black Opals,* and *Saturday Evening Quill,* as well as the only issue of *Fire!!* He guest-edited a special "Negro Number" of the journal *Carolina Magazine* at the University of North Carolina in 1927. His work was included in the anthologies *The New Negro,* edited by Alain Locke; *Ebony and Topaz,* edited by Charles S. Johnson; and *Caroling Dusk,* edited by Countee Cullen. He never published a book of his poems.

Hokku

My soul like a tree
Sways above dry-leaf Autumn:
Be kind, oh wind-god.

*

Like cherry blossoms
Dancing with the passing wind—
My shattered hopes.

*

Last night I saw you
A dream rose, and I your stem
Showing you the sun.

*

O apple blossoms
Give me your words of silence!
Yes, your charming speech.

*

My soul is the wind
Dashing down fields of Autumn:
O, too swift to sing.

*

The wind is a comb
Fixing clouds about the moon
In a strange coiffure.

*

My ears burn for speech
And you lie cold and silent.
Supinely cruel:
Look at the white moon
The sphinx does not question more.
Turn away your eyes.

Frank Smith Horne

August 18, 1899 – September 7, 1974

Frank Smith Horne is best known as a member of President Franklin D. Roosevelt's "Black Cabinet." An optometrist who trained at the City College of New York, the University of Southern California, and the Northern Illinois College of Ophthalmology, Horne briefly practiced as a doctor before becoming president of Fort Valley High and Industrial School in Georgia. He moved to DC in 1936 to take a series of government appointments, including assistant director of the Division of Negro Affairs of the National Youth Administration and director of the Office of Race Relations for the U.S. Housing Authority.

Horne began his affiliation with the Harlem Renaissance in 1925, winning second place for his poem "Letters Found near a Suicide" from the *Crisis*. Other poems were published in *Opportunity* and the anthology *The New Negro*. In 1963, he published a limited edition volume of poems in London, titled *Haverstraw*.

Horne left DC in 1955 for New York City, where he founded the National Committee Against Discrimination in Housing and served on the New York City Housing Redevelopment Board. He helped to raise his niece, the singer and actress Lena Horne.

To a Persistent Phantom
I buried you deeper last night
You with your tears
And your tangled hair
You with your lips
That kissed so fair
I buried you deeper last night.

I buried you deeper last night
With fuller breasts
And stronger arms
With softer lips
And newer charms
I buried you deeper last night.

Deeper . . . ay, deeper
And again tonight
Till that gay spirit
That once was you
Will tear its soul
In climbing through . . .
Deeper . . . ay, deeper
I buried you deeper last night.

❖ BIBLIOGRAPHY ❖

Alexander, Eleanor. *Lyrics of Sunshine and Shadow: The Tragic Courtship and Marriage of Paul Laurence Dunbar and Alice Ruth Moore*. New York: New York University Press, 2001.

Allen, Gay Wilson. *The Solitary Singer: A Critical Biography of Walt Whitman*. New York: Macmillan, 1955.

Asch, Chris Meyers, and George Derek Musgrove. *Chocolate City: A History of Race and Democracy in the Nation's Capital*. Chapel Hill: University of North Carolina Press, 2017.

Babcock, William Henry. *Legends of the New World*. Boston: R. G. Badger, 1919.

Banning, Kendall. *The Phantom Caravan*. Chicago: Bookfellows, 1920.

Beauchamp, Tanya Edwards, and Kimberly Prothro Williams. *The Anacostia Historic District*. Rev. ed. Washington, DC: Historical Society of Washington, DC, 2006.

Bennett, Paula Bernat, ed. *Nineteenth-Century American Women Poets: An Anthology*. Malden, MA: Blackwell, 1998.

———, ed. *Palace-Burner: The Selected Poetry of Sarah Piatt*. Champaign: University of Illinois Press, 2001.

Bibb, Eloise A. *Poems*. New York: Monthly Review Press, 1895.

Bierce, Ambrose. *The Collected Writings of Ambrose Bierce*. Edited by Clifton Fadiman. New York: Citadel, 1946.

———. *Poems of Ambrose Bierce*. Edited by M. E. Grenander. Lincoln: University of Nebraska Press, 1995.

Botta, Anne C. *Memoirs of Anne C. Botta Written by Her Friends, with Selections from Her Correspondence and from Her Writings in Prose and Poetry*. Edited by Vincenzo Botta. New York: J. S. Tait and Sons, 1894.

Boyd's Directory of Washington and Georgetown. Washington, DC, multiple years.

Brooks, Noah. *Washington, D.C. in Lincoln's Time.* Chicago: Quadrangle, 1971.

Brooks, Walter H. *The Pastor's Voice.* Washington, DC: Associated Publishers, 1945.

Brown, Solomon G. *Kind Regards of Solomon G. Brown.* Washington, DC: Smithsonian Institution Press, 1983.

Burroughs, John. *Wake-Robin.* New York: Hurd and Houghton, 1871.

Byars, J. C., ed. *Black and White: An Anthology of Washington Verse.* Washington, DC: Crane, 1927.

Callow, Philip. *From Noon to Starry Night: A Life of Walt Whitman.* Chicago: Ivan R. Dee, 1992.

Carter, Charles Carroll, William C. DiGiacomantonio, and Pamela Scott. *Creating Capitol Hill: Place, Proprietors, and People.* Washington, DC: United States Capitol Historical Society, 2018.

Cary, Francince Curro, ed. *Washington Odyssey: A Multicultural History of the Nation's Capital.* Washington, DC: Smithsonian Books, 2003.

Chronicling America: Historic American Newspapers. The Library of Congress digital collections. http://chroniclingamerica.loc.gov/.

Clark-Lewis, Elizabeth, ed. *First Freed: Washington, D.C. in the Emancipation Era.* 2nd ed. Washington, DC: Howard University Press, 2002.

Clifford, Carrie Williams. *Race Rhymes.* Washington, DC: R. L. Pendleton, 1911.

———. *The Widening Light.* Washington, DC: Walter Reid, 1922.

Cooper, Anna Julia, ed. *The Life and Writings of the Grimké Family.* Privately printed, 1951.

Cosentino, Andrew J., and Henry H. Glassie. *The Capital Image: Painters in Washington, 1800–1915.* Washington, DC: Smithsonian Institution Press, 1983.

Cromwell, John W. "The First Negro Churches in the District of Columbia." *Journal of Negro History* 7, no. 1 (January 1922): 64–106.

Crosby, Caresse. *Poems for Harry Crosby.* Paris: Black Sun, 1930.

Cullen, Countee, ed. *Caroling Dusk: An Anthology of Verse by Negro Poets.* New York: Harper and Brothers, 1927.

Davis, Bertha Gerneaux, Mark Winton Woods, and Harriet Winton Davis. *Verses by Three Generations.* College Park: University of Maryland Press, 1921.

District of Columbia Public Schools Archives. Sumner School Museum and Archives, Washington, DC.

Douglass, Frederick. *The Life and Times of Frederick Douglass, Written by Himself.* 1881. New York: Carol Publishing Group, 1995.

Frederick Douglass Papers. Library of Congress, Washington, DC.

Dunbar, Paul Laurence. *The Collected Poetry of Paul Laurence Dunbar.* Edited by Joanne M. Braxton. Charlottesville: University of Virginia Press, 1993.

Paul Laurence Dunbar Collection. Dayton Metro Library, Dayton, OH.

Dunbar-Nelson, Alice. *Give Us Each Day: The Diary of Alice Dunbar-Nelson.* Edited by Gloria T. Hull. New York: Norton, 1984.

Alice Dunbar-Nelson Papers, 1895–1942. University of Delaware Library, Newark, DE.

The Charles E. Feinberg Collection of the Papers of Walt Whitman. Library of Congress, Washington, DC.

Fitzpatrick, Sandra, and Maria R. Goodwin. *The Guide to Black Washington.* Rev. ed. New York: Hippocrene, 1999.

French, Benjamin Brown. *Witness to the Young Republic: A Yankee's Journal, 1828–1870.* Edited by Donald B. Cole and John J. McDonough. Hanover, NH: University Press of New England, 1989.

Furgurson, Ernest B. *Freedom Rising: Washington in the Civil War.* New York: Knopf, 2004.

Gatewood, Willard B. *Aristocrats of Color: The Black Elite, 1880–1920.* Fayetteville: University of Arkansas Press, 2000.

Gilbert, Anne Kelledy. *The Angel of the Battlefield and Other Poems.* New York: H. Vinal, 1928.

Gillette, Howard, Jr., ed. *Southern City, National Ambition: The Growth of Early Washington, D.C., 1800–1860.* Washington, DC: American Architectural Foundation and George Washington University Center for Washington Area Studies, 1995.

Glyndon, Howard. *Idyls of Battle and Poems of the Rebellion.* New York: Hurd and Houghton, 1864.

Green, Constance McLaughlin. *The Secret City: A History of Race Relations in the Nation's Capital.* Princeton, NJ: Princeton University Press, 1967.

———. *Washington: A History of the Capital, 1800–1950.* Princeton, NJ: Princeton University Press, 1962.

Greenwood, Grace. *Poems.* Boston: Ticknor, Reed, and Fields, 1851.

Hamalian, Linda. *The Cramoisy Queen: A Life of Caresse Crosby.* Carbondale: Southern Illinois University Press, 2005.

Harrold, Stanley. *Subversives: Antislavery Community in Washington, D.C., 1828–1865.* Baton Rouge: Louisiana State University Press, 2003.

Hay, John. *Poems.* New York: Houghton, Mifflin, 1871.

Hornaday, William Temple. *Old-Fashioned Verses.* New York: Clark and Fritts, 1919.

Hull, Gloria T. *Color, Sex and Poetry: Three Women Writers of the Harlem Renaissance.* Bloomington: Indiana University Press, 1987.

Hunter, Alfred. *The Washington and Georgetown Directory.* Washington, DC: Kirkwood and McGill, various years.

Jacob, Katheryn Allamong. *Capital Elites: High Society in Washington, D.C. after the Civil War.* Washington, DC: Smithsonian Institution Press, 1995.

Johnson, Andre E., ed. The Henry McNeal Turner Project. University of Memphis. www.thehenrymcnealturnerproject.org/.

Johnson, Georgia Douglas. *An Autumn Love Cycle.* New York: H. Vinal, 1928.

———. *Bronze.* Boston: B. J. Brimmer, 1922.

———. *The Heart of a Woman.* Boston: Cornhill, 1918.

Johnson, James Weldon. *James Weldon Johnson: Writings.* New York: Library of America, 2004.

Jones, Judy Yaeger, and Jane E. Vallier, eds. *Sweet Bells Jangled: Laura Redden Searing, A Deaf Poet Restored.* Washington, DC: Gallaudet University Press, 2003.

Key, Francis Scott. *Poems of the Late Francis S. Key, Esq.* New York: Robert Carter and Bros., 1857.

Leech, Margaret. *Reveille in Washington, 1860–1865.* New York: Harper and Brothers, 1941.

Lewis, Tom. *Washington: A History of Our National City.* New York: Basic, 2015.

Litchfield, Grace Denio. *Collected Poems,* New York: Putnam's Sons, 1913.

Logan, Rayford W., and Michael R. Winston, eds. *Dictionary of American Negro Biography.* New York: Norton, 1982.

Lowe, Gail S., ed. *East of the River: Continuity and Change.* Washington, DC: Smithsonian Institution Anacostia Community Museum, 2010.

Luria, Sarah. *Capital Speculations: Writing and Building Washington, D.C.* Durham: University of New Hampshire Press, 2006.

Martin, Rev. J. Sella. *The Hero and the Slave: Founded on Fact.* Boston: W. F. Brown, 1870.

Masur, Kate. *An Example for All the Land: Emancipation and the Struggle over Equality in Washington, D.C.* Chapel Hill: University of North Carolina Press, 2010.

McGuire, William. *Poetry's Catbird Seat: The Consultantship in Poetry in the English Language at the Library of Congress, 1937–1987.* Washington, DC: Library of Congress, 1988.

McHenry, Elizabeth. *Forgotten Readers: Recovering the Lost History of African American Literary Societies.* Durham, NC: Duke University Press, 2002.

McQuirter, Marya Annette. *African American Heritage Trail, Washington, DC*. Washington, DC: Cultural Tourism DC, 2003.

Menard, John Willis. *Lays in Summer Lands*. Edited by Larry Eugene Rivers, Richard Matthews, and Carter Brown Jr. Tampa, FL: University of Tampa Press, 2002.

Miller, Joaquin. *Selected Writings of Joaquin Miller*. Saratoga, CA: Urion, 1977.

May Miller Papers. Rose Library Archives, Emory University, Atlanta, GA.

Mills, Cynthia. *Beyond Grief: Sculpture and Wonder in the Gilded Age Cemetery*. Washington, DC: Smithsonian Institution Scholarly Press, 2014.

Mirick, Edith, ed. *District of Columbia Poets*. New York: Henry Harrison, 1932.

Moore, Jacqueline M. *Leading the Race: The Transformation of the Black Elite in the Nation's Capital, 1880–1920*. Charlottesville: University Press of Virginia, 1999.

National Intelligencer archives. Library of Congress, Washington, DC.

O'Toole, Patricia. *The Five of Hearts: An Intimate Portrait of Henry Adams and His Friends 1880–1918*. New York: Ballantine, 1990.

Paulding, James Kirke. *The Backwoodsman: A Poem*. Philadelphia: M. Thomas, 1818.

Payne, Daniel Alexander. *The Pleasures and Other Miscellaneous Poems*. Baltimore: Sherwood, 1850.

———. *Recollections of Seventy Years*. Nashville, TN: Publishing House of the A.M.E. Sunday School Union, 1888.

Piatt, John James. *Poems in Sunshine and Firelight*. Cincinnati: R. W. Carroll, 1866.

Pierpont, John. *The Anti-Slavery Poems of John Pierpont*. Boston: Oliver Johnson, 1843.

Proctor, John Claggett. *Proctor's Poems*. Washington, DC: self-published, 1950.

———. *Washington: Past and Present*. Vol. 1. New York: Lewis Historical Publishing, 1930.

Rankin, Jeremiah Eames. *Broken Cadences: An Ode in Three Parts*. Boston: Our Day Publishing, 1889.

Renehan, Edward J., Jr. *Burroughs and Whitman: Comrades in Letters and Life*. Web exhibit, 2008. Vassar College Libraries, Archives and Special Collections. "Walt Whitman & John Burroughs: Literary Comrades."

Roberts, Kim. *A Literary Guide to Washington, D.C.: Walking in the Footsteps of American Authors from Francis Scott Key to Zora Neale Hurston*. Charlottesville: University of Virginia Press, 2018.

———. "Georgia Douglas Johnson." *Beltway Poetry Quarterly* 13, no. 4 (Fall 2012).

——. "Walt Whitman, Civil War Nurse." *American Journal of Medicine* 118 (July 2005).

——. "Whitman in Washington (1863–1873)." *Beltway Poetry Quarterly* 4, no. 4 (Fall 2003).

Roberts, Kim, and Martin G. Murray. "Whitman in DC: Gay DC Walking Tours," Rainbow History Project, 2005.

Roberts, Kim, and Dan Vera. *DC Writers' Homes.* Web exhibit, 2011, with regular updates. www.dcwriters.org.

Roome, Lilian Pike. *Gen. Albert Pike's Poems.* Little Rock, AK: Fred W. Allsopp, 1900.

Roses, Lorraine Elena, and Ruth Elizabeth Randolph. *Harlem Renaissance and Beyond: Literary Biographies of 100 Black Women Writers, 1900–1945.* Cambridge: Harvard University Press, 1990.

——, eds. *Harlem's Glory: Black Women Writing, 1900–1950.* Cambridge: Harvard University Press, 1996.

Samuels, Ernest. *Henry Adams.* Cambridge: Harvard University Press, 1989.

Sandweiss, Martha A. *Passing Strange: A Gilded Tale of Love and Deception across the Color Line.* New York: Penguin, 2009.

Schaffner, M. A. "A Good Opinion of Bierce." *Beltway Poetry Quarterly* 9, no. 3 (Summer 2008).

Scheyer, Ernst. *The Circle of Henry Adams: Art & Artist.* Detroit: Wayne State University Press, 1970.

Sherman, Joan R. *African-American Poetry of the Nineteenth Century: An Anthology.* Champaign: University of Illinois Press, 1992.

Simmons, William J. *Men of Mark: Eminent, Progressive and Rising.* Cleveland: George M. Rewell, 1887.

Sluby, Paul E. *Bury Me Deep: Burial Places Past and Present in and Nearby Washington, D.C.* Temple Hills, MD: P. E. Sluby, 2009.

Smithsonian American Art Museum, Art Inventories Catalog. http://siris-artinventories.si.edu.

Smithsonian Anacostia Museum and Center for African American History and Culture. *The Black Washingtonians: The Anacostia Museum Illustrated Chronology.* Hoboken, NJ: Wiley and Sons, 2005.

Speyer, Leonora. *Fiddler's Farewell.* New York: Knopf, 1926.

Spofford, Harriet Prescott. *In Titian's Garden and Other Poems.* Boston: Copeland and Day, 1897.

Stafford, Wendell Phillips. *Dorian Days.* New York: Macmillan, 1909.

Stedman, Edmund Clarence, ed. *An American Anthology, 1787–1900.* Boston: Houghton Mifflin, 1900.

Todd, Charles Burr. *The Story of Washington: The National Capital.* New York: Putnam's Sons, 1889.

Toomer, Jean. *Cane.* New York: Liveright, 1923.

Warren, Ina Russelle, ed. *The Poets and Poetry of Washington.* Buffalo, NY: Charles Wells Moulton, 1895.

Washington Republican archives. Library of Congress, Washington, DC.

Watson, Steven. *The Harlem Renaissance: Hub of African-American Culture, 1920–1930.* New York: Pantheon, 1995.

West, Aberjhani, and Sandra L. West. *Encyclopedia of the Harlem Renaissance.* New York: Fact on File Books, 2003.

Whitman, Walt. *Memoranda during the War.* Edited by Peter Coviello. Oxford: Oxford University Press, 2004.

———. *Walt Whitman: Complete Poetry and Collected Prose.* New York: Library of America, 1982.

Willard, Emma Hart. *The Fulfillment of a Promise.* New York: White, Gallaher and White, 1831.

Williams, Lida Keck. *The Life and Works of Paul Laurence Dunbar.* Washington, DC: Austin Jenkins, 1907.

Wills, Garry. *Henry Adams and the Making of America.* Boston: Houghton Mifflin, 2005.

Woodress, James. *A Yankee's Odyssey: The Life of Joel Barlow.* Philadelphia: Lippincott, 1958.

Wylie, Elinor. *Collected Poems of Elinor Wylie.* New York: Knopf, 1932.

Yale Collection of American Literature. Beinecke Rare Book and Manuscript Library, Yale University, New Haven, CT.

❖ INDEX ❖

Adams, Clover, xxi, 18, 212, 237–38, 239–41, 263

Adams, Henry, xix, xxi, 16, 18, 212–15, 229, 237, 239–41

Adams, John Quincy, xx, 6, 31–34

Adams, Louisa, 48–50

Agg, John, 6, 47–49

Aldrich, Thomas Bailey, 111–12

Alexander, Lewis Grandison, 16, 21, 316–18

Allen, Elizabeth Akers, 7, 13, 100–105

Ames, Mary Clemmer, 7, 163–64

Andrews, Annulet, 244–45

Arlington National Cemetery, xxi, 45, 46, 90–91, 109–10, 173, 178, 179, 238–39, 289, 293

Arts Club of Washington, 212, 293

Auslander, Joseph, 18–19, 315–16

Babcock, William Henry, 231–33

Bailey, Gamaliel, 10, 68, 85, 156

Bailey, Margaret Lucy Shands, 10, 68–69, 85, 156

Banning, Kendall, 19, 179–80

Barlow, Joel, 25–29

Barney, Natalie Clifford, 271–73

Benét, William Rose, 294

Benson, Carl, 143–44

Bierce, Ambrose, xix, 12, 222–25, 229

Blaine, James G., 16, 125, 156

Bohanan, Otto Leland, 303–4

Bonnin, Gertrude Simmons, 269–71

Botta, Anne Lynch, 7, 184–88

Bowen, Arthur, xx, 8, 72–74

Boyle, Esmerelda, 17, 218–19

Bradley, Mary Emily Neeley, 161–62

Bristed, Charles Astor, 143–44

Bronson, Ruth Muskrat, 312–15

Brooks, Walter H., xx, xxii, 16, 126–27

Brown, John, 275

Brown, Solomon G., 12, 149–55

Brull, Mariano, 297–98

Bruncken, Herbert Gerhard, 306–8

Bulwer-Lytton, Edward Robert, 195–96

Burke, Margaret Louisa Sullivan, 7, 162–63, 168

Burroughs, John, 108, 203–5

Charles, Emily Thornton, 7, 230–31

Claudel, Paul, 253–55

Clay, Henry, 184

Cleveland, Rose Elizabeth, 20, 145, 165–68

Clifford, Carrie Williams, 15, 16, 21, 241–44

Congressional Cemetery, 51, 62, 183

Coppin, Fanny Jackson, xx, 14, 113–15

Cranch, Christopher Pearse, 138–39

Crosby, Caresse, 298–300

Custis, George Washington Parke, 45–47

Dahlgren, Madeleine Vinton, 5, 16, 90, 147–49
Dall, Caroline Healey, 6, 145–46
Davis, Bertha Gerneaux, 19, 177–79
DC Public Schools, 6, 10, 14, 16–17, 39, 88, 94, 175, 177, 203, 259, 262, 273, 281, 286, 302, 303, 306, 308, 316
Deans, Jennie, 140
Dodge, Mary Abigail, 156–59
Dodson, Owen, 309
Dorsey, Anna Hanson, 141–43
Douglass, Frederick, xx, 11, 13, 74–79, 191, 261–62
Dunbar, Paul Laurence, xix, 16, 18, 259–62, 266
Dunbar-Nelson, Alice Moore, 19, 21, 259, 266–69, 276

Ensley, Newell Houston, xx, 16, 169–70

Fauset, Jessie Redmon, 16, 19, 21, 286–88
Fillmore, Millard, 140
Fort Myer, 176–77
Fortune, T. Thomas, xx, 15, 16, 129–32
French, B. B., 15, 62–63

Gallaudet University, 14, 118, 120–21, 202
Gates, Isabel Likens, 176–77
Gath, 108, 189, 219–21
Georgetown Female Seminary, 6, 52, 145
George Washington University, 6, 138, 170, 288
Gilbert, Anne Kelledy, 18, 19, 237–39
Glenwood Cemetery, 90, 105, 163
Glyndon, Howard, 7, 118–21
Greenwood, Grace, 7, 9, 10, 68, 85–87, 108, 184

Grimké, Angelina Weld, 16, 21, 281–83
Grimké, Charlotte Forten, 10, 14, 15, 205–10, 281, 283

Halpine, Charles G., 7, 192–93
Hamilton, Gail, 10, 156–59
Hansbrough, Mary Berri Chapman, 12, 264–66
Hawkins, Walter Everette, 16, 289–92
Hawthorn, Emily, 7, 230–31
Hay, John, xx, 213, 215–18, 249
Hornaday, William Temple, 150, 235–37
Horne, Frank Smith, 21, 318–19
Hovey, Richard, 245–47
Howard, O. O., 12, 14, 16, 91–94
Howard University, xxi, 16, 20, 88, 91, 126, 129, 174–75, 190, 225, 226–27, 242, 257, 276, 289, 293, 303–4, 316
Hughes, Langston, 286

Jackson, Andrew, 73
Jacob, Mary Phelps, 298–300
James, Alice Archer Sewall, 255–56
Jefferson, Thomas, xxi, 4, 5, 25, 35, 50, 213
Jiménez, Juan Ramón, 284–85
Johnson, Georgia Douglas, 21, 241, 273–76, 308
Johnson, James Weldon, xix, 19, 21, 256–59
Johnson, Robert Underwood, 234–35
Joyce, John A., 12, 121–25

Keckley, Elizabeth, 13–14
Kennedy, Thomas, 34–37
Key, Francis Scott, xix, xxi, 8, 38–42, 73
King, Horatio, 14, 15, 90, 183–84
Ku Klux Klan (KKK), 20, 64

Law, Thomas, 6, 29–31
Lee, Muna, 3, 304–6
Lester, Miriam, 168–69

Library of Congress, xxii, 5, 18, 50–51, 62, 74, 79, 259, 300–301, 315
Lincoln, Abraham, xxi, 3, 7, 12, 13, 15, 18, 62–63, 70, 124, 126, 131, 135–36, 159, 160–61, 215, 219, 244
Lincoln, Jeanie Gould, 127–29
Lippincott, Sarah Clarke, 7, 85–87
Litchfield, Grace Denio, 233–34
Locke, Alain, 20, 241, 286, 317

MacLeish, Archibald, xx, 300–301
Madison, James, 42, 51, 213
Marquis, Don, 277–81
Martin, John Sella, xx, 10, 11, 94–100
McCreery, John L., 105–6
Menard, John Willis, 108, 115–17
Meredith, Owen, 195–96
Miller, Cincinnatus Heine, 210–12, 229
Miller, Joaquin, 210–12, 229
Miller, Kelly, 16, 17, 19, 174–76
Miller, May, 175, 309
Mirick, Edith B., 237, 288–89
Monroe, James, 48, 49
Mount Vernon, 18, 45, 171, 172–73

National Association for the Advancement of Colored People (NAACP), 19, 129, 175, 241, 256–57, 286
Nealy, Mary E., 89–91

Oak Hill Cemetery, 68, 122–25, 128
O'Donoghue, Marian Longfellow, 168–69
Ohl, Maud Andrews, 244–45
Old Soldiers' Home, 12, 128
O'Reilly, Miles, 7, 192–93

Paulding, James Kirke, 37–38
Payne, Daniel Alexander, 11, 17, 135–37
Payne, John Howard, 124
Paynter, John Henry, xx, 5, 11, 173–74
Peet, Mary Toles, 201–2
Perse, Saint-John, 301

Piatt, Donn, 189–90, 197, 219
Piatt, John James, 107–8, 189, 197–99
Piatt, Sarah Morgan Bryan, 15, 107–11, 197
Pierpont, John, 9, 59–61
Pike, Albert, 12, 20, 64–67
Poe, Edgar Allan, 121, 184–85, 232–33
Popel Shaw, Esther, 21, 308–12
Proctor, John Claggett, 19, 247–49

Rankin, Jeremiah Eames, 16, 190–92
Rock Creek Cemetery, xxi, 18, 48, 164, 176, 212–13, 230, 237–38, 240–41, 248, 263, 265
Rock Creek Park, 18, 203, 210
Roosevelt, Theodore, 21, 170, 203, 215, 235

Schayer, Julia Von Stosch, 221–22, 262
Searing, Laura Redden, 7, 14, 118–21
Slade, William, 10, 11, 70–71
Smith, Margaret Bayard, 4
Smith, Samuel Harrison, 4–5, 29
Smithsonian Institution, 4, 6, 9, 11–12, 29, 79, 145, 149, 153–55, 235
Sparrow, Louise Kidder, 293
Speyer, Leonora, 18, 221, 262–64
Spofford, Harriet Prescott, 199–201
Spring-Rice, Cecil Arthur, 18, 239–41
Stafford, Wendell Phillips, 19, 170–73
St. Elizabeths Hospital, 12, 265, 301
Stoddard, Charles Warren, 229–30
Story, Joseph, xx, 5, 42–45
Sumner, Charles, 2, 159, 207–8, 227–29
Swisshelm, Jane Grey, 7, 13, 140–41

Terrell, Mary Church, 241
Thompson, Eloise Bibb, 16, 276–77
Toomer, Jean, 16, 21, 301–3
Townsend, George Alfred, 108, 189, 219–21
Turner, Henry McNeal, 11, 159–61
Turner, Nat, 130–31

U.S. Congress, xxi, 2–4, 5, 6, 7, 9, 11–12, 14, 15, 16, 18, 20, 33–34, 35, 47–48, 59, 62, 65, 107, 115, 122, 135, 140, 164, 185–87, 189, 192, 197, 220–21, 273, 305–6

Vashon, George Boyer, 3, 16, 88–89

Walden, Alfred Islay, xx, 16, 225–29
Washington Navy Yard, 5, 6, 8, 73, 147
Watterston, George, xx, 5, 29, 50–52
Webster, Daniel, 7, 49, 185–87, 193

White House, 5, 6, 12, 13, 20, 35, 70, 86, 135–36, 149, 165, 195, 215
Whitman, Walt, xix–xx, 13, 79–85, 111, 198–99, 203, 229, 232
Whitney, Helen Hay, 249–50
Willard, Emma, 6, 7, 52–55
Willard Hotel, 13
Wilson, Woodrow, 19, 191
Woodworth, Eliza, 18, 193–95
Wordsworth, William, 208–9
Wylie, Elinor, 293–97

Zitkala-Ša, 269–71